THE LIMITS OF EMPIRE

THE LIMITS OF EMPIRE

SUB-IMPERIALISM AND PUKHTUN RESISTANCE IN THE NORTH-WEST FRONTIER

SAMEETAH AGHA

Orient BlackSwan

THE LIMITS OF EMPIRE: SUB-IMPERIALISM AND PUKHTUN RESISTANCE IN THE NORTH-WEST FRONTIER

ORIENT BLACKSWAN PRIVATE LIMITED

Registered Office
3-6-752 Himayatnagar, Hyderabad 500 029, Telangana, India
e-mail: centraloffice@orientblackswan.com

Other Offices
Bengaluru, Bhopal, Chennai, Guwahati,
Hyderabad, Jaipur, Kolkata, Lucknow, Mumbai,
New Delhi, Noida, Patna, Visakhapatnam

First published by Orient Blackswan Private Limited 2020

ISBN 978-93-5287-996-0

Maps cartographed by
Sangam Books (An imprint of The Agricultural Development Commercial Credit And Industrial Investment Company Private Limited)

Maps

Typeset in
Minion Pro 10.5/13
by Le Studio Graphique, Gurgaon 122 007

031780

Printed in India at
Akash Press, Delhi

Published by
Orient Blackswan Private Limited
3-6-752 Himayatnagar, Hyderabad 500 029, Telangana, India
e-mail: info@orientblackswan.com

For my brother, Agha Iqbal Ali
and
my father, Agha Ashraf Ali

CONTENTS

ABBREVIATIONS

DoA	Directorate of Archives
FF	Foreign Frontier
GoI	Government of India
GoP	Government of Punjab
IOR/BL	India Office Records and Private Papers, British Library
K.W.	Keep With
NAI	National Archives of India
NWFP	North-West Frontier Province
PGoI	Proceedings of the Government of India
PGoP	Proceedings of the Government of Punjab
Sec F	Secret Frontier
&c.	archaic alternative form of et cetera or etc.

FIGURES AND TABLES

Figures

Tables

PUBLISHERS' ACKNOWLEDGEMENTS

For granting permission to reproduce copyright material in this volume, the publishers thank the following:

Oxford University Press, for 'Inventing a Frontier: Imperial Motives and Sub-imperialism on British India's North-West Frontier', in *Fringes of Empire: Peoples, Places, and Spaces in Colonial India*, eds. Sameetah Agha and Elizabeth Kolsky, India: Oxford University Press, 2009. Reproduced with permission of Oxford University Press India, © Oxford University Press 2009. An excerpt of this has been used in 'Mapping the Frontier'.

Indian Historical Review and SAGE Publications, for 'Sub-imperialism and the Loss of the Khyber: The Politics of Imperial Defence on British India's North-West Frontier', first published in *Indian Historical Review* 40(2): 307–330, December 2013, by SAGE Publications India Private Limited, All rights reserved. Copyright © SAGE Publications India Private Limited, 2013. It is available at: https://doi.org/10.1177/0376983613499682. An excerpt of this has been used in 'The Deliberate Creation of the "Blackest Day"'.

Routledge, Taylor & Francis Group, for 'Deciphering the Maizar Military Tribunal, 1897: Civil-military Tensions and Pukhtun Resistance on the North-West Frontier of British India', in *Culture, Conflict and the Military in Colonial South Asia*, eds. Kaushik Roy and Gavin Rand, Routledge India, 2018. An excerpt of this has been used in 'Constructing the 1897 Revolt'.

Palgrave Macmillan, for 'Demystifying "Millenarianism": Oral Historical Evidence of Pukhtun Resistance and Colonial Warfare in the North-West Frontier of British India', in *Resistance and*

Colonialism: Insurgent Peoples in World History, eds. Nuno Domingos, Miguel Bandeira Jeronimo and Ricardo Roque, Palgrave Macmillan, 2019. An excerpt of this has been used in 'The Uprising in Swat'.

ACKNOWLEDGEMENTS

This book has been many years in the making. It started out as a doctoral dissertation at Yale University. Four years of transcontinental archival research and travel in the North-West Frontier Province and Federally Administered Tribal Areas (now Khyber Pukhtunkhwa) were made possible by the John M. Olin Fellowship, Smith-Richardson Grant, Yale Center for International and Area Studies Grant and by the generous support of Yale's International Security Programs. At Yale, I am grateful to William Foltz for his encouragement and the late Robin Winks for his support and guidance when the project was just beginning. I owe a special debt to Paul Kennedy for his mentorship, support and guidance over the years.

I am grateful to the staff and custodians of many institutions: the India Office Records of the British Library, London; National Archives of India, New Delhi; Punjab Government Archives, Civil Secretariat, Lahore; Directorate of Archives, Peshawar; and the Pashto Academy, Peshawar. I also thank the political agent, Khyber (1995), for allowing me to consult files in the Khyber Political Agency, and the political agent and assistant political agent, North Waziristan (1995), for the same privilege in their jurisdiction.

So many people helped and looked after me during my research and travels in Peshawar and Khyber Pukhtunkhwa that it is impossible to name them all. In particular, I must thank Sehyr Saigol and Naseem Saigol for facilitating my travels to Peshawar and for their hospitality in Lahore. In Peshawar, when I was still developing a road map of where and how to go about finding Pukhtun oral accounts, I benefited from the advice of Taqweem-ul-Haq, Qalandar Mohmand,

Rahimullah Yusufzais, Nawaz Tahir, Latif Afridi, Zulfiqar Gilani, Taki Bangash and Afrasiab Khattak. I am indebted to the numerous people of Swat, Buner, Khyber, Mohmand and North Waziristan for their help, hospitality and openness in conversing with me. Behroz Khan was of invaluable help as we literally went from door to door in Swat and Buner and finally found Haji Nawab Khan, the oldest living participant/witness of the revolt in Malakand. I am also indebted to Behroz for helping me with translations of testimonies gathered in Swat and Buner. I cannot thank Babri Gul Wazir enough for working with me for months in London to translate testimonies gathered in North Waziristan, and for instructing me in a vocabulary and concepts that were passing out of usage. I am grateful to the extended family of Khan Abdul Ghaffar Khan for hosting me in Peshawar. I am indebted to the guidance and mentorship of the late Eqbal Ahmad and for his warm hospitality in Islamabad.

For some years this book fell into hiatus. In recent years, as I returned to recasting and completing the study, I am grateful of the support of several colleagues and friends. At Pratt Institute, I would like to thank Ric Brown, Gregg Horowitz, Ivan Zatz-Diaz, Kumru Toktamis, May Joseph, Luca Lucic, Randy Donowitz, Nancy Seidler, Sophia Babb and Suzanne Verderber. A sabbatical in 2014 and Mellon research grants from Pratt Institute's Social Science and Cultural Studies and the School of Liberal Arts and Sciences helped greatly towards the completion of this book. I am indebted to Jason Rodgers, Nicholas Dease, Caroline Skelton and the amazing staff at Pratt Library Brooklyn for all their help and their prompt attention to my insatiable requests for inter-library loans.

Beyond Pratt, I have benefited from the advice and kindness of many scholars and friends. In particular I would like to thank Kaushik Roy, Gavin Rand, Douglas Peers, Shah Mahmoud Hanifi, John Butt, Naveen Seth and David Goodman for the many insightful comments.

Excerpts used in this book have previously appeared in the following publications: *Resistance and Colonialism: Insurgent Peoples in World History*, eds. Nuno Domingos, Miguel Bandeira Jeronimo and Ricardo Roque (Palgrave Macmillan, 2019); *Culture, Conflict and the Military in Colonial South Asia*, eds. Kaushik Roy and Gavin Rand (Routledge India, 2018); *Indian Historical Review* 40(2): 307–330,

December (SAGE Publications, 2013); and *Fringes of Empire: Peoples, Places, and Spaces in Colonial India*, eds. Sameetah Agha and Elizabeth Kolsky (Oxford University Press, 2009). I thank the volume editors and publishers for granting permission to reproduce excerpts from the above.

I am grateful to Anjali Aggarwal Gupta, Moyna Mazumdar and the amazing editorial team at Orient BlackSwan, and especially Roopa Sharma for her continued patience and support.

No words of gratitude can adequately express the extent to which I owe this book, and so much else, to the love, support and detailed involvement of my family in my intellectual projects—my father Ashraf, the most brilliant historian I know, for instilling in me a love of history; my sister Hena, for her impeccable editorial advice and for our writing hermitages; my brother Iqbal, for turning my barriers into technical details to be overcome; Steven, for the much needed and welcome excursions; and my son Cailean, for being a sweetheart and wading with me through the voluminous mass of papers and books strewn all over our living space. And in loving remembrance of my mother Sufia, who with her grace and gentle compassion taught us to look for details that would otherwise remain submerged; and my brother Shahid, our beloved witness who turned poetry into history, and history into poetry.

INTRODUCTION

> 'Maizar...A piece of treachery unequalled on the Frontier.'
>
> H. W. Mills (1897: 23)

> 'So treacherous was this attack, and so utterly at variance with the Pathan code of honour that frontier officers found the greatest difficulty in ascertaining the exact cause.'
>
> C. C. Davies (1932: 93)

> 'The Maizar attack was not a premeditated act of treachery.'
>
> Ruling of the Maizar tribunal (December 1897)[1]

> 'The English came and wanted to occupy our land. They were aggressors and they were cruel. We would not allow them to occupy our land and that is why we fought them. That is why we sacrificed ourselves and killed them also. They wanted to take our own land from us, so what do you expect.'
>
> (Malik Abdul Wadud, Sadda Khan's great grandson,
> quoted from an interview with the author,
> Maizar, Tochi, North Waziristan, 1995)

These contrasting and conflicting accounts about an attack that was the opening scene of one of the biggest armed revolts against the British Empire forms the central problematic that segues into the themes explored in this study. On 10 June 1897, a large military garrison was attacked in Maizar, in North Waziristan. According to official and contemporary accounts, the British officers and soldiers were received hospitably by the Wazir tribes and then suddenly attacked while resting. Casualties were heavy, leading to shocked outrage in the press. The event described as an act of 'treachery', 'revolting even to the Afghan', is the official story, how Empire presented and explained itself publicly. This imperial narrative which has largely been preserved within historiography till today is part of a discourse conceptualised here as *imperial explanations*.

Emerging from the colonial archive, the third quote is constitutive of the inner workings of Empire in the North-West Frontier and completely contradicts the first two statements. A trial—the Maizar Military Tribunal—was held a few months later to investigate the Maizar attack and to try the accused tribesmen. The British military tribunal established without doubt that there was nothing 'treacherous' in the attack. The detailed proceedings of the trial are contained within the colonial archive, yet any mention of the trial or its verdict has been omitted from the annals of the colonial history of the North-West Frontier. This missing history of Empire as it actually functioned in the Frontier is conceptualised here as *sub-imperialism*.

The fourth quote above, the 'Pukhtun voice', points us towards another history that lies submerged, that of colonial *resistance* in the Frontier. Sub-imperialism and resistance are constitutive of a silenced history that is at the heart of the colonial encounter in the North-West Frontier. At the intersection of these lie the limits of Empire.

* * *

The 'North-West Frontier' was an imperial creation, its geography and terrain represented and given form through British colonial expansion in the nineteenth century. In 1898, amidst a heated debate in the House of Commons, Lord Roberts declared:

> A Frontier, more than 1,000 miles in length, with a belt of huge mountains in its front, inhabited by thousands of warlike men, over whom neither we nor any other Power had control, and with a wide impassible river in its rear, seemed to me then, as it does now, an impossible Frontier...[2]

Roberts' view was characteristic of colonial representations of the region and its inhabitants—an 'intractable', 'barren', 'mountainous' terrain peopled by 'independent' though 'barbaric', 'warring' tribes in 'a state of permanent rebellion against the world'.[3] In 1849, the

British conquered Punjab and took possession of territories of the Sikh kingdom. The 'North-West Frontier' referred to the mountainous borderland area beyond the Indus that lay between the previously Sikh-held, and now British administered, territories and the kingdom of Kabul or Afghanistan. While the North-West Frontier has 'no claim as a separate physiographic entity',[4] its status as a frontier was a continual project in the making that occurred largely within the context of imperial military expansion that, in turn, was met by the fiercest colonial resistance to be found anywhere in the British Empire.[5] Between 1849 and 1947, the area was the scene of perpetual violence and warfare—over a hundred punitive military expeditions known as 'butcher and bolt' or 'burn and scuttle', named after the pattern of tactics the colonial military employed, were sanctioned against the different tribes. Armed colonial resistance was in great part responsible for the recurring orientalist tropes and images of the tribes (especially the Pukhtuns, the biggest demographic group) as 'barbaric', 'bloodthirsty', 'warring' and 'recalcitrant'.[6] The biggest within this history of resistance was the revolt of 1897.

In the summer of 1897, the trans-Indus borderland exploded in rebellion against British occupation. Tribes revolted from Waziristan to Swat. The extent of the area involved was unprecedented. Further, it pointed to an attempt at coming together by the different tribes in the area, something that had never happened before. In fact, a cornerstone of British policy had been to rely on the assumption that the different tribes would not be able to sink their internecine quarrels and combine against the British. As far back as 1855, Temple had estimated the strength of the tribes at some 200,000 fighting men, but then immediately pointed out:

> The aggregate may appear large but it is to be remembered, that only a very small portion of these forces would ever be arrayed against at one time and in one place—it is but rarely that even two or three Tribes can combine against us. ...Anything approaching to a general combination is a contingency quite beyond the range of probability (Temple 1856: 53).

However, that is what seemed to have happened. The commander-in-chief declared in a speech that the involvement of '200-000 first rate fighting men' and the dates of the various risings indicated 'an identity

Figure 1: North-West Frontier Region

Source: Redrawn from C. C. Davies (1932).

of design and a unity of purpose never before discernible in the history of frontier disturbances'.[7] Military outposts were attacked and

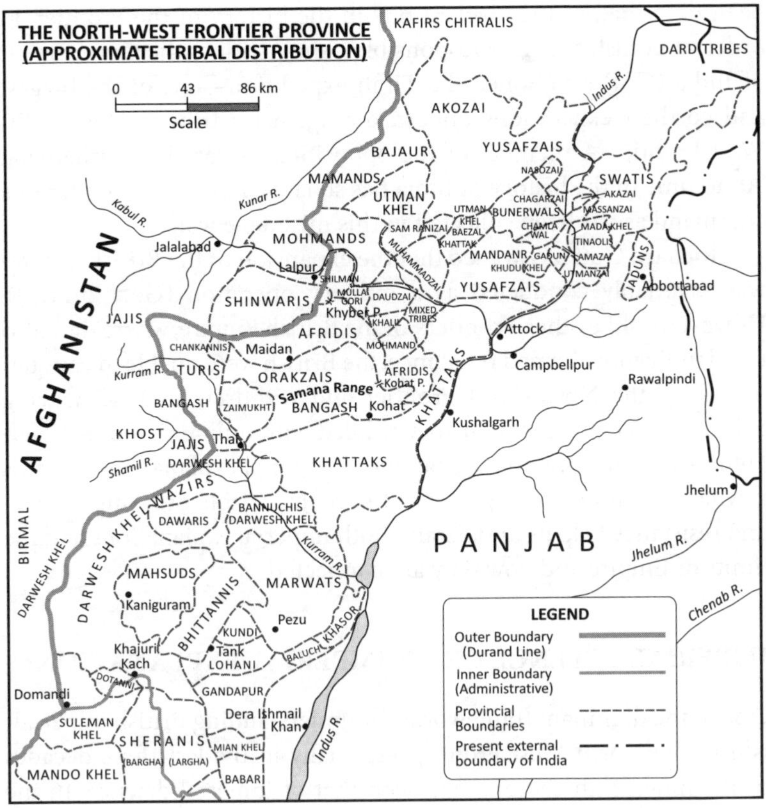

Figure 2: Approximate tribal distribution

Source: Redrawn from C. C. Davies (1932).

garrisons were besieged. On 10 June, a large British military escort was attacked in northern Waziristan and suffered heavy casualties. On 27 July, fortified posts were attacked in Malakand and Chakdara and the garrisons there were besieged for several days. On 9 August, the Mohmands attacked Shabkadar and burnt the village of Shankargarh. By the end of the summer, the British had deployed three field forces simultaneously to suppress the uprising. One of these was the Malakand Field Force, involving some 10,000 troops, which became famous for the presence of one of its young subalterns, Winston Churchill. On 25 August 1897, the British lost the Khyber Pass—a day that has been described as the blackest day in the history of the Frontier. In order to punish the tribe responsible—the Afridis—the Government of India (GoI) sanctioned the Tirah expedition—one of the biggest and costliest expeditions undertaken against a tribe in the North-West Frontier. A member of the opposition declared in Parliament: 'At no time in the history of India has so large a force been under one command as has been collected in this miserable war.'[8]

Richard Gott has argued that the expansion of the British Empire was invariably conducted as a military operation (Gott 2011: 2). However, unlike other 'Frontiers' of the British Empire, where they also faced indigenous armed resistance, the British were unable to conquer or 'pacify' the North-West Frontier and withdrew in 1947, leaving behind a violent colonial history riddled with military failures. These failures were integral to the shaping of imperial explanations and this is where the limits of Empire start to become visible. Sub-imperialism and resistance help us understand both imperial explanations and the limits of Empire and how they are connected.

IMPERIAL DEFENCE OR AN IMPERIAL EXPLANATION?

One of the dominant frameworks for understanding British imperialism in the North-West Frontier, especially in the last three decades of the nineteenth century, has been that of imperial defence. In the nineteenth century, imperial defence was an ever evolving term that never really signified a concerted, coherent policy for the British Empire as a whole. However, the term 'gained a specific meaning in the last decades of the nineteenth century when it came to be applied to an integrated system of defence for the home islands, the overseas territories whether formally or informally held, and the commercial and strategic links between them' (Killingray 1999: 342). Within this scheme, as has been pointed out by the giants of the history of imperialism, the security of India loomed large.[9] Charles Dilke, among other contemporary statesmen who wrote on the question, emphasised that the problem of the security of India was distinct and 'wholly different in its nature from the British Imperial Defence question' as it existed elsewhere in the Empire (Dilke and Wilkinson 1892: 350).[10] The reason for its distinctness was the existence of a large land frontier which was conterminous with Russia, seen as the main competitor to England in Asia.[11]

The inner workings of Britain's imperial rivalry with Russia and the prevailing Russophobia among British statesmen are not our concerns here. Was British fear of a Russian invasion of India real or imagined, manipulated by colonial figures to serve ulterior agendas, and what were the actual motives that guided the British statesmen in London and India are issues that have been debated at length and have been the subject of several noteworthy studies.[12] However, in the last three decades of the nineteenth century, it was the North-West Frontier that emerged as key to the defence of British India. Through all the imperial debates and squabbles, there was very little doubt that securing the region for Indian defence was important but the issue was to determine what was needed in order to achieve this.

Within the Indian empire, the debate waged on how best to secure the Frontier.[13] In fact, for the continuously expanding British Empire through the nineteenth century in India, the question now was: What was and should be its Frontier? Implicit within this problematic is the question of limits which, if recognised, would spell an end to continuous imperial expansion. The result was the birth of the concept of the 'scientific frontier' (Harris 1966). The Scientific Frontier, mainly the formulation of Lord Roberts, was an imaginary line connecting the Afghan cities of Kabul, Ghazni and Kandahar. The problem was that this 'perfect line of defence' lay in Afghan territory, outside the British Empire. As Leslie Harris put it: 'How to arm a frontier that lay in its entirety within the confines of another state, whose ruler, though technically a friend and ally, was jealous of his independence and would under no conditions countenance the peace-time occupation of his territory by British forces?' (1966: 70). Stopping short of annexation of Afghanistan, the forward policy that was undertaken in the 1890s was the incoherent result of this imperial problematic.

In a nutshell, the scheme to secure the frontier was to 'push forward by all the key passes leading from the Indus to the Kabul–Kandahar line, and to construct advanced military posts from which the "scientific frontier" could be readily occupied' (ibid.: 71). Therefore, the 'most important development in the plans for the defence of

India concerned the approach to the tribes who lived astride lines of communication between Afghanistan and India' (Johnson 2003: 740). Not only did the key to the entire scheme of imperial defence and securing the frontier involve securing the major passes and mountain routes that lay in the North-West Frontier but a crucial component of this scheme was also enlisting the tribes that inhabited the region as allies.

It is important to note that this geopolitics was mainly espoused and played out at the higher echelons of government and bore little upon how Empire actually functioned on the Frontier. This understanding of imperial defence lays out statements of policies and the rationalisations behind them. As such, imperial defence was perhaps the grandest, most overarching imperial explanation that functioned to provide a justification for expansion. Further, this top-down model of imperial defence does not tell us how the forward policy functioned on the ground or its engagement with, and impact on, the inhabitants of the region. This study reveals how the complex dynamics of 'securing the routes' and 'enlisting the tribes as allies' actually functioned. In order to do so, we need to turn to sub-imperialism.

SUB-IMPERIALISM

Two interrelated arguments about Victorian imperialism lead us into the concept of sub-imperialism. In their seminal article, 'Imperialism of Free Trade', Gallagher and Robinson (1953) challenged the then prevalent idea of mid-Victorian indifference to Empire followed by a sudden expansion in the late nineteenth century, or the Hobson/Lenin thesis of the 'new imperialism', evidenced especially in the spectacular partition of Africa (Hobson 1902; Lenin 2013). In contrast, they brought forth the concept of 'informal empire' and claimed a continuity to imperial expansion throughout the Victorian era. In confronting the paradox of expansion when the official stated policy was against annexation, symbolised most by the phrase 'millstone round our neck', they brought the periphery into sharp focus—'the local factor'.[14] Around the same time period, J. S. Galbraith (1960, 1963) converged to a similar position in his 'turbulent frontier' or 'man on the spot' thesis. Again, confronting the contradiction between stated aims of non-annexation and actual events, he attributed British expansion to the pull exerted by 'turbulent frontiers' (areas of disorder adjacent to British imperial authority) and to the wide powers exercised by imperial viceroys (man on the spot) in an era of primitive communications—it was the man on the spot who was the key agent of imperial expansion. Gallagher and Robinson, and Galbraith thus shifted the focus in imperial historiography away from the metropole as the main driving force and towards the periphery, ultimately paving the way for what may be termed sub-imperialism.

Since then, sub-imperialism has followed two trajectories. The first definition and usage lies within Marxian political economic, especially dependency, theories analysing the international system after the Second World War. Ruy Mauro Marini, a Brazilian sociologist, conceptualised sub-imperialism in the 1960s and defined Brazil as sub-imperialist: 'It is not a question of passively accepting North American power (although the actual correlation of forces often leads to that result), but rather of collaborating actively with imperialist expansion, assuming in this expansion the position of a key nation' (Marini 1965: 22). Within this framework, the concept generally refers to a go-between or collaborator between the core (imperialist) and the dominated (periphery): '...sub-imperialist actors are conceived as intermediaries in the relations between center and periphery when they are simultaneously both dominant and dominated units; more dominated than dominant, however' (Varynen and Herrera 1975: 165).[15]

The second usage pertains to and is located within the broader history of (British) imperialism. While the term sub-imperialism has been invoked in the last several decades by historians of imperialism, its meaning is more often implied while the concept has yet to be further clarified, explained and theorised (Elridge 1978; Metcalf 2007). In 1976, Robin Winks used it to refer to those examples of informal control 'which involved a colony itself acquiring preeminent power in another area, as Queensland sought over Papua from 1884 to 1906 or South Africa would in a variety of circumstances' (1976: 546). In recent decades, the term has appeared across different histories of imperialism (Elridge 1978; Metcalf 2007; Wong 1997; Roberts 1962;

Jackson 2012). At times, the term may not be used directly but we can see histories that reflect the construct (drawing from the frame of the pioneers mentioned above). This does not rule out the fact that histories might arrive at similar conclusions without any reference to the term (Blyth 2003). However, the influence of the pioneers is evident in the types of histories that are illustrative of sub-imperialism (Blyth 2003; Simpson 1996; Yapp 1980). Broadly, we can surmise its meaning especially from the kinds of histories it is used in illustrating—empire within empire, man on the spot, role of periphery within imperialism.

Noteworthy among more recent works that explore the concept is that of John Darwin who has argued that British expansion throughout the nineteenth century was chaotic and incoherent and driven less by the government in London and more by sub-imperial interests: 'The decisive causes of British expansion in India were to be found not in the urgings from home but in the uniquely favourable environment in which Anglo-Indian sub-imperialism took root' (Darwin 2009: 17). In 'Imperialism and the Victorians', Darwin (1997) makes a powerful case for the need to move beyond conventional hypothesis and existing historiography to explain the 'seemingly random course of Victorian imperialism'. In addition to reinforcing the role of the 'man on the spot' in driving British expansion, Darwin introduces the concept of 'bridgehead'—'the hinge or "interface" between the metrople and a local periphery"—as a useful way to understand the 'baffling shape of Victorian Empire':

> If we look at Victorian expansion world-wide, strategic imperatives and/or commercial need offer at best only partial explanations for the character and timing of British intervention. The crucible variable was the 'bridgehead': the purchase achieved by British interests on their zone of operation.... Only by reconstructing more fully the functioning and interaction of these bridgeheads at home and abroad will we be able to explain properly the erratic, unpredictable, tentative, opportunistic but ultimately insatiable progress of Victorian imperialism (Darwin 1997: 642).

Within the frame established by this tradition of scholarship, this study conceptualises the space where the actual colonial encounter takes place as the arena of sub-imperialism and uses the lens of microhistory to further reveal its mechanics. This study will show that sub-imperialism is not a facet of imperialism but it is how imperialism functions on the Frontier. Of relevance here is not only the significance of the man on the spot as a cause in imperial expansion, but also the role played by the man on the spot in the colonial encounter which shapes imperialism on the Frontier. Viewed from Whitehall, India may seem like a sub-imperial centre with viceroys or commander-in-chiefs as the 'man on the spot', but viewed from a remote geographic periphery such as the Frontier, the sub-imperial centre appears more as the core rather than the periphery. So while we have biographies and histories of 'men on the spot' such as Wolseley and Kitchener, we know little of figures such as Herbert William Gee or Sadda Khan—the men who functioned within and shaped the colonial space of the Frontier.[16] Employing sub-imperialism as a conceptual construct to explicate the contexts and mechanics of on-the-ground imperialism opens up the space for revisiting military history. Most importantly, a microhistory of sub-imperialism brings into sharp focus the silenced history of resistance on the Frontier.

MICROHISTORY

Microhistory can be described as a historiographical practice that arose, at least in its deliberate, self-conscious form, in the 1970s in Italy.[17] While they encompass diverse material and their theoretical references are varied and eclectic, microhistories share certain common features. 'Microhistory as a practice is essentially based on the reduction of the scale of observation, on a microscopic analysis and an intensive study of the documentary material' (Levi 1991: 99). Though scale in itself is not the main issue, underlying the reduction of scale is the unifying principle of microhistorical research that 'microscopic observation will reveal factors previously unobserved' (ibid.). As Levi points out: 'Phenomena previously considered to be sufficiently described and understood assume completely new meanings by altering the scale of observation. It is then possible to use these results to draw far wider generalizations although the initial observations were made within relatively narrow dimensions and as experiments rather than examples' (ibid.: 102).

Another characteristic of microhistory is its approach towards the problem of narrative. Breaking with the authoritarian form of discourse adopted by historians who present reality as objective, microhistory incorporates into the main body of narrative the procedures of research and its documentary limitations. In contrast to interpretive anthropology to which it bears some resemblance, microhistory considers social differentiation essential. 'Individuals constantly create their own identities, and groups define themselves according to conflicts and solidarities which, however cannot be assumed a priori but result from dynamics which are the object of analysis' (Levi 1991: 109). Finally, it deals with the problem of selecting important areas for examination—the idea of seeing the subjects of traditional history in 'one of their localized variations...in order to discern meanings which have previously evaded explanation' (Levi 1991: 114). Microhistory rejects post-structuralist relativism and, for what is important here, attempts to bring forth the silenced stories and unheard voices of dominant narratives.

This study did not start out as a microhistory. I was not familiar with the term or the field (if it can be called that). The study evolved towards microhistory somewhat intuitively. I set out to research an event, the 1897 revolt, which hardly existed within historiography in comprehensible historical detail. I viewed the revolt as an aspect of the colonial encounter in the North-West Frontier. And to tell that story, all the voices had to be brought forth. Very simply, I wanted to know what happened and why. This is because the colonial official story which seeped into historiography was not history. Larger narratives based on minimal evidence would only lead to an incomplete picture. Finding evidence emerged as crucial, leading to an unusually longer period of research, and the scale of the study started to become smaller based on the evidence. Thus, instead of the whole revolt, which comprised more attacks (such as the Mohmand uprising) and the numerous military expeditions that followed, this study focuses on three episodes. Evidence at the sub-imperial level brings forth diverse voices of Empire that were suppressed and are thus missing in the historical record to reveal mechanics of imperialism in the Frontier. It is important to note that such imperial agents held different notions of how Empire should function, a point that is lost in seeing the Empire generally as a coherent monolith in the Frontier. A microhistorical examination of sub-imperial evidence in the colonial archive along with accounts gained from Pukhtun oral tradition lead us towards the story of colonial resistance in the Frontier. It is important to note that both the sub-imperial evidence and Pukhtun oral tradition largely corroborate each other.

UNDERSTANDING RESISTANCE IN COLONIAL WARS

Ranajit Guha claims that a 'conjuring trick' of colonialist historiography was to make 'resistance disappear from the political history of India under colonial rule' (Guha 1997: 89). Nowhere is this more evident than in the historiography of colonial North-West Frontier. Throughout the colonial presence, Pukhtun resistance was continuous and fierce, manifest in various forms, the most prominent of which were collective armed rebellions such as the one examined here. However, the 1897 revolt was in some ways the most 'spectacular manifestation' of resistance in the North-West Frontier and is thus significant to furthering our understanding of the phenomenon as a whole.[18] The British did not succeed in conquering and administering the Pukhtuns. In colonial literature, Pukhtun acts that challenged colonial authority were generally represented as works of 'fanaticism' or as typical features to be found among 'barbaric' and 'warlike' people.[19] This tendency has continued in historiography on the Frontier and in much of the recent counter-insurgency (COIN)-centred literature. The postcolonial Pukhtun has yet to come into being as does the history of colonial resistance in the Frontier.[20] So how do we approach the question of writing the history of resistance in the North-West Frontier? The question is all the more daunting because first and foremost evidence has to be recovered in order for such histories to even become possible.

In recent decades, especially since the 1960s, a considerable literature has developed towards advancing our understanding of colonial resistance. Within Indian historiography there has been an attempt, beyond the nationalist struggles, to write resistance into colonial history. The Subaltern Studies project is its most notable and significant example. James Scott in different works 'drew attention to less organized, more pervasive, and more everyday forms of resistance' (Ortner 1995: 175). Under the frame of millenarianism, Michael Adas (1979) has analysed the relationships between the rise of prophetic leaders and violent protest as 'key examples of social protest against the conditions resulting from colonial rule'.[21] Perhaps the most exciting and persistent research into colonial resistance has come out of African studies (Ranger 1967; Isaacman 1977; Comaroff and Comaroff 1997). One of the reasons for this has been the use of oral testimonies in African social history which, as Allina-Pisano points out, 'with few exceptions' is 'history from below' 'through the lens of a resistance paradigm' (Allina-Pisano 2003: 188). 'Oral data have been commonplace in the writing of African history since at least the early 1970s, and these data were key in helping to center African historical actors on the stage of history. Informants' accounts of resistance to colonial conquest helped rewrite the opening act of the colonial era from an African perspective' (ibid.: 190). 'In these voices we hear history read from below' (ibid.: 194).

A central question within what have been termed resistance studies is that of definition—what constitutes resistance and how is it to be conceptualised and theorised? Initially 'Resistance' started out as the binary opposite of 'Domination' while being idealised and romanticised. Over time it became more ambiguous and the neat binary became murky, especially when confronted with colonial 'collaborators'. Critiques have pointed out the limits of resistance as a category and suggested viewing the colonial experience as a field of 'negotiation': 'Domination and resistance can be seen as end-points along a power-laden continuum of experience. There is a full range of human action which spans that distance and in between the poles there lies a very crowded spectrum of human interests, goals and needs' (Allina-Pisano 2003: 193).

As this study will show, Pukhtun resistance encompassed multiple forms of action including opposition, negotiation and collaboration. Yet, in the North-West Frontier, the more overwhelming evidence points us to a consistent and unambiguous opposition to British imperialism expressed in myriad modes from cutting wires and opposing the building of roads to individual attacks and collective armed rebellions. However, merely reclassifying and interpreting such acts as resistance is not sufficient. What was the historical context that led to specific acts of opposition? When and how did negotiation and collaboration occur? Who were the actors involved and what were their motives for acting as they did?

A microhistorical approach towards the colonial archive reveals the sub-imperial level of the 1897 encounter which makes the history of resistance visible. Pukhtun oral tradition corroborates sub-imperial evidence and brings in Pukhtun narratives of the revolt.

THE 1897 REVOLT IN HISTORIOGRAPHY

The origins of the historiography on the 1897 revolt lie in contemporary sources—official histories and what we can term semi-official—written mainly by officers and war correspondents. The most famous among these is Churchill's *Story of the Malakand Field Force* (1898), which continues to be referenced constantly.[22] The dominant ways that such accounts have portrayed the revolt are that it was 'sudden', 'treacherous' and 'fanatical'. This is clearly evident in H. W. Mills' work that was written to bring together official and journalistic accounts to 'form a narrative of the leading features of the present frontier disturbances' (Mills 1897). The Maizar attack is described as a 'defiance of British authority by a piece of treachery unequalled on the frontier' which had its explanation in a 'miserable tribal story of lying and deceit to attain private ends—a true Pathan procedure' (ibid.: 5). The uprising in Swat is attributed to the preaching of a Mad Mullah whose 'excited appeals to the fanaticism which exists in every Pathan were responded to in a manner little short of marvelous' (ibid.: 35). The loss of the Khyber Pass was 'universally held to be the worst blow our prestige could suffer on the north-west frontier' and the disaffection of the Afridis the work of 'yet another of those pestiferous fanatics whose presence on our frontier is always a menace to peace and order' (*The Risings on the North-West Frontier* 1898: 106, 108). Abounding in orientalist colonial tropes, such accounts shared the outrage of the government and largely reproduced and overlapped with the official narrative. Ranajit Guha has shown that such texts were written by those who had most to fear from such acts of insurgency and are thus complicit within the colonial project—'they only make sense as a code of pacification for the colonial regime which was a complex of coercive intervention by the state and its proteges' (Guha 1983: 15). He describes such writings as the prose of counter-insurgency.

There is an overlap and element of continuity of this paradigm and discourse within the secondary literature.[23] Ranging across a longer period of time and including writing from the popular to the more academic, the revolt appears in two types of writings. It is mentioned in passing or described in general histories of the Frontier whose main framework is the North-West Frontier as an imperial 'problem' or 'challenge' or 'migraine'. It also appears in operational military histories with the aim to provide direct lessons in colonial warfare (at least in accounts dated to 1947) (Callwell 1911; Skeen 1932; Nevill 1912). Most accounts still rely on the same tropes of 'treachery' and 'fanaticism' to explain the revolt and the same narrative remains intact.

Let us consider an early example of what might be considered, on the surface, to be a more academic account. Cuthbert Collin Davies wrote *The Problem of the North-West Frontier, 1890–1908* in 1932. A Welshman who had served on the North-West Frontier, Davies also held a distinguished first from the University of Wales and a doctorate from Cambridge. He later became Reader in Indian history at Oxford University. Davies ascribes the 1897 risings to 'the active forward policy pursued in the nineties and the influence of fanaticism' (Davies 1932: 94). The tribes looked upon the military advances of the 1890s as encroachments into their territory and a threat to their independence and therefore broke out. Fanaticism is explained thus: 'The chief part played by fanaticism was the way in which the frontier mullahs used it to stir up the latent passions of the turbulent tribesmen' (ibid.: 98).

A similar well-respected account is Olaf Caroe's *The Pathans* published in 1958. Caroe describes the revolt as a sudden outbreak. Without mentioning 'fanaticism', he discusses British penetration of tribal areas accompanied by demarcation of the Durand line, the passage and stationing of troops in some of the most fertile valleys—forward moves which the tribes regarded as 'a deliberate menace to a long cherished independence' (Caroe 1958: 387). However, he immediately wants to justify this: 'A menace indeed it was, but not deliberate. Every move had been forced upon authority either by tribal depredations or by the need to oppose disruptive influences' (ibid.). Here we can witness Guha's magistrate turned into historian, who feels compelled to justify policy. At the same time, merely invoking the forward policy in generalised terms does not suffice as a historical explanation for one of the biggest revolts against the British Empire.

Again, as Guha (1983) has pointed out, such secondary discourse, while assuming some distance in time from the event, still draws on the official narrative and serves a transformative function of turning the narrative of policy justification of the first into history in the second. While it might exhibit some sympathy for the insurgents, ultimately it absorbs the concerns and objectives of the colonial regime. This is not surprising as many of the authors of this type of historiography are colonial administrators (civil and/or military) turned into historians. The two discourses—the official narrative and secondary discourse—are also embedded in each other and interpenetrate and sustain each other.

Finally, we come to the more recent literature spurred by ongoing international intervention in the region. While popularised accounts that rehash the old narratives continue well into the present, let us consider the more scholarly recent writings.[24] Akbar Ahmed, an anthropologist who has written much on the Frontier and also served as an administrator there, describes the revolt in Swat as 'millenarian movements'—'meaning a spontaneous, universal and historically short-lived, native reaction to economic or political stimulus, expressed through the presence of foreign troops and administrators' (Ahmed 1976: 105). Without using 'fanatical', he sees the revolt as a religious reaction: 'The British penetration of hitherto untouched and sequestered areas, harbouring some of the fiercest, and enthusiastically Islamic fighting tribes of the subcontinent, was seen as a direct physical threat to moral and religious values and the immediate cause of the uprisings' (ibid.: 107). While studies of movements characterised as millenarian under colonial rule have yielded some useful insights (Adas 1979), in the case of Swat, as is evidenced in Chapter 4, the concept is not entirely applicable nor does the mere description help us understand its complex history. Religion on its own is not an explanation neither is it a full representation of why the attack occurred in Swat.

Without the same tropes, the structural narrative continues on in scholarly studies. In a 2000 study on Waziristan, Alan Warren uncritically repeats the entrenched colonial era narrative and sums up the Tochi attack as: 'Tribal Maliks invited Gee and the officers of his escort to sit down to a meal, and then sprang a premeditated ambush' (Warren 2000: 28). What is troubling about some of these histories is that they introduce blatant historical inaccuracies. For example, Christian Tripodi on the Tochi attack states that, 'a party of British and native troops accompanying William Gee, PA Tochi, was attacked by Datta Khel Wazirs, smarting over the imposition of a fine the previous year, and *Gee was killed*... His death now inflamed matters and the Wazirs simply added fuel to a fire that stretched the length of the Frontier' (Tripodi 2011: 88; emphasis added). Tripodi introducing Mr Gee's death is blatantly erroneous and does not exist in any account, even the biased contemporary colonial ones. In fact, the historical construction of what took place in Tochi is substantially drawn from Mr Gee's communications after the attack, which exist in plain sight all over the colonial historical record. Diverse in tone and emphasis, the historical account remains intact.

While the relevance of the region as an international hotspot or 'the most dangerous place in the world' has led to a growth of writings, it is precisely its view as a 'problem' that has led to much of the resurgence in this scholarship.[25] Much of this literature is aimed towards current powers who are engaged in COIN in the region, so they can learn from lessons unlearnt and mistakes of the past. This in great part adds to the ongoing basic structure of the 1897 revolt as a colonialist construction.[26] In the case of the Frontier, the third level of discourse, which is the most distant from the event, not only remains complicit with the colonial agenda but within this historical accuracy is also not much of significance. In 1899, an author described the vista of the North-West Frontier as 'too remote for human sympathy' (Robertson 1899: 1). This borderland ever present in international relations continues as a problem to be solved but 'too remote' for even historical accuracy. How many would catch the death of H. W. Gee as erroneous or distinguish North Waziristan from South Waziristan in such narratives? According to Guha, such narratives' 'downright refusal to look at the evidence that is there' stems from the fact that much of this literature is still trapped in the paradigm which inspired the ideology of the first two discourses. 'It follows in each case from a refusal to acknowledge the insurgent as the subject of his own history' (Guha 1983: 38), and incorporates the rebel as an ideal rather than in his real historical specificity. It is distanced from the prose of counter-insurgency only by a 'declaration of sentiment'.

The historiography on the revolt provides a limited view and is not a history that explains the history of the revolt. In his seminal revisionist history of the British–Maori wars, James Belich states that 'we must first know what happened, how and why' (Belich 1986: 12). The opening problematic in this chapter clearly suggests the importance of doing so. This also leads us towards a context—the context of recent history but not seen merely from the forward policy perspective but from a sub-imperialist one, which brings missing events to light that do help explain what happened and why, and provide the much needed missing context.

This study shows that historical evidence does not support the 1897 revolt as a sudden, spontaneous, treacherous or fanatical rebellion. It was the culmination of a continuous resistance against imperial occupation. The forward policy in abstract generalised terms does not explain what occurred. It is only by turning attention to the actual nature of imperialism as it occurred on the ground, sub-imperialism, that this history starts to become coherent.

METHODOLOGY, RESEARCH AND SOURCES

Empire in the Frontier has written its own history the way that it has wanted to, and the ensuing imperial explanations have remained largely dominant and endured within existing historiography. This history has not been scrutinised or probed the way it ought to.[27] However, the imperial archive, even 'as the supreme technology of the late nineteenth-century imperial state' (Stoler 2002: 87), is bigger than its explanations and this archival evidence provides a basis for undermining the dominant imperial explanation.[28] In order to obtain this evidence, we have to go to the microhistorical level. An extensive microhistorical examination of the archives reveals a sub-imperial dynamic which is missing in imperial explanations. And this sub-imperial layer leads us towards reconstructing the history of Empire as it actually functioned on the Frontier, in contrast to its claims. The evidence comprising this dynamic in the case of the 1897 revolt will be examined in detail within the body of this study.

Not satisfied that imperial explanations such as 'fanaticism' and 'treachery' constituted historically adequate explanations in understanding the revolt, my research for this book started out in the main archives that contain the colonial records: the India Office Records and Private Papers at the British Library (IOR/BL) in London, and the National Archives of India (NAI), Delhi. The archives contained a voluminous mass of documentation on imperial debates, communications surrounding policy, military and political reports, and private papers of notable statesmen and their views on the Frontier. The Frontier 'problem' loomed large within this information and especially the 1897 revolt as Empire tried to grapple with the military failures that had taken place. By 1897, there was a remarkable flow of information within Empire centrally through telegrams, reflecting multiple perspectives. It started to become evident that there was not a clear-cut monolithic policy around the Frontier. Through all this information a fundamental question emerged: How did the variety of perspectives and the imperial squabbling actually get translated and implemented through the chain of command to the Frontier? In other words, what did this overwhelming mass of documentation that I waded through reveal about what actually occurred on the ground during this time?

It was in the NAI and the Directorate of Archives (DoA) in Peshawar that documents containing confidential communications became visible that started to outline a different narrative. Going beyond the official explanation, information flows within the lower echelons of Empire started to bring into focus how Empire actually functioned rather than how it stated it did.[29] Unanswered questions in the historiography such as the 'loss of the Khyber' were addressed far more fully within this evidence. Central figures in this history that were missing in historiography surface here. In unravelling the sub-imperial politics we find a consistent pattern of misrepresentations and misinformation within the Empire on the Frontier. Further, the mechanics of sub-imperialism also reveal collaboration and resistance as integral parts of the story of the revolt. Most importantly, the colonial archive did not corroborate existing historiography. One example that forms the opening of this book (and will be examined in detail in Chapter 3) should suffice. Colonial archival evidence shows that in contrast to official and existing historiography, in the case of the Maizar attack, a tribunal was held to examine the causes of the attack and try Madda Khel prisoners. After a lengthy investigation, the tribunal unanimously ruled that 'there was nothing in the way of treachery in the attack'.[30] The tribunal as well as its ruling are completely absent in historiography. Imperial explanations of treachery not only silence resistance, but in excluding the colonial archive they also deny British imperial history on the Frontier. The question as to why this evidence has not made it into the historiography is examined in the conclusion in Chapter 6.

A second source for this study was fieldwork undertaken in the Frontier—specifically in Waziristan, Swat and Khyber. There were two dimensions to my research while in the Frontier. The first involved researching written sources on the revolt which led me to the offices of the political agents (see Figures 3 and 4). The offices

Figure 3: Record keeper at the office of the Political Agent, North Waziristan Political Agency

Note: All photographs in this volume are taken by the author, in 1995.

Figure 4: Records at the office of the Political Agent, Khyber Political Agency

of the political agents are not archives as such and not open to the public or to researchers. It was unusual for me to be able to consult material contained therein. With respect to the colonial period there are some remarkable documents (sometimes original handwritten ones with notes scribbled next to them) that reveal direct aspects of encounters with the tribes. There are also original petitions and letters from the tribesmen that provide an insight into the Pukhtun view. However, these documents had not been preserved and were suffering due to lack of attention, and were stored in cupboards and sacks. With handkerchiefs over their faces, the record keepers and staff in Tochi and the Khyber pulled out sacks that had not been opened in decades and lamented their decay. If organised and preserved, they would have constituted an invaluable historical source.

The second aspect involved over a hundred interviews conducted with people in the Frontier and collecting memories of the revolt preserved in the oral tradition. The Pukhtuns do not have a comparable written archive where they have represented themselves. Yet, they have a history and I was determined to find their views on this war. Not trained in anthropology, I did not have a blueprint on how to conduct this research. Further, I was not researching their customs and rituals, I was investigating a war nearly a 100 years old.

In Federally Administered Tribal Areas (FATA), the richest source of the Pukhtun view of the British–Pukhtun encounter was contained in Pukhtun oral tradition. Until 1995 (which is the last time I was in the region), this tradition kept history alive mostly in the form of Tapas and Charbettas—forms of Pukhtun poetry and verse as well as stories passed down through generations. Even at the time, the ones that deal with the British period were not remembered by younger Pukhtuns and were mostly narrated by certain elder tribesmen (see Figure 5). So I went in search of the oldest tribesmen I could find (Figure 6). What I turned up with was startling (Figure 7). Not only was I able to obtain remembered accounts of the revolt but I was also able to interview two persons who were young participants/witnesses of the 1897 uprising. Though scarcely weighted in balance to the colonial archive, it formed an invaluable aspect of this study. However scant and uneven, it provided a glimpse into the history that has been excluded and highlighted what this history might have consisted of.

Figure 5: Author with tribal elder

Figure 6: Author travelling with armed escorts in North Waziristan

For a historian concerned with the accuracy of facts, Pukhtun oral history corroborated many features of the archival sub-imperial evidence. A remarkable feature of this narrative was that what had

Figure 7: Author interviewing Haji Nawab Khan

taken me three years to reconstruct from the archive was in cases very similar to what was provided in Pukhtun accounts. It also brought forth the missing Pukhtun voice and gestured towards a submerged history. This study does not claim to do justice to this history because in order to do so it would have to become a different project—a history of the Pukhtuns on their own terms. But I was writing the history of a colonial encounter—a war as it actually happened. However, an important part of Pukhtun history is that it is not a linear narrative. Rather, it is lived, dynamic history. The 1897 revolt is not viewed in isolation but as an episode in a continuous and multifaceted struggle and engagement with the British which involved collaboration and resistance.

OUTLINE OF THE BOOK

Very simply, this book is the untold story of the 1897 revolt. It shows the complex ways in which imperial explanations were constructed, functioned, and have continued to dominate the historical record of the 1897 revolt. Through a microhistorical examination of three major events in the revolt (Tochi, Swat and Khyber) and through providing new evidence, sub-imperialism and resistance emerge as key features of the colonial encounter in the North-West Frontier that help us understand the limits of Empire. Imperial explanations also exist internally and play a role in the shaping of imperialism on the Frontier. Chapter 1, though not a microhistory, is a critical re-examination of the period leading to the 1897 event. Chapter 2 presents the structure of the 1897 revolt that corresponds largely to how the historical event has been constructed. Imperial explanations were integral to constructing this view of the revolt. Chapters 3 and 4 focus on the revolt in Tochi and Swat, respectively. In the case of Tochi, sub-imperialism brings into view military failures, military occupation, civil–military tensions and the establishment of a tribunal whose findings falsify the colonial narrative. Oral accounts corroborate sub-imperial evidence and bring forth Pukhtun views on the reasons behind the attack and how it occurred. In Chapter 4, sub-imperialism shows an attempt to misrepresent the reality on the ground and again traces how discontent and resistance to the occupation of Swat evolved to develop into the revolt. In the process, the importance of local politics and the role of middle-men within this occupation is highlighted. Chapter 5 focuses on the loss of the Khyber Pass. Imperial explanations shift here as the discontent of the tribes and their intention to attack were communicated to the authorities well before the attack occurred. Further, the fort was held by a group of levies recruited for and working for the British. The chapter follows sub-imperial decision-making to reveal the circumstances around the fall of the Khyber. Chapter 6 offers some concluding remarks on how the colonial encounter in the Frontier emerges as a result of this counter-history and illustrates the limits of Empire.

NOTES

1. Trial on Madda Khel Prisoners, 27 December 1897, Proceedings of the Government of India (PGoI), Sec F, September 1898, NAI.

2. House of Commons, Debates, 10 March 1898, p. 1226, IOR/BL.

3. An early official account carrying such representations and reproduced quite frequently in contemporary colonial literature can be found in Temple (1856). For other contemporary examples, see Andrews (1937), Coxe (1878), Mills (1897) and Pennell (1909).

4. Dichter (1967: 6). Dichter states that the point is made clear by the fact that the region shares various geomorphological characteristics with adjacent and what have been considered strictly as 'physical regions'.

5. Politically, the term 'North-West Frontier' was used to refer to territories which were carved into the North-West Frontier Province (1901–2010), and areas within the independent tribal belt. Both regions became part of Pakistan in 1947. The tribal belt was referred to as Federally Administered Tribal Areas (FATA). Comprising seven tribal agencies (Bajaur, Mohmand, Khyber, Orakzai, Kurram, North Waziristan and South Waziristan) and six frontier regions (Bannu, Dera Ismail Khan, Kohat, Lakki Marwat, Peshawar and Tank), FATA continued to have a special 'semi-autonomous' status within the Pakistani state. The North-West Frontier Province was renamed Khyber Pukhtunkhwa in 2010. In 2018, FATA were merged with Khyber Pukhtunkhwa (see Figures 1 and 2).

6. Colonial tropes and representations continue to be reproduced in subtle, and overt, versions in recent literature. See, for example, Richards (2003), Swinson (1967) and Barthorp and Anderson (1996).

7. Sir George White, quoted in *The Risings on the North-West Frontier*, p. 1.

8. The Earl of Northbrook, 7 March 1898, *Parliamentary Debates*, Commons (1898), (IOR/BL).

9. The most influential among these were Robinson and Gallagher who provided a seminal thesis by arguing that British expansion, especially the 'scramble for Africa', was ultimately motivated by concern for the defence of key routes to India. See Robinson and Gallagher (1961).

10. Notable among other major contemporaries who wrote on the question was Field Marshall Frederick Roberts who went on to hold the position of the commander-in-chief of India. For instance, see Roberts (1897). Burroughs (1999) claims that the motive behind many of these writings was to influence policy.

11. The other land frontier within the British Empire was in Canada which did not generate the same cause for alarm as the US was viewed as a peaceful neighbour not likely to invade Canada whereas Russia was an 'autocracy with untold millions of men who are ready to march at one man's will' (Dilke and Wilkinson 1892: 350).

12. See Gillard (1977); Ingram (1979, 1981); Singhal (1963); Yapp (1980); Menon (1957). In the more popular genre, the 'Great Game' has been covered by Hopkirk (1992), and Meyer and Brysac (1999). For more recent works, see Sergeev (2013) and Ewan (2010). For a related study, see also Sunderland (2004).

13. For contemporary views, see Andrew (1885); Boulger (1879); Hamley (1879), Hanna (1895, Vol. 1). For a more recent view, see Johnson (2003). The motives underlying the debates have been described as competition among imperial statesmen for key posts and as a pretext for self-aggrandisement. See Preston (1976) and Beckett (2005).

14. This argument was fleshed out especially in *Africa and the Victorians* where Robinson and Gallagher (1961) claimed that it was African politics that had played a crucial role in British expansion in the region. The phrase 'millstones around our neck' is William Gladstone's in reference to the 'wretched colonies' (Malmesbury 1885).

15. South Africa and even Iran in the period of the Shah have been defined as sub-imperialist, and more recently the definition has been extended to BRICS (Brazil, Russia, India, China and South Africa). This is similar to the role of the semi-periphery within Immanuel Wallerstein's (2006) world-systems analysis.

16. The little attention paid to key local actors is not just unfortunate, but it is striking how lacking in relevance that layer of crucial history is within colonial historiography on the Frontier. This may also explain how, for example, authors such as Christian Tripodi have introduced inaccuracies surrounding Herbert W. Gee and the Maizar attack. This is discussed later in this chapter.

17. However, there were works written in a microhistorical vein that preceded this rise, such as Tolstoy's *War and Peace* (1904) and Stewart's *Pickett's Charge* (1959). For discussions of the concept, see Levi (1991); Ginzburg (1993). For examples of outstanding works of microhistory, see Ginzburg (1976); Davis (1983).

18. I borrow the phrase from Terence Ranger (1967) as he contextualises the revolt of 1896/97 in southern Rhodesia in his classic study on African colonial resistance.

19. Of course, this is somewhat of an oversimplification. There were exceptions to this tendency and upon a close reading of the official colonial narrative, we find within it subtle (and sometimes not so subtle) criticisms of the imperial project on the Frontier. Pursuing lines of inquiry opened up by such clues is potentially one way to identify and begin to address the historical gaps that prevent us from undertaking a historical reconstruction of the motives and actions of Pukhtun actors. For example, in the aftermath of the revolt, the opposition in the House of Commons criticised government policy during the Fall of the Khyber and its violation of the agreement with tribes in Swat which led to occupation of the valley (House of Commons, *Parliamentary Debates (1898)*, IOR/BL). However, such criticisms did not

make a significant impact towards altering the dominant narrative preserved within historiography.

20. Some recent works are a promising foray in this direction by providing more nuanced views of colonial rule in the Frontier. See for example, Condos (2016); Rand (2018); Bayly (2016). While still to be fully realised within the colonial military history of the North-West Frontier, recent scholarship coming out of the New Military History of Colonial South Asia provides important directions. See Roy and Rand (2018); Roy (2008, 2015); Omissi (1990); Peers (1995); Moreman (1998).

21. The uprising in Swat, discussed in Chapter 4, has been described as a millenarian revolt by Akbar Ahmed (1976), and Adas' (1979) descriptions of such movements seem to share some similarities with Swat.

22. Others include: *The Risings on the North-West Frontier* (1898); Mills (1897); James (1898); Fincastle and Elliott-Lockhart (1898). A handful of others deal with the Tirah expedition, which is not part of this study.

23. Examples of these include: Andrews (1937); Atteridge (1899); Barton (1939); Bird (1909); Davies (1932); Egerton (1899); Nevill (1912); Skeen (1932); Wylly (1912); Younghusband (1898); Miller (1977); Richards (2003).

24. For popular accounts, see, for example, Meyer and Brysac (1999); Stewart (2007). For the more scholarly, see Ahmed (1976). See also Ahmed (1983); Beattie (2002); Roe (2010); Tripodi (2011); Warren (2000); Johnson (2011). Johnson has also written a book on the 1897 revolt with the promising words 'Pashtun Perspectives' in the title. But the evidence he provides (letters of mullahs who led the attacks that were presented in colonial accounts and circulated by the press at the time) leaves the basic construction of the event intact and in keeping with the dominant narrative even while it may attempt at a more sympathetic way of understanding the motives in the revolt (see Johnson 2009).

25. The following are examples of the writings that have emerged from the framework of counter-insurgency aimed largely to be useful to the US and other Western powers engaged in military operations in Afghanistan: Jones (2010); Williams (2008); Tripodi (2008); Striegher (2013); Qazi (2011); Peceny and Bosin (2011); Johnson (2013); Jagadish (2009); Hoffman (2009); Hilali (2013); Egnell (2010); Catignani (2012).

26. An exception within the literature on the revolt is David Edwards' examination of the role of the 'Mad Mullah of Swat' within the 1897 uprising, in particular the relationship between the moral authority of the mullahs and the reason for the failure of the revolt. While Edwards' focus is different from mine and, as he claims himself, the evidence presented not conclusive, he does raise important questions such as pointing to the internal factors that

may have undermined the Mullah's chances of success in the revolt (Edwards 1996).

27. While there have been some attempts to critique this (Hanifi 2011; Hopkins 2008), such efforts have not yet extended to colonial military history of the North-West Frontier. The postcolonial Pukhtun has not yet come into being.

28. See Stoler (2002). In this article, Stoler points out that scholars need to move from 'archive-as-source to archive-as-subject'. Her advice is primarily aimed at anthropologists turning to history; however, historians who are engaged in using the archive as a source for evidence need to do both as the archive cannot be dismissed for writing colonial history.

29. By 1897, a complex political machinery existed on the Frontier. Until 1878, dealings with the trans-frontier tribesmen were conducted by the deputy commissioners of the six districts who were under the two commissioners of Peshawar and Derajat, who in turn acted under the orders of the Punjab Government. In 1878, Khyber became a political agency when a special officer was appointed there. In 1892, Kurram became an agency and in 1895 the political agency of Malakand was created, also known as Dir, Swat and Chitral Agency. In 1895–96, political agencies were created in North and South Waziristan. All these reported to the Government of Punjab (GoP), except Malakand, which was placed directly under the Government of India (GoI). The GoP was supposed to carry out the policy formulated by the GoI. The communication between the political agents, their superiors, Punjab and the GoI, which further reported to the secretary of state in London, is contained in thousands of telegrams, letters and reports. The India Office Library contains documents (described more fully in the Bibliography) that provide information about how the higher level of this chain of command functioned. However, it is the Proceedings of the Government of India (PGoI) and the Proceedings of the Government of Punjab (PGoP) that contain confidential and secret documents that provide a detailed and comprehensive view as to how the British functioned on the Frontier. The Foreign Frontier (FF) branch of these Proceedings can be found in the India Office Records, British Library (IOR/BL), London, but the crucial documents are mostly contained in the Secret Frontier (Sec F) branch and the K.W. (Keep With) attached with the files. These are contained mostly in the NAI, Delhi, the DoA, Peshawar, and to a lesser extent in the Punjab Government Archives, Civil Secretariat, Lahore. While there is an overlap in much of the material, there are documents which are only to be found in one place. Often it is these documents that provide the missing link.

30. Trial on Madda Khel Prisoners, 27 December 1897, PGoI, Sec F, September 1898, NAI.

1

MAPPING THE FRONTIER
The Making of an Imperial Geography

The North-West Frontier was an imperial creation. Yet, it was never stable and neither was it easy to define. Throughout the nineteenth century, through all the policy debates and within the imperial literature, it remained difficult to define. Since there was no clear boundary and there was a refusal to accept the geographic barrier of the Indus as the boundary, the imperial question of the Frontier was largely fought in policy matters about imperial expansion and limits of Empire. Part of the imperial problem of defining the 'North-West Frontier' as an ideal and a practice arose from resistance to expansion. Thus mapping, demarcating and imperial debates were continual projects of rule in the trans-Indus borderland.

British policy in the North-West Frontier in the nineteenth century has been interpreted as one of non-interference or close-border policy until 1878, and a more active forward policy from 1880 onwards. The official axiom underlying both policies was non-annexation. However, there was a huge disjuncture between stated policy and actions on the ground. While the close-border policy (also known as 'masterly inactivity' by its critics) claimed non-interference and a desire for peace, numerous military punitive expeditions were sanctioned against the tribes and heavy fines imposed on them in this period. In the 1880s, the colonial government became more aggressive while still claiming non-interference and non-annexation. The Durand Line, delineating spheres of influence between Afghanistan and British India, was established as the new boundary in 1893. Through the 1890s, roads were opened and military outposts and garrisons established from Zhob to Chitral. Although the GoI officially maintained that it had no desire to annex the Frontier and only wanted to foster close and friendly relations with the tribes, by 1896 George White, commander-in-chief, summed up the forward policy of the last decade candidly, '...the Gomal has been traversed by our troops from Domandi to its eastern gate, and has since been rendered safe by the *conquest and occupation of Waziristan*: the Tochi has been annexed and direct communication opened between it and Bannu'.[1] All this time the colonial authorities continued to represent to Whitehall that they in no way desired annexation.

INVENTING THE NORTH-WEST FRONTIER (1849–89)

In 1849 the British annexed Punjab from the Sikhs and as a result got control of the trans-Indus Frontier districts of Hazara, Peshawar, Kohat, Bannu, Dera Ismail Khan and Dera Ghazi Khan. Historically, the Indus River, 1,800 miles long, marked the boundary between India and Central Asia. 'For a thousand years the influence of Hinduism has stopped at its banks; geographically, culturally, and ethnographically India is the country "south-east of the Indus and south of the Himalayas"' (Swinson 1967: 15). While India stops at the Indus, the plains continue for another 50 miles. The edge of the plains or the trans-Frontier districts came to mark the administered boundary. The problem for the British, as they laid claim to these districts, was that this administered border line had never been clearly defined. After the British took over the trans-Frontier districts, the line of frontier was

> held to extend from a point on the River Jhelum, half-way between the hill sanitaria of Abbotabad and Murree, running due north with the Kaghan ranges into the high Himalayas, nearly to Chilas, and then descending to the south till it touches the Indus where that river emerges from the hills at Torbeyla (Griffin 1883: 1–2).

Lepel Griffin, secretary to the GoP, acknowledged in a report that this frontier line was not strictly defined and 'the boundaries shown on maps is merely that of the topographical survey, the limits of which were influenced by considerations of departmental convenience, and not of general policy' (Griffin 1883: 2). It was also recognised that the Sikhs had possessed little influence in the trans-Indus tracts and their administration there had been of the loosest type. Between this ill-defined administrative border line and Afghanistan lay a mountainous terrain that extended from Chitral and the Pamirs in the north to the Sulaiman Mountains and the Gomal Pass in the south, and was inhabited largely by the Pukhtun tribes. Ethnographically and geographically, the area had close ties with Afghanistan. The Pukhtuns speak the same language as Afghans and use the term 'Afghan' or 'Pukhtun' interchangeably when referring to themselves.[2] Politically, the Pukhtuns have been independent, while acknowledging a loose allegiance to Kabul. The Pukhtuns are organised on an intensely democratic basis and do not have a stable institution of political authority:

> Most tribes, it is true, recognize certain groups of *maliks* and elders as representatives of the tribe in dealing with tribal questions; they are not, however, invested with authority in any form. Real authority rests with the whole body of tribesmen, and the agreements or decisions reached by the *maliks* are frequently repudiated by the junior members of the tribe (Barton 1939: 18).

Law in Pukhtun society is determined by a code of honour referred to as Pukhtunwali. The main institutions of Pukhtunwali are (a) Badal: revenge or vendetta; (b) Melmastia: hospitality to guests; (c) Nanawatai: law of asylum, especially when an enemy comes to sue for peace; (d) Jirga: tribal assembly of elders that is called on to decide conflicts and regulate issues.[3]

During the first three decades after they took over Punjab, the British recognised the independence of the tribes and claimed that they sought no territorial aggrandisement. Their main goal was to secure peace and order on the Punjab Frontier, or as Richard Temple, secretary to the chief commissioner, stated in 1856, the British government '*only* wants, and is resolved to have, tranquility on the Frontier' (Temple 1856: 57; emphasis in original).

Administration of the trans-Frontier territory was under the jurisdiction of the GoP. The three northern districts of Hazara, Peshawar and Kohat formed the commissioner-ship of Peshawar, and the three southern ones of Bannu, Dera Ismail Khan and Dera Ghazi Khan that of the Derajat. The commissioner of Peshawar, under the lieutenant governor, also conducted negotiations with the Kabul court. The Punjab government never had a policy of its own towards Kabul and merely carried out the policy laid out by the GoI. Each district was governed by a deputy commissioner, who reported to the commissioner of the division. The control of the civil, political and police arrangements of the districts of their division lay with the commissioners, under the direct orders of the Punjab government. In these early decades, the district commissioners also dealt with issues pertaining to the independent tribes across the border, as no special agency existed until 1878 for dealing with the tribal areas.

While it was claimed in the first few decades that the government desired nothing other than peace on its border, no less than 38 military expeditions were undertaken against the tribes during this time (see Table 1.1). These expeditions were also called 'butcher and bolt' or 'burn and scuttle'. If all the British government wanted was peace on the border and had no territorial aggrandisement in mind, why were these expeditions undertaken? The authorities justified that these were forced upon them due to the depredations committed by the independent tribes in British territory and against British subjects. This claim, which formed the basis of Punjab policy in the Frontier areas, has remained largely unquestioned. For example, Davies, who had access to some of the early British documents and whose book is considered a significant work on the Frontier, wrote:

> Every endeavour was made to cultivate friendly relations, but, when kindness and conciliation failed, when the tribesmen continued to murder our subjects and to harass our borders, then the ultimate sanction was force. It was our bounden duty to protect our own; and for this reason, and this alone, can punitive expeditions be considered justifiable (Davies 1932: 25).

Richard Temple, secretary to the chief commissioner of Punjab, wrote a report in 1855 on the relations of the British government with the tribes on the Frontier. This document has become a crucial source for the history of Britain's initial encounters on the Frontier and is referred to repeatedly. Therefore, it is important to discuss some

Table 1.1: Military expeditions against tribes (1849–79)

S. No.	*Year*	*Tribe*	*Type of Expedition*	*Troops Employed*
1	1849	Yusufzai	British	1,500
2	1849	Baizais	British	2,300
3	1850	Afridis	Independent	3,200
4	1851	Miranzai	British	2,050
5	1851–52	Mohmands	Independent	1,597
6	1852	Mohmands	Independent	700
7	1852	Ranizais	Independent	3,270
8	1852	Utman Khel	Independent	2,200
9	1852	Darwesh Khel Wazirs	Independent	1,500
10	1852	Kaghan	British	850
11	1853	Hassanzais	Independent	3,800
12	1853	Shiranis	Independent	2,800
13	1853	Kasranis	Independent	600
14	1853	Afridis	Independent	1,500
15	1854	Michni Mohmands	Independent	1,600
16	1855	Miranzai	British	3,700
17	1855	Rabia Khel Orakzais	Independent	2,300
18	1856	Turis	Independent	4,896
19	1857	Bozdar	Independent	2,640
20	1857	Yusufzais Border	Independent and British	3,015
21	1858	Hindustani Fanatics	Independent	4,877
22	1859	Kabul Khel Wazirs	Independent	5,237
23	1860	Mahsuds	Independent	6,796
24	1863–64	Hindustani Fanatics	Independent	9,000
25	1866	British villages of Utman Khel	British	4,182
26	1868	Black Mountain Tribes	Independent	12,544
27	1869	Bizoti Orakzais	Independent	2,038
28	1872	Dauris	Independent	1,786

(contd)

Table 1.1 (contd)

S. No.	*Year*	*Tribe*	*Type of Expedition*	*Troops Employed*
29	1877	Jowaki Afridis	Independent	1,750
30	1877–78	Jowaki Afridis	Independent	7,400
31	1878	Utman Khel	Independent	280
32	1878	Ranizais	Independent	860
33	1878	Utman Khel	Independent	875
34	1878	Zakha Khel Afridis	Independent	2,500
35	1878	Powindahs, Sulaiman Khels	Independent	640
36	1879	Zakha Khel Afridis	Independent	3,750
37	1879	Mohmands	Independent	600
38	1879	Zaimukht	Independent	3,226

Source: Proceedings of the Government of India, Secret Frontier, 1889, National Archives of India.

Note: The British referred to tribes within the administered territories as 'British' and tribes beyond the administered line as 'Independent'. Therefore, the type of expedition has been classified as 'British' or 'Independent'.

points that are contained in his report. Describing the conduct of the tribes towards the British, he charges them with the following:

> They have kept up old quarrels, or picked new ones, with our subjects in the Plains and Valleys near the Frontier; they have descended from the Hills and fought these battles out in our Territory: they have plundered and burnt our villages and slain our subjects; they have committed minor robberies and isolated murders without number; they have often levied black mail from our villages; they have intrigued with the disaffected everywhere, and tempted our loyal subjects to rebel, and they have for ages regarded the Plain as their preserve and its inhabitants as their game. When inclined for cruel sport, they sally forth to rob and murder and occasionally to take prisoners into captivity for ransom. They have fired upon our own Troops, and even killed our own Officers in our own Territories. They give an asylum to every mal-content or proclaimed criminal, who can escape from British justice. They traverse at will in our Territories, enter

> our villages, trade in our markets; but few British subjects, and no servant of the British Government, would dare to enter their country on any account whatever (Temple 1856: 56–57).

In contrast, according to Temple, the British government recognised their independence, claimed that it sought no fiscal or territorial aggrandisement, did not extend its jurisdiction beyond the old limits of the Sikh dominions, abstained from interference in or connexion with their affairs, threw its markets open to them, and so on. In other words, the conduct of the British towards the tribes was one of 'kindness' and 'conciliation'.

> But when kindness, conciliation and confidence, all fail; when outrages from their serious character, or from their constant repetition, exceed the bounds of toleration; when the blood of our subjects cries from the ground; when our Territory has been invaded, and our sovereign rights flagrantly violated, and all this in the utter absence of provocation; then we either make reprisals from, or lay an embargo upon, or use military force against, the offending Tribe or section of Tribe (ibid.: 58–59).

British policy for several decades was based upon the following system. When reprisals were made, cattle and men were seized, property detained as security and men as hostages. A message was sent to the tribe and if they did not come to terms, then the property would be sold. During an embargo, the mouths of passes belonging to the tribe would be closed and watched to the extent possible. Any person and property belonging to the tribe in British territory would be seized and markets would be closed for the tribe. Finally, the government would resort to military expeditions. These entailed destroying houses, seizing cattle and grain, and burning crop fields. Needless to say, the entire tribe would be punished for the offence of a few. Temple claimed that these punitive expeditions were 'absolutely necessary' and justified them thus:

> If reprisals and embargo prove insufficient, or cannot be adopted in a particular case, as may sometimes happen, then what but an expedition remains? When an expedition is undertaken, then if the enemy were to assemble in force and take up a position and offer battle, they could be attacked and defeated, and their discomfiture might suffice as a punishment, without any

> further measure. In that event the affair would be conducted after the manner of regular warfare. In civilized warfare, force is directed against the armed enemy and his defensible positions, but not against his country and subjects, who may be morally unconcerned in the hostilities and innocent of offence. *But this is not civilized warfare;* the enemy does not possess Troops that stand to be attacked, nor defensible posts to be taken, nor innocent subjects to be spared. He has only rough Hills to be penetrated, robber fastnesses to be scaled, and dwellings containing people, *all of them to a man, concerned in hostilities. There is not a single man of them who is innocent*... [Their] villages and grain are the resources and sinews of guerilla warfare and the basis of operations. They are as much the property of the enemy as the stores, convoys, arms and munitions belonging to an army in the field. The latter would *never* be spared; why should the former? (Temple 1856: 60)

The reason for these expeditions was that they were forced upon the British due to the offences committed by the tribes against British subjects while, in these early decades, the British abstained from interference. This was what the authorities claimed and what later writers have accepted as well. Inside these early imperial explanations we witness built-in limits as to how Empire was functioning. Many of these offences and crimes are described by Temple. However, his discussion of these offences and depredations clearly establishes that many tribes objected to the enforcement of the administrative boundary and that it led to the creation of an artificial division, which was resisted not only by the independent hill tribes but also by tribes living in the plains now regarded as British subjects.

Through the example of salt, an issue that arose repeatedly, and would be represented as one of the grievances of the Afridis in their attack on the Khyber in 1897, we can examine Empire through the layer of imperial explanations that focused on tribal raiding and violence as a cause for imperial punitive expeditions.[4] The issue centred around the British takeover of the trans-Indus salt mines situated in the Southern Khattak hills near the villages of Bahadurkhel, Kurruck and Lutumur. The Sikhs never managed these mines at all and farmed them out to some local chief and left him to collect what he could. However, after 1849, the British seized possession of these mines and fixed a duty on the salt excavated at the mines. Temple claimed that this duty was fixed 'not so much with a view to obtaining revenue as to asserting our sovereign rights in this respect' (Temple 1856: 50), and reasoned that the tax should not press upon the hill tribes. However, he described many offences committed by different tribes that clearly were connected with the salt issue. In February 1850, a party of sappers and miners working on a road were 'cut to pieces' by some Afridis. After stating that the chief cause for this was probably the 'innate ferocity' of the Afridis and their distrust of a civilised government, Temple then alludes to the fact that it was supposed by some that the increased taxation of salt and the construction of a road through the Kohat Pass were circumstances of provocation. While he admits that the British salt tax 'was indeed higher than the former taxes', this did not seriously injure the Afridis as 'this was the only duty'. However, the Afridis saw things differently and would again and again bring up grievances connected with the salt tax. Again the Kabul Khel Wazirs in the autumn of 1850 launched an 'audacious attack on Buhadoorkheyl and its salt-mines. For this purpose they assembled in considerable force and induced many of the Khuttuk villages round Buhadoorkheyl itself to league with them' (Temple 1856: 29). Temple dismisses that they should have a grievance with regard to salt, but then says the following:

> Being, like the Afreedees, largely engaged in the salt-carrying trade, they doubtless had perceived the political importance of the mines, and the great influence which accrued to the British Government from the possession of them. For the same reasons the Khuttuks envied their masters the command of these valuable resources, and would have been glad, if in co-operation with the Wuzeerees, they could have secured the possession (Temple 1856: 30).

In fact, it was not just the hill tribes but some of the plains tribes too that committed offences that clearly stemmed from the salt issue. After annexation, the British not only took over control of the salt mines but also established a Preventive Line along the left bank of the Indus, as far as British jurisdiction extended, to prevent trans-Indus salt from crossing into the Punjab. In autumn of 1851, Mr Carne, the uncovenanted head of the customs department, wanted to visit this border with the view to extend this line. The board of administration objected and warned him against visiting the area. Against this advice, Carne proceeded to reconnoitre the border anyway. He and another gentleman with him were murdered by a band of armed Hassanzais. The Hassanzais were a British subject tribe from the plains (*Frontier and Overseas Expeditions from India*, 1: 102).

This is important to note as it calls into question the hard and fast difference between the hill and plains tribes set up by the British and generally reinforced within historiography.[5] It also disrupts the imperial explanation for expeditions against hill tribes—protection of British subjects, that is, plains tribes from the predatory hill tribes. Clearly, several tribes of the plains and the hills who were engaged in the salt mines and salt trade resented British control of the mines, the raising of the salt tax and the establishment of the preventive line. Many other 'offences' committed by the tribes in these early years continuously call into question the distinction between the hill and plains tribes that was reinforced through claiming the administrative line as a boundary.

Members belonging to the same tribe could be found both in the hills and the plains. Tribes moved back and forth, especially the hill tribes. For example, the Wazirs would move to the plains and cultivate there in the colder months and as the heat approached they would reap their crops and retire into the mountains. Of course, tribes were also closely connected by marriage and other alliances. Describing the people of Buner, Temple says that they seemed to be on good terms with their neighbours, the people of Swat. 'In 1849 they aided some British subjects at Loondkhor, in Eusufzye, who refused to pay revenue' (Temple 1856: 7). This incident and several others that he describes bring to light the fact that many expeditions were not undertaken to 'protect the British subjects' from the savage hill tribes but against these British subjects themselves who resisted British encroachment and the enforcement of the administrative line. Further, it is clear that both the hill and the plains tribes resisted the enforcement of the administrative line and regarded British presence as a political encroachment. The alternative for the British was either to retreat to the Indus, to push forward or to stay where they were. Despite figures who argued for holding the line at Indus, which was a natural boundary, the British stayed put as at this point they could not move forward. The strategic pros and cons of the Indus Frontier were much debated. But finally the argument against holding the boundary at Indus came down to the fact that withdrawal or retreat would mean a 'loss of prestige'. And at the time they did not have the resources to move forward. In this early period, we see Empire grappling with its internal limits.

Interestingly, even the most ardent advocates of the close-border policy, who thought it was wiser not to move forward, later turned apologetic and defended their policy by arguing lack of resources. Thus, in 1897, Sir Lepel Griffin defended the policy adopted by the Punjab government in the early years from its critics, the Forward men. Referring to one in particular, he stated:

> He considered that the *civis Britannicus* should be able to wander over the Afridi hills as securely as in Bond Street, a much-to-be-desired ideal. But these things cost money; and the Punjab Government had no money. It ruled the poorest and most backward province in India with a revenue inadequate to meet the necessary expenses of a civilized administration. Every rupee for frontier defence was squeezed with the greatest difficulty out of the Government of India. We had neither roads nor railways. I have ridden up and down the frontier many times from Hazara to Sind, and have a vivid remembrance of the stony or sandy track and the slippery mud of the Derajat, impracticable in wet weather for guns or camels. And, as the Punjab Government was poor it was unable, even if it had wished, to favour a forward policy, which is a luxury for the rich (Griffin 1897: 510).

So for the time being, the British remained where they were and claimed that their policy was one of non-interference in the 'countries beyond' and towards the independent hill tribes. These debates and tensions bring out competing definitions of Empire that demonstrate its internal limits which it was attempting to combat.

THE FORWARD POLICY: IMPERIAL CONTRADICTIONS

In 1886, Commander-in-Chief of India Frederick Roberts declared in a memorandum that the advance of Russia in Central Asia called for a new policy. At stake was the defence not just of the North-West Frontier but of the Indian Empire itself. It was essential for the British to have command of the northern passes and to be able to see 'the other side of the hill'. Roberts proposed that it was essential in any scheme for the defence of the North-West Frontier to have the tribes who occupied the intervening countries as allies:

> It is of such vital importance that we should get hold of the tribes, that I strongly advise a reconsideration of the policy which has guided us during the last 38 years, and which has resulted in our knowing little more about our neighbours in the hills, that we did when first we occupied the Panjab, and in our being absolutely uncertain as to whose side they would be upon, in the impending struggle between Russia and England. Such an unsatisfactory state of affairs should not be allowed to continue longer.[6]

Thus ensued a series of correspondence which led to a debate between the GoI and Punjab on the state of affairs in the Frontier and the called for departure in policy. The new more 'active' policy that the GoI insisted upon adopting has been called the forward policy. It is important to consider this policy in some detail as it was undertaken in the years preceding the 1897 tribal revolt and was viewed by some politicians, especially those of the opposite party, and by some scholars as one of the causes of the revolt.[7]

The new policy called for bringing the tribes that inhabited the Frontier region under British influence and enlisting them as allies for the purposes of imperial defence. The tribes that the British were most concerned with consisted of the 'independent or semi-independent communities' that held the 'chain of almost impenetrable mountains' immediately outside the British administrative frontier line. The British divided these tribes into three broad divisions. The first consisted of people of Dard origin who had no affinity of race with the Pathans though they were Muslim. The second division stretched from Dir and Kohistan on the north to the country of the Kakars on the south and was inhabited by the Pathans. The third division consisted of Baluch tribes and stretched from the Kakar country to the sea and westward reaching as far as the Persian Frontier.

It was the second or the Pathan division that concerned the British most as they regarded it as being the strongest and most important of the three:

> It contains several great tribes, such as the Afridis, Orakzais, and Waziris, inhabiting a rough mountainous country; and with the exception of a few non-Pathan Swatis and Kohistanis in the north, and some of the softer Pathan tribes in the south, all its million and a quarter or more of inhabitants belong to hard untamed races. They are fanatical, brave, fairly armed, and inured to hardship and warfare from their childhood; and they can turn out at least 200,000 very formidable fighting men.[8]

British relations with Pathan tribes were conducted, up to this point, by officers of the Punjab frontier districts, with the aid of two special political officers—Colonel Warburton stationed in the Khyber and an assistant stationed at Thal.

The conditions in the first and third divisions were viewed by the GoI as being fairly satisfactory. The Gilgit Agency was re-established in 1889 and this gave the British effective political control of the first division.[9] In 1877, British troops occupied Quetta, and the Baluchistan Agency was established. The Agency consisted of a governor-general's agent and five other officers. Again, Baluchistan had been brought under political and military control. As the viceroy declared in 1889: 'The third, or Baluch division, is in hand already. We have run railways and roads through the country, and are managing it, directly or indirectly, with considerable success.'[10]

The problem lay with the Pathan division:

> With regard to the second or Pathan division, we find a totally different state of things. Except at one or two points, e.g., Kurram and the Khyber, our officers cannot cross the frontier; the tribes are thoroughly independent; and our own territory is frequently troubled by their raids. Except the Khyber we have no roads, and of course we have no railways, through their country; and though some of their men enlist in our regiments, and many live on our side of the border, we cannot be said to have gained any controlling influence over them.[11]

This was the central issue that is strewn all across the imperial historical record. It also demonstrates internal limits and the inability of Empire to accept those limits. Many in the GoI thought it appalling that British control stopped at the foothills and the area beyond was off-limits. Of course now the question seemed to have gained a certain legitimacy—as any forward move could be justified on the ground of its being necessary for imperial defence. Various schemes were discussed.[12] Underlying the discussions lay the sentiment on the part of those in India who desired an active policy on the Frontier that the Punjab government was critical of a policy that advocated annexation of the tribes beyond the administered boundary.

After much internal debate, the GoI arrived upon the conclusion that at this stage it was best to effect the policy of pushing British influence across the frontier through the Punjab government. On 17 October 1889, a letter was sent to the authorities in Punjab. The letter again emphasised:

> The Government of India cannot consider its present relations with the trans-frontier tribes on the Punjab border as either suitable or satisfactory, and the absence of any friendly understanding between them and the neighbouring British Officers may at any time prove a source of serious danger and anxiety. The country within a day's ride of one of our most important garrisons is indeed almost a *terra incognita*, and there is no security for British life a few miles beyond the border. Punitive expeditions have been frequent, but have been attended with very few permanent results, and there is probably no other spot in the world where, after 35 years of peaceful occupation, a great civilized power has obtained so little influence over its semi-savage neighbours or has acquired so little knowledge of them.[13]

In effecting this policy, the GoI felt that it was important that British control be established in the Kurram valley and that lines of communication, such as the roads through Dir to Chitral and through the Tochi and the Gomal passes, be thoroughly explored. At the same time, the GoI stated that 'nothing in the way of annexation was required or should be attempted nor should any step be taken likely to lead to a collision'.[14] The execution of this policy would be entrusted to the GoP and therefore the views of the lieutenant governor of Punjab upon the subject were requested.

The GoP sent a lengthy letter and a memorandum recorded by J. B. Lyall, the lieutenant governor of Punjab, in reply to the GoI's communication on the departure in policy. Lyall protested the strong terms in which the letter of GoI described the defects in the relations of the Punjab government with the tribes and condemned its system of management. He then proceeded to explain the system of the Punjab government in dealing with the trans-Frontier tribes and why it had adopted such a system. The tribes not only of the second division but of the border districts of Peshawar, Kohat, Bannu and a strip of Dera Ismail Khan were ethnographically part of Afghanistan. The North-West Frontier Gazetteer of 1887 and certain maps prepared by the GoI had been prepared upon the theory that Pathan border tribes were distinct in race from the Pushtu-speaking tribes to the country west of them—the latter being Afghans, while the former were not—and that the country they occupied was not geographically or ethnologically part of Afghanistan. This, he alleged, was a 'new theory, and one entirely without foundation'.[15] Not only the hill lands of the border tribes but also the open fertile lands that now formed the districts of Peshawar, Kohat and Bannu were politically part of Afghanistan till the Sikhs annexed them. He pointed out that:

> The fact that these border tribes are independent or semi-independent is nothing new; they were so when the Afghan boundary extended to the Indus, and when there were Governors of the Amir of Kabul in Peshawar and Kohat, and they were so still earlier when the whole of Afghanistan was part of the Mogul Empire. And, in fact, it is not only these border tribes which are semi-independent; the same position has generally been held by the mountain tribes in most parts of Afghanistan. The Amirs or rulers of the country only fully held, taxed, and governed the more fertile and comparatively open tracts, while the mountain tribes were mainly left to govern themselves owing to the difficulty of coercing them, and the little revenue to be got out of them. This position was not understood by the ruler of the country or the mountain tribes to imply that the country of the latter was not part of his kingdom, or that they were completely independent of him. On the contrary, as I said before, these mountain tribes, including those which we call border tribes, used to say that they were Afghans, and the

> Amir of Kabul their Amir, though they repudiated his right to levy taxes from them, or to appoint officers to interfere in their internal affairs.[16]

Lyall argued that this new departure in policy would be regarded by the Amir as 'unfair and aggressive' and the same view would be taken by his subjects and tribes on the border. He agreed that from a military point of view it was desirable to be able to depend upon the goodwill and assistance of the border tribes in case of a Russian advance; however, he pointed out that 'if at such a crisis the Amir and his Afghans are hostile, or even only unfriendly and distrustful, our hold on these border clans will in my opinion be exceedingly precarious'.[17] The GoI acknowledged in reply to Punjab that

> the cultivation of closer intercourse with the tribes, whose territory borders upon that of the Amir, may at times give rise to troublesome questions between our officers and those of the Amir, or between the tribes owing allegiance to the British Government and those connected with Kabul; and may be viewed with apprehension by a ruler as suspicious of foreign intervention as his Highness.[18]

Despite this admission, the GoI was adamant upon pursuing the new policy and reiterated that recent affairs had 'rendered it absolutely necessary to abandon the policy of non-intervention in the affairs of the frontier tribes'.[19]

In 1896, the GoI reviewed with satisfaction the results of the forward policy. Commander-in-Chief George White summed up the progress made since 1889:

> 1) Zhob has been brought under our protection; the long dreaded Sherani hills including the Takht-i-Suleiman, at which the Punjab Frontier Force had been looking for 40 years since the annexation of the Punjab, have been turned and the tribes, who formerly found safe sanctuary in their fastnesses, have been dominated and brought under control: 2) the Gomal has been traversed by our troops from Domandi to its eastern gate, and has since been rendered safe by 3) the conquest and occupation of Waziristan: 4) the Tochi has been annexed and direct communication opened between it and Bannu: 5) the

> Dir-Chitral route has not only been opened as a tribal postal route to Chitral, but a British right of way has been established and British forces have moved from the Peshawar valley to Chitral, and from Chitral to the Peshawar valley along roads held on our interests by tribal levies. ... 7) the Durand Mission has settled a line of influence between Afghanistan and India, and it now remains to us but to safeguard the interests thus secured to us against Afghan repudiation of a bargain which entailed on us the payment of an extra subsidy of six lakhs a year, besides gifts of arms and numerous other benefits.[20]

These forward moves were undertaken in order to foster close and friendly relations with the tribes so as to render India safe in event of foreign aggression. At the same time, the GoI continued to declare that it desired in no way to interfere with the independence of the tribes or to annex their territories. Underneath this imperial contradiction was the fact that the forward policy allowed for the expansion of Empire on the ground but one that was not declared or acknowledged as such.

NOTES

1. G. S. White, 15 June 1896, 'Administration of the Frontier Districts of the Punjab and the Management of the Trans-Frontier Tribes', PGoI, Sec F, NAI, August 1896; emphasis added. The full quote from White is given later in the chapter.

2. The British referred to them as Pathans. The word Pathan is viewed to be a corruption but is still used at times, though Pukhtun is the correct term.

3. While this evokes a static and fixed code of colonial cultures that has come under scrutiny in recent decades, it is generally presented as such in colonial and much of the subsequent literature on the Frontier. Interestingly, during my fieldwork in the Frontier, it was almost always presented as such by the many Pukhtuns whom I interviewed and others whom I spoke with and got to know.

4. In his thorough and insightful study on irrigation in the Indus basin, David Gilmartin's discussion of water on the Baloch Frontier highlights inter-tribal relationships and flows surrounding the resource, and thus also challenges the division between the plains and trans-Frontier spaces. See Gilmartin (2015).

5. See, for example, Ahmed (1980).

6. Frederick Roberts, 'Extract from a Memorandum on the Desirability of Making a Military Road through the Kohat Pass', 17 August 1886, PGoI, Foreign Frontier (FF), NAI, 1887.

7. See Parliamentary debates 1898 (IOR/BL) when the opposition charged the government's policy as a cause of the revolt. See also Davies (1932) and Ahmed (1976).

8. Lord Lansdowne, 'Proposed New Arrangements for the Administration of the N. W. Frontier Districts and the Management of the Trans-Frontier Tribes', PGoI, Sec F, NAI, 1889.

9. For an account of the British in Gilgit, see Keay (1979).

10. Lansdowne, 'Proposed New Arrangements'.

11. Ibid.

12. As far back as 1877, Lord Lytton had proposed a great Frontier Chief Commissionership to deal with the trans-Frontier tribes and to administer the frontier districts of Punjab. In another proposal, the commander-in-chief recommended that the political work of the Frontier should be placed under the orders of a single high officer reporting directly to the GoI. In one way or another, all these schemes revolved around removing the authority of the Punjab government so that the GoI had more power.

13. 'From—The Secretary to the GoI, Foreign Department, To—The Secretary to the GoP', 17 October 1889, PGoI, Sec F, NAI, 1889.

14. Ibid.

15. J. B. Lyall, 'Confidential Note, "Arrangements for the Better Administration of the Punjab Frontier Districts and Management of the Trans-Frontier Tribes"', PGoI, Sec F, NAI, October 1890. This imperial debate and Lyall's opposition to the GoI's deliberate misclassification is a direct and vivid example of colonial knowledge being produced in order to create a basis for justifying a policy of expansion and for laying claim to the Amir's territories. While there is a substantial and growing literature on colonial knowledge since Said's *Orientalism* (1978) and Cohn's *Colonialism and Its Forms of Knowledge* (1996), of related relevance here are Peers (2005) and Hopkins (2008: 11–33). For wide-ranging case studies that present different approaches to the study of colonial knowledge, see Roque and Wagner (2012).

16. Lyall, 'Confidential Note'.

17. Ibid.

18. 'From—W. J. Cuningham, Esq., Offg. Secretary to the GoI, Foreign Department, To—H. C. Fanshawe, Esq., Offg. Chief Secretary to the GoP', 16 June 1890, PGoI, Sec F, NAI, October 1890.

19. 'To—The Right Hon'ble Viscount Cross, G.C.B., Her Majesty's Secretary of State for India, From—Governor General in Council', 7 October 1890, PGoI, Sec F, NAI, October 1890.

20. White, 'Administration of the Frontier Districts of the Punjab'.

2

CONSTRUCTING THE 1897 REVOLT

Military Failures and Imperial Explanations

This chapter presents the official narrative of the attacks in Tochi, Swat and the Khyber that became public at the time.[1] This narrative has continued to be reproduced within the literature on the 1897 revolt.[2] Since this narrative has endured as the authoritative account of what occurred and is the basis for constituting the 1897 revolt in its historical version, it is important to consider it in some detail. How this account deals with the questions implicit within this narrative is examined critically. Also considered here are the questions that these accounts leave out. These unanswered questions are then taken up in the following three chapters.

THE 'MAIZAR OUTRAGE'

The attack in Maizar, a group of villages in Tochi in North Waziristan, is considered to be the first outbreak of the 1897 revolt on the North-West Frontier of India. On 10 June, a British military party was 'suddenly and treacherously' attacked in Maizar. This attack was considered by the British to have signalled the great tribal revolt of 1897 in the Frontier.

The British divided Waziristan into northern and southern Waziristan for political and administrative purposes. The main inhabitants of Waziristan are the Darwesh Khels, the Mahsuds, the Dauris and the Bhittanis. The Darwesh Khels and the Mahsuds are Wazirs proper, but the name now refers to the former; the latter call themselves 'Mahsid'. The country is rugged and mountainous with little fertile land. The Tochi valley and Spin plains are the only large areas suitable for cultivation (Figures 8 and 9). In 1895/96, the

Figure 8: Tochi Valley

Figure 9: Tochi River

political agencies of North and South Waziristan were established with headquarters in Datta Khel and Wana respectively.

The basic facts of what occurred in Maizar were presented as follows[3]: Mr H. W. Gee was the British political officer stationed in the Tochi valley. On 10 June 1897, Mr Gee went to Maizar with a large military escort—300 men from the 1st Sikhs Infantry and 1st Punjab Infantry, two guns of No. 6 Bombay Mountain Battery and twelve sabres of the 1st Punjab Cavalry. The object was to fix a site for a new military outpost and also to realise a fine that had been imposed upon the tribesmen some months back. The tribal maliks, the headmen through whom the British dealt with the tribes, showed every sign of friendship and food was provided for the officers and soldiers. After the meal, the troops were resting under some trees and the pipers of the 1st Sikhs started playing for the benefit of the villagers. Suddenly, a hubbub arose in the village, and from the top of a tower a man was seen to wave a sword. The villagers started clearing off and firing at once commenced on the troops. A 'desperate fight' occurred and the escort had to beat a retreat. The British troops were pursued for 4 miles until reinforced from the nearby military post of Datta Khel (see Figures 10 and 11). Casualties suffered by the British were heavy; three British officers, 22 men of the native ranks and two followers were killed, while three other British officers and 24 men were wounded.

The attack was perceived as a disaster and an embarrassment. A large military party that had gone well prepared was taken by surprise and had to beat a retreat. How were they caught off guard? Did they have no premonition of the attack? And what led the tribes to attack them in the first place? These were some of the immediate questions raised in the press as the attack became public.

Gee, who survived the attack, sent a telegram to the British authorities describing the attack as cowardly and treacherous. The troops were at rest, after lunch, when they were 'suddenly rushed by a large body of tribesmen' (*The Risings on the North-West Frontier* 1898: 3). Another report sent by authorities in Tochi stated that the cause of such treachery was not clear: 'The fact that they attacked a party who had just eaten food with them—contrary to all Pathan codes of honour—renders the matter additionally hard to explain' (ibid.: 9).

Figure 10: Entrance to Military Headquarters, Datta Khel

Note: The structure has been unaltered since 1897. This photograph was taken in 1995.

Figure 11: Inside Datta Khel Military Headquarters

Note: A few local levies lived here at the time of the author's visit in 1995.

However, what Gee concluded with certainty was that the attack was premeditated and had been carefully planned beforehand. Thus, the attack was established as being treacherous and provoked outrage from all quarters:

> The Madda Khel had deliberately planned the attack on Colonel Bunny's detachment and had carried it out in the most treacherous way. Their offence was clearly defined and their punishment needed to be exemplary. A tribal rising of the ordinary kind, or a raid upon an outpost, is not of material consequence in the borderland. Such disturbances are more or less to be expected whenever our troops occupy positions beyond the old frontier line. But the Maizar affair was of an entirely different complexion, for it involved a breach of hospitality and could only have been successful by cunningly contrived treachery (*The Risings on the North-West Frontier* 1898: 23).

This was the version that became public at the time. However, notwithstanding the 'treachery', there was criticism from the press because one of the main duties of a political officer in the Frontier was to gauge the attitude of the tribesmen. But the unpreparedness of Gee and his escort could be explained if the attack was so sudden and treacherous in nature that they were lulled into a feeling of security and then attacked. This is how contemporary accounts generally explained what happened. Thus, H. W. Mills, a contemporary British writer, stated:

> Correspondents wrote as if the Political Officer and the military officers with him at Maizar were imbeciles to have trusted the Madda Khel at all. Yet Colonel Bunny was an officer intimately acquainted with the Pathan character, thoroughly experienced in the manners and customs of frontier tribesmen, and generally cautious in his dealing with the tribesmen: but he must have been deceived by Sadda Khan's hospitality. ... It remained for a comparatively small section of the Darwesh Khel to break the peace at Maizar and to signalise its defiance of British authority by a piece of treachery unequalled on the frontier, and perfidy in setting at nought the laws of hospitality of a sort revolting even to Afghan sentiment (Mills 1897: 23).

The question of the failure of the political officer and the military expedition is subsumed here by dramatising treachery and invoking the code of hospitality. Consequentially imperial explanations function (in this case with the emphasis on 'treachery') to render the question of motive as irrelevant. The questions that would help us understand what occurred at Maizar start to be suppressed and we are left with an incomplete historical record. If the code of hospitality is a fixed inviolable code, as is suggested by this imperial understanding, then the logical question points towards the circumstances that would have led to this exceptional violation. Contemporary writers speculated on this question but did not really give an answer. The usual trope of 'fanaticism' was offered as an explanation since the attack took place during the month of Muharram. But Muharram is observed by Shia Muslims and the Madda Khels are Sunnis, so this view had to be discounted. Fanaticism is occasionally mentioned but its relation to the outbreak was never clearly established: 'Whether the Madda Khel were to any great extent influenced by fanaticism other than that due to the constant preaching of their Mullahs, cannot be said' (Mills 1897: 20). Lacking motives, even 'patriotism' was mentioned as a cause: 'In some quarters it was suggested that patriotism pure and simple had inspired the tribesmen to attack the escort, but it is difficult to realise the occasion for such hostility. The country has always, although within the sphere of our political influence, been treated with conspicuous leniency' (ibid.: 22). Almost all later writers have presented the attack at Maizar in a similar fashion. For example, Davies wrote: 'So treacherous was this attack, and so utterly at variance with the Pathan code of honour, that frontier officers found the greatest difficulty in ascertaining the exact cause' (1932: 93). In conclusion, he states:

> The relative importance of fanaticism, Afghan and other intrigues, and the feeling of unrest engendered by discontent at tribal allowances, as causes of the Maizar outrage, will perhaps never be definitely determined, but it seems certain that the exaggerated reports of this affair, disseminated by anti-British mullahs, did tend to affect the rest of the border—to some extent Maizar heralded the approaching storm (Davies 1932: 94).

This view of the 'Maizar outrage' as a sudden and treacherous attack has held till today. What caused such treachery is not answered clearly either by contemporary or later writers. Further, the facts presented regarding the attack itself raise the following questions: (a) If the object of the visit of Mr Gee and the military party was to 'realize' a fine, then why were the troops dining in the village and playing music for the benefit of the tribesmen? If the object was a friendly one, then why did the political officer take a big military escort with him? (b) Why were the officers and troops not better able to defend themselves? Their military performance did not go unnoticed: 'At first there was much murmuring in some quarters, and in Calcutta it was suggested that the escort had been utterly demoralized and that something like a *sauve qui* peut had followed' (Mills 1897: 16). Nevill raised the question more critically:

> The position taken up by the escort was, tactically speaking unsound; the attractions of shady trees for breakfast seem to have overridden more important considerations. The troops had arrived in Maizar nominally as an escort to the Political Officer, but practically to compel the payment of a fine which the tribesmen had resisted for a long time as, in their opinion unjust; consequently, the most hospitable of welcomes was hardly to be expected, and there must be a reason or motive for a phenomenon or action of an unnatural kind (Nevill 1912: 221).

There was also the question of ammunition failure and the fact that the gunners continued to fire blank:

> Artillery fire may be ineffective from a variety of causes, but when the cause is the use of blank, as in the example in question, it is almost certain that, so far from frightening the enemy, the only result will be to advertise the otherwise possibly unrecognized fact that the supply of shell is exhausted, or nearly so, and all the moral effect of the guns—their most valuable asset—will be lost (ibid.: 222).

Writing a few years after the attack, Nevill points to the unpreparedness of the troops as well as the fact that the reason for the attack remained deliberately ignored. In the process, the role of the political officers on the spot is also called into question. However, this line of questioning is not picked up in other writings about the Maizar attack. Rather than focus on the military failure of the escort, curiously enough, most writers instead applaud the 'gallantry' and 'admirable conduct' of the troops. What was admirable about troops beating a retreat?

Strangely, the retreat itself is turned into something admirable: 'With bullets raining upon them and with their British commanders all *hors de combat*, the retirement was carried out in the most orderly and admirable fashion' (Mills 1897: 16). The GoI officially endorsed this view. The commander-in-chief of the British Indian army recorded his appreciation of the heroic conduct of officers and men, and declared that 'the action was a deed of arms second to none in the annals of the British army'.[4] Later, rewards and medals of honour were bestowed on many of the officers and soldiers for their bravery.

The 'Maizar outrage' remained intact as a case of treachery that was 'contrary to all Pathan codes of honour', but the cause of such treachery was never really explained.

The next attacks occurred in Swat and have been viewed as part of an unexpected wave of fanaticism that swept through the Frontier and was inspired by a 'Mad Mullah'.

THE UPRISING IN SWAT: 'FANATICISM' AND A 'MAD MULLAH'

Swat takes its name from the river and comprises the valley that follows the course of the river from Panjkora to the village of Ain (Figure 12). The upper portion of the valley from Ain to Landakai is known as Bar (upper) Swat and from Landakai downwards to the village of Kalangai is known as Kuz (lower) Swat (*Frontier and Overseas Expeditions from India*, 1: 321). The Swat valley is fertile and highly cultivated. The inhabitants of Swat are the Akozais, a division of the Yusufzais tribe. The valley is divided into five districts, which receive their name from the five clans of the Akozais—Baizai, Ranizai, Khadakzai, Abazai and Khwazazai.

British troops entered Swat for the first time in 1895. They entered the country because they needed a passage to Chitral to help a besieged garrison there. At this time, the government announced to them that they only wanted right of passage to reach Chitral and had no intention of interfering in their country. However, the 'Swatis allowed their fanaticism to carry them away' (ibid.: 363) and opposed the British entering their country. In September 1895, an agency was instituted in Swat with headquarters at Malakand and a secondary

Figure 12: Swat Valley

post created at Chakdara. A levy system was established and increased allowances were granted to the Khans of Swat, foremost among them being Muhammad Sharif Khan, the Khan of Dir. The new arrangements appeared to be satisfactory and 'all signs of hostility on the part of the people quickly disappeared' (*Frontier and Overseas Expeditions from India*, 1: 363). In 1896, factional fights took place and some unrest was caused by the activities of the Khan of Dir. The mullahs and other religious leaders 'attempted to stir the fanaticism of the people, but no serious disturbance resulted; and the condition of the valley was on the whole satisfactory' (ibid.: 364). While there was some friction caused by factionalism early in 1897, Major Deane, the Political Agent in Swat, reported that the tribes had accepted their being under government influence in 'good spirit' (ibid.: 365). Nevill described the situation in Swat as such: 'After the conclusion of the Chitral Campaign, the arrangements made with the tribes inhabiting the Swat Basin were of so satisfactory a character, and the indications of a new era of unprecedented were so full of promise, that the gathering of a wave of fanaticism in this quarter was as unexpected as it was to be deplored' (Nevill 1912: 223). Viscount Fincastle, one of the officers posted in the Malakand, later wrote in a book:

> During the eighteen months that had elapsed since the occupation of the pass by our troops, life at the Malakand had flowed in the ordinary channels of a frontier post; leave was given to officers who could be spared from their duties, and the remainder of the garrison occupied their leisure hours with polo and other amusements. The 26th of July opened with no more eventful occurrences in prospect than the ordinary routine of the preceding months; it was little suspected that the apparent calm was to be so soon and so rudely disturbed (Fincastle and Elliot-Lockhart 1898: 27–28).

In the middle of July in 1897, some 'excitement' was caused in lower Swat by the appearance of a man called the 'Mad Mullah' who was attempting to 'arouse the fanaticism of the Swat tribes' and preach against the British, but according to these accounts, this was not thought to be important.

The basic facts of the attacks on Malakand and Chakdara have been presented as follows[5]: On the afternoon of 26 July, the officers from the Malakand and Chakdara posts played polo, unaware of any impending trouble. The villagers near the ground appeared 'quite friendly'. Towards evening, however, 'disquieting reports' of the Mad Mullah's movements reached Major Deane (*Frontier and Overseas Expeditions from India*, 1: 367). He requested Colonel Meiklejohn to hold troops in readiness and sent a telegram to Mardan for a reinforcement of troops. At this point it was reported that the Mullah was moving down the valley with a gathering of about 400 or 500 men. Further news indicated that the Mullah's gathering was increasing as he was joined by people from all the villages that he passed through. Colonel Meiklejohn arranged to despatch a force at midnight to hold the Amandara pass—a pass commanding the road to Chakdara, 5 miles from Malakand. His intention was to command the pass and to move the next day with the rest of his brigade to disperse the enemy. 'The astonishing rapidity, however, of the movements of the tribesmen, and the astounding manner in which their numbers grew, rendered these movements impossible' (Fincastle and Elliot-Lockhart 1898: 30). Close to 10 pm, reports were received that the Fakir was close at hand with a large number of men and intended to attack the Malakand. The alarm was sounded and the troops had hardly reached their positions when the onslaught started.

The advancing tribes drove back the piquets, captured the serai, overran the bazaar within British lines and penetrated the Commissariat godown, killing the Commissariat officer Lieutenant Manley. The Crater Camp held by Sappers and Miners was repeatedly attacked and in one of these charges the tribes succeeded in capturing a large quantity of ammunition. The attack lasted till 4.30 am when the tribesmen retired, carrying off their dead and wounded. British casualties during this night were one officer and 22 non-commissioned officers and men killed, and five officers (of whom two died subsequently) and 31 men wounded.

The next day, troops in the North Camp, which had not been seriously attacked the previous night, were sent in pursuit of the enemy. The troops had not got very far when they saw a large gathering of the tribesmen advancing. The guns and infantry were ordered to retire at once as it was decided that the North Camp could no longer be safely held. These retiring troops were directed to concentrate in the Crater Camp. However, they abandoned their tents and stores in the North Camp as they were too heavy to transport. These were soon captured by the tribes and the remainder burned by them that evening. All during the day large bodies of tribesmen were seen gathering over the hills and occupying the surrounding heights with their 'gaily-coloured standards' (Fincastle and Elliot-Lockhart 1898: 42). Meanwhile, a regiment of the 24th Punjab Infantry and Guides Cavalry arrived from Mardan to reinforce the troops in Malakand.

It had become clear by now that this attack was not a 'local disturbance' but a combined rising of most of the neighbouring country in an attempt to drive the British out of Swat (*Frontier and Overseas Expeditions from India*, 1: 371). It was also evident that the attack was by no means over, so steps were taken to improve the 'defensive arrangements'.

The tribes attacked at 8.30 pm on 27 July 27 and maintained the attack throughout the night. They commenced the attack with a 'vigorous assault' on a fortified enclosure at the north-east corner of the Crater Camp. The enclosure was held by 25 men of the 31st Punjab Infantry under a native officer, Subadar Saiyid Ahmed Shah. He and his small garrison made a gallant defence until the tribesmen cut their way through the wall and set fire to the door. The troops were forced to evacuate and in the subsequent engagement with the tribesmen nine were killed and 10 wounded, including the officer. Severe fighting occurred on the right flank held by piquets of the 45th Sikhs and Guides Infantry. The tribesmen succeeded in forcing an entrance to one piquet when four men were killed and 17 wounded on the British side. Fincastle, describing the attack of that night, states:

> It was a veritable pandemonium that would seem to have been let loose around us. Bands of Ghazis, worked up by their religious enthusiasm into a frenzy of fanatical excitement, would charge our breastworks again and again, leaving their dead in scores after each repulse, while those of their comrades who were unarmed would encourage their efforts by shouting with much beating of tom-toms and other musical instruments (Fincastle and Elliot-Lockhart 1898: 45–46).

At dawn, Lieutenant Climo delivered a counter-attack on the tribesmen with two companies of the 24th Punjab Infantry supported by the fire of two guns and 'inflicted great loss on them' (ibid.: 46). That day the tribesmen kept up a 'desultory fire' on the camp while the troops were strengthening the defences and demolishing the bazaar and serai, which were to be abandoned. Towards evening the tribes could be seen 'swarming down the hills' to the attack. The attack started as soon as it was dark and the whole night passed in 'hard fighting' (ibid.: 47). The tribes, using the same tactics, withdrew at daybreak and could be seen on the neighbouring hills. But pursuit was impossible due to the 'exhausted condition' of the troops (*Frontier and Overseas Expeditions from India*, 1: 373).

On 29 July, more troops were sent to reinforce the Malakand garrison—the 11th Bengal Lancers, the 35th Sikhs, 38th Dogras and some men of the Guides. It was a fearful march in the intense heat and the troops arrived at Dargai exhausted, 21 of them having died of heat apoplexy. So they were halted at Dargai the next day to rest. On the night of 29 July, the tribesmen attacked again. They made a 'fierce assault' on the water piquet on the flank and a good deal of hand-to-hand fighting occurred. However, at 3 am the attack suddenly ceased. It was reported later that the Mad Fakir who had personally led the last assault was wounded in the hand and had retired to Landakai. At daylight the tribesmen were seeing carrying their dead and wounded.

On the night of 30 July, the tribes attacked again but with less vigour. It was reported that the wounding of the Mullah had had a disheartening effect on the tribesmen. The next day, Colonel Reid arrived in Malakand with the troops from Dargai. Shots were fired into the camp but no night attack occurred. On 1 August, Colonel (now Brigadier-General) Meiklejohn decided to send some troops to relieve the garrison at Chakdara, which had been attacked simultaneously since 26 July. The troops moved towards Chakdara with orders to seize the Amandara pass. However, tribesmen were gathered to oppose the troops and stopped them from passing through. After a skirmish the troops withdrew to the camp.

On 30 July, the GoI sanctioned a force to relieve the beleaguered garrison at Malakand. The following order was issued: 'The Governor-General in Council sanctions the despatch of a force, to be styled the Malakand Field Force, for the purpose of holding the Malakand and the adjacent posts, and operating against the neighbouring tribes as may be required' (Fincastle and Elliot-Lockhart 1898: 54). On 1 August, Major-General Sir Bindon Blood arrived at the Malakand and assumed command. The force included the troops that had originally formed the garrisons of the Swat posts, along with the reinforcements. The next day a large force was despatched to relieve the garrison at Chakdara, which had been under siege since 26 July. Communication between Malakand and Chakdara had been interrupted since 27 July, the telegraph wire had been cut by the tribesmen and the signalling tower was under constant attacks. However, on 1 August, Chakdara was able to send a short message containing the words, 'help us'.

The fortified post at Chakdara had been constructed in 1895, 10 miles from Malakand to protect a suspension bridge across Swat River. Chakdara was a smaller garrison and on the eve of the outbreak consisted of 20 men of the 11th Bengal Lancers and 180 men of the 45th Sikhs under Lieutenant Rattray. On 26 July he had been playing polo with the other officers of Malakand when he received an urgent message that large number of tribesmen with standards were moving towards Chakdara. Rattray along with another British officer rode back to the fort 'through gradually increasing crowds of natives, who, strangely enough, allowed these two officers to pass unharmed through their midst, although a few hours later these same men were engaged in a desperate and fanatical assault on our posts' (Fincastle and Elliot-Lockhart 1898: 66).

The attack commenced that night, when the tribes rushed the west side of the fort with ladders, attempting to gain an entrance into the inner enclosure but were repulsed. The next day troops of the 11th Bengal Lancers under Captain Wright arrived and the latter assumed command at Chakdara. On this day the tribes had surrounded the fort and occupied the neighbouring heights from where they kept up a 'desultory but harassing' fire on the fort. The signalling tower, with a few men trapped inside, was cut off from communication with the fort.

> By this time the tribesmen, ever impressionable and impulsive as children, had been worked up by the discordant din of their own tom-toms to the highest pitch of fanatical frenzy, and occasionally from out of the shifting crowd that swarmed over the slopes of the adjacent hills, a small body of wild-looking Ghazis, drunk with anticipated success, would dash up to the walls of the fort, there to meet with that death which, coming from the hands of the infidel, qualified them for an immediate entrance into the joys of Paradise (Fincastle and Elliot-Lockhart 1898: 69–70).

Over the next few days the attacks continued, with more and more tribesmen arriving to join their brethren. On 30 July, they occupied the civil hospital, which lay between the signal tower and the fort from where they were able to fire with 'complete impunity' into the outer enclosure of the fort. Interior communications within the fort became impossible. 'The increased numbers of the enemy, and the cautious manner in which they were now pushing forward under cover of entrenchments, in contrast to the frenzied recklessness of their former open attacks, greatly augmented the difficulties of the garrison' (*Frontier and Overseas Expeditions from India*, 1: 380). Matters looked so serious that on 1 August Captain Wright decided to send a message to Malakand asking for assistance. Due to the difficulty of signalling, 'a sepoy had to climb out of the port-hole of the tower carrying a helio' and managed to send 'help us', being exposed to fire the whole time (ibid.). The reply stating that a relief force would be sent the next day was never received. Much like the unpreparedness of the troops in Maizar, British military failure is clearly visible in Swat.

On 2 August the tribes attacked during the day in a 'most determined manner', numbering about 8,000 to 10,000. They carried ladders and bundles of grass, which would enable them to cross the wire entanglements that surrounded the fort in an attempt to capture the post at all costs. Though a large number of tribesmen were seen to fall, the 'combined fire of the small arms and the maxim and 9-pr. gun was barely sufficient to check the onward rush' (*Frontier and Overseas Expeditions from India*, 1: 380). Just as the position of the defenders was becoming 'critical', the relieving column appeared on the Amandara ridge. The tribes continued to press their attack until the squadrons were close, when they started retreating in small parties. Lieutenant Rattray made a sortie against the hospital, which was held by about 30 tribesmen. In one account, they 'fled' being pursued for half a mile, and in another they were 'shot down' as they tried to escape.[6] The cavalry of the relieving force attempted to pursue the tribesmen but 'owing to their horses being done up and the heavy ground over which they had to pursue, they were obliged to return after going a comparatively short distance' (Fincastle and Elliot-Lockhart 1898: 75). The crisis was over. The village of Chakdara was burned, and the next day the force marched to Amandara, where the troops were met by Sir Bindon Blood, escorted by 500 rifles. The force searched villages on the way looking for enemy but these were found deserted. On 3 August, most of the troops had returned to Malakand.

In the face of the military unpreparedness and the resulting besieged garrisons, most accounts emphasise the 'sudden-ness and fanaticism' of these attacks. 'Fanaticism' is also seen as a cause of the above attacks. Nevill wrote:

> To some extent the North-West Frontier tribes of India present an anomaly to the world in their methods of warfare. At times they show all the characteristics of well-armed but unorganized adversaries, at others the latent fire of the untamed barbarian blazes forth, and no epithet but savage can be applied to the class of warfare which is the result. The desperate and repeated attacks on the garrisons of Malakand and Chakdara are conspicuous examples of the savage side of the methods of war

> practised by the Muhammadan tribes inhabiting the north-western borderland of India. It is true that the attacks were delivered at night and not in broad daylight as in the Sudan, but they were renewed with greater persistency. There is no instance in the military history of the Egyptians or Sudanese in which temporary insanity brought on by religious fervour has lasted more than twenty-four hours. Before Malakand and Chakdara the tribesmen were religious maniacs for eight days, and advanced to the attack with a bravery which fully entitled those that fell to any reward that such a death may bring (Nevill 1912: 249–50).

The fanaticism of these attacks is attributed to the 'Mad Mullah'. He appeared in Swat in July and claimed to work miracles and announced that he would drive the British away from Malakand and Chakdara in eight days:

> His excited appeals to the fanaticism which exists in every Pathan were responded to in a manner little short of marvellous: his progress from Landakai to Thana and thence to Aladand, both villages in view of Chakdara post, must have been a triumphal one; the villagers flew to arms our levies hastily retired, except such as joined his standard; all the headmen, with one solitary exception, were carried away by the popular enthusiasm, and by nightfall a resolute body of tribesmen were on the move to attack the Malakand, while another party turned their attention to Chakdara (Mills 1897: 35).

However, the question of what caused such 'fanaticism' was not really answered. Thus, Mills concluded:

> This possible and probable explanation of the rising only added, however, to the difficulties of fully explaining the origin of the unprecedented outbreak. What was the lever which moved the 'mad fakir.' Was it fanaticism pure and simple? If not who was responsible for the laying of the train and for the preliminaries which ended in the convulsion around the British outposts? These questions still remain unanswered (ibid.).

A correspondent, however, did point to the fact that all was not right in Upper Swat. The Khan of Dir attempted to extend his authority in Upper Swat. However, the writer does not discuss how this played a role in the revolt: 'Exactly how far he pursued a forward policy is not for the present purpose worth inquiring into' (*The Risings on the North-West Frontier* 1898: 38). Later writers have essentially presented the same picture of the attacks. They focus on 'fanaticism' and how the 'mad fakir' roused the fanaticism of the tribesmen. Some of them have embellished the narrative by introducing something that is not mentioned in contemporary accounts—an intoxicant called *bhang*. For example, Davies states: 'Thousands of tribesmen whose ferocity was heightened by religious enthusiasm flocked to join him [the fakir]. Drunk with *bhang*, maddened by fanaticism, they fell upon our positions in the Malakand' (Davies 1932: 97).

This view of the attacks as 'sudden' and 'fanatical' again leaves many questions unanswered. If this fanaticism was roused by the 'Mad Mullah', what caused the people to follow a 'lunatic'? Why were the garrisons not better prepared to deal with the attacks? Malakand and Chakdara were strongly fortified military posts, yet they could not move out against the tribesmen. The troops acted on the defensive while under attack. The North Camp was abandoned, and the tribes succeeded in capturing a large quantity of ammunition at Malakand. The garrisons were besieged and could not hold their own; in fact it is certain that the posts would have fallen to the tribesmen if they had not been reinforced. These obvious questions are not dealt with in colonial historiography. Instead we have imperial explanations that focus on the suddenness and fanaticism of the attacks, leaving crucial questions unanswered.

BRITISH INDIA'S 'BLACKEST DAY' ON THE FRONTIER

From the imperial standpoint, 25 August 1897 has been described as the blackest day in the history of the Frontier.[7] It was on that day that the British lost the Khyber. The loss of the Khyber Pass, described as a place of 'great antiquity, and of great importance', and whose 'preservation is undoubtedly of the very greatest importance to what is known as the prestige of the Government of India',[8] was a big blow to British imperial reputation. 'The fall of such impregnable fortresses as Ali Musjid and Landi Kotal, and the securing of the Pass was universally held to be the worst blow our prestige would suffer on the north-west frontier' (Mills 1897: 108). And it was in order to recover this prestige that the British sanctioned one of the biggest military undertakings, since the uprising and war of 1857, against the Afridi tribe, the inhabitants of the Khyber. The Tirah expedition would lift the veil from Tirah—the summer home of the Afridi tribe, a lush and fertile valley that they considered inviolable and inviolate and which had never been penetrated by an Englishman, and thus recover British prestige.

The Afridi tribe inhabits the country between the Khyber–Kabul route, the Safed Koh mountains to the west and south of Peshawar. They are divided into eight clans—the Kuki Khel, Malikdin Khel, Kambar Khel, Kamrai, Zakha Khel, Sipah, Aka Khel and Adam Khel. The first six are collectively known as the Khyber Afridis. The Aka Khel live to the south of the Bara River and the Adam Khel occupy the hills between the Peshawar and Kohat districts. The last are regarded as a separate community. In 1879, following the second Afghan war, the British undertook negotiations with the Khyber Afridis regarding the Khyber Pass. By the Treaty of Gandamak concluded with Afghanistan, the British took over the security of the Pass. The British offered to pay allowances to the Afridis in return for their keeping the Pass open. Before that the Afridis had received allowances from the court in Kabul. In 1881, the headmen of the Khyber Afridi clans affixed their seals to an agreement with the British, undertaking to maintain order in the Pass in return for allowances. The Khyber Rifles, a local militia of about 550 men, was raised to maintain the security of the Pass. They were to be appointed and dismissed by the headmen of their clans who would report their arrangements to the political officer at Jamrud. Thus, Khyber became the first political agency on the Frontier. The Afridis, in general, were regarded by the British as among the best fighters on the Frontier. 'The Afridis are men of fine physique and grand fighting qualities' (Mills 1897: 105). 'The Afridis are collectively the finest and best armed race of dare-devil Afghans of our border, and are believed to have a united fighting strength of not less than from 25,000 to 28,000 men' (ibid.). Therefore, the possibility of the Afridis joining the revolt in 1897 was, for the British, something to be reckoned with.

On 23 August, a lashkar composed of about 10,000 Afridis commenced an attack upon Ali Masjid and Fort Maude. By that evening the tribes had succeeded in capturing these posts and had burnt the British forts there. The next day an attack was made on the fortified serai at Landi Kotal, further up the Khyber. The attack continued until the next morning, by which time this post was also captured, looted and burnt. A great quantity of ammunition stored at Landi Kotal fell into the hands of the Afridis.

In contrast to the previous attacks, it could not be argued that the attack on the Khyber was sudden. It became public that British officials had been receiving information of an Afridi rising since early August. Further, the Afridis had communicated their grievances to the authorities:

> They [the Afridis] were posing as something more than religious fanatics. Their leaders had intimated to the authorities at Peshawar that certain concessions were desired from the Government of India. These were the withdrawal of all troops from the Swat Valley and the Samana Range, the rectification of the salt tax, and the rendition of all Afridi women living in British territory. Given these terms their fighting men would return to their homes (*The Risings on the North-West Frontier* 1898: 109–10).

It was also known that the Afridis and Orakzais had entered into a war alliance so that they could deliver two simultaneous attacks.[9] But the Orakzais were waiting for the Afridis to attack the Khyber before moving themselves. This gave the British even more time to prepare: 'Instead of descending upon us swiftly and suddenly as the Swatis and the Mohmands had done, they were by their hesitancy giving us an opportunity to make better defensive preparations' (ibid.: 110). Given that British garrisons had been attacked throughout the Frontier, it was acknowledged that further risings amongst the tribes not yet implicated were to be feared and this imposed on the government the necessity of taking precautionary measures on a large scale (*Frontier and Overseas Expeditions from India*, 2: 68). Troops started arriving in Peshawar since the middle of August. On the eve of the attack, General Elles had at his disposal 18 squadrons of cavalry besides infantry, two Batteries Royal Horse Artillery, two Field and one Mountain Batteries—a force consisting of between 11,000 and 12,000 men.

The question arose, with such a formidable force mobilised to fend off an Afridi rising, how could the Khyber fall into the hands of the tribes so easily—a loss that was universally regarded as a great disaster? While most accounts ignore this obvious question even when they describe the number of British troops being mobilised, one contemporary author did not. H. W. Mills stated:

> In the plains of India no one ever dreamed that the Khyber Pass could fall into the hands of the tribesmen with such an army close at hand, but by the 23rd the whole Pass from Ali Musjid to Landi Khana was in the possession of the Afridis... At the time the Pass was attacked (and it was known for days before hand that an attack was imminent), there were 9,500 British and native troops at Peshawar, Fort Bara and Jamrud, and not a man was moved to help the Khyber Rifles, who were waiting for assistance from the *Sirkar* whose salt they had eaten and in whose good faith they had implicit trust (Mills 1897: 107, 114).

In face of outrage and criticism from the newspapers, the government claimed that the force was not well-equipped to move into the Khyber: 'Any active operations into the Khaibar were rendered impossible by scarcity of transport, all transport immediately available having been requisitioned for military operations in progress in other parts of the frontier' (*Frontier and Overseas Expeditions from India*, 2: 71). While Mills did not consider this a convincing plea, he did not attempt to offer an explanation of why the Khyber was not defended in face of ample warnings. This question has remained unanswered both in contemporary and in more recent accounts.

The three attacks discussed here all demonstrate major imperial military failures. These accounts that will become the historical basis for the literature on the 1897 revolt work to suppress fundamental questions about the reasons behind the attacks and serve as justifications for the failures and more so as cover-ups for how empire was functioning in the Frontier. Immediately, the question of why the attacks occurred in Maizar and in Swat is important because the tribes were key allies within the scheme of imperial defence as formulated under the forward policy. In the case of the Khyber, the central question is not why (as the Afridis had already communicated their grievances to the authorities before the attack) but how could a strategic post that was key within imperial defence be allowed to fall and not even attempt to be reinforced. However, imperial explanations point us not only to imperial interests but also to sub-imperial workings of empire.

Reading between the lines of such accounts, it is evident that there are cracks between such external imperial explanations. In the case of Tochi, as is pointed to by Nevill's criticism, even as the rest of his account falls in with the official story, there is an attempt by the local officers to conceal what occurred. In the case of Swat, as we shall see again, there is a misrepresentation of the reality on the ground. However, even from the imperial side, and as the next chapters shall show, these imperial explanations consisted of carefully selected pieces where other men on the spot and other narratives were deliberately left out. A complex play of civil–military tensions, the man on the spot, and imperial decision-making and competing definitions of Empire will show how the limits of Empire functioned internally, and that Pukhtun resistance was an integral part of that history.

NOTES

1. See Mills (1897) and *The Risings on the North-West Frontier* (1898).
2. See, for example, Davies (1932); Ahmed (1976); Miller (1977); Warren (2000); Tripodi (2011); Richards (2003); Barthorp and Anderson (1996).
3. The particulars of the attack were furnished by Mr Gee who survived the attack. His version of the events surrounding the attack was made public and widely circulated at the time. This view resonates across the literature ranging from popular histories to the more scholarly. From the colonial to more recent accounts, the basic narrative of what occurred in Maizar has remained intact. For recent examples, see Stewart (2007); Roe (2010); Warren (2000); Tripodi (2011). Some of these accounts also contain glaring historical inaccuracies. For example, Stewart claims that the attack occurred in South Waziristan (2007: 110). Tripodi tells us that 'Gee was killed' in the attack and his death 'inflamed matters' (2011: 88). Beyond the uncritical repetition of entrenched colonial-era narratives, historical distortions such as these highlight the marginality and historical insignificance of events and their details within the dominant historiography on the colonial Frontier.

4. Quoted in *The Risings on the North-West Frontier* (1898: 19).

5. Contemporary accounts that describe the attacks in Malakand and Chakdara present largely the same narrative. For the following paragraphs, see *Frontier and Overseas Expeditions from India*, Vol. 1; and Fincastle and Elliot-Lockhart (1898).

6. Fincastle and Elliot-Lockhart (1898) mention that they 'fled', while in *Frontier and Overseas Expeditions from India*, Vol. 1, it is stated that they were 'shot down'.

7. Cited in Swinson (1967: 242).

8. The Under Secretary of State for India, 7 March 1898, *Parliamentary Debates*, Lords (1898) IOR/BL, London.

9. The Orakzais are a tribe closely connected to the Afridis. In summers the Afridis move to Tirah, a high plateau, which is inhabited by the Orakzais.

3

THE MAIZAR ATTACK

Imperial Cover-Up and the Politics of Occupation in North Waziristan

The first section in this chapter is based on new archival evidence drawn from confidential and secret documents that brings forth previously unknown facts surrounding the Maizar attack. As will become clear, information about the attack was misrepresented in an effort to conceal not just the military failure of the visit to Maizar, but also the fundamental failure of the forward policy in Waziristan. This sub-imperial-level evidence reveals civil–military tensions following a military expedition to punish the inhabitants of Maizar, the Madda Khel, that lead to the remarkable and unprecedented establishment of a military tribunal to try the prisoners accused of plotting the attack. The findings of the tribunal contradict the man on the spot's representations of the attack and its causes. However, both the tribunal and its rulings are missing from the historiography of the Frontier. The role of Herbert William Gee and other political officers, explanations and misrepresentations, civil–military tensions, and the establishment and rulings of the tribunal form one layer of sub-imperialism uncovered in this section.

Evidence from this sub-imperial level necessitates going back to the occupation of Waziristan to uncover the causes of the attack. In the second section, sub-imperialism reveals the competing agendas behind internal imperial explanations, the expansion and functioning of Empire under the forward policy that led to the occupation of North Waziristan, and brings into focus the continuous Pukhtun resistance to that occupation. Oral Pukhtun accounts corroborate this narrative and bring forth an element of Pukhtun perspective of the Maizar attack and its causes.

SUB-IMPERIAL POLITICS AND THE MAIZAR ATTACK

As the political officer stationed in North Waziristan, Gee was the British government's man on the spot. He conducted dealings in Tochi and he kept them informed of the temper of the tribesmen. This was the essential duty of a political officer. On 10 June 1897, immediately after the attack, he sent a brief telegram to the government authorities in Punjab and Simla. He mentioned that he had gone to Maizar for the 'purpose of fixing site for post and realization of fines'.[1] He and his escort were 'suddenly attacked while resting under the trees at Maizar in a most cowardly and treacherous manner'.[2] He advocated immediate retaliatory measures on the Madda Khels.

The GoP had not been informed of Gee's intention to visit Maizar. At this point, authorities both in Punjab and Simla, considering this attack a serious matter, asked Gee to furnish a detailed report on the attack, its causes and his reasons for going to Maizar. Further, the GoI questioned the GoP on whether they had any premonition of the Madda Khel outbreak.

Over the next few days, Gee sent the following pieces of information to the governments. He had gone to Maizar to select a final site for the building of a new military post somewhere between Maizar and Sheranni,[3] and to arrange the payment of a fine. The fine referred to had been imposed on the tribes due to the murder of a *muharrir* (scribe, clerk), Honda Ram, of the nearby Sheranni post in June 1896. At the time of his visit, Gee had believed the valley to be quite peaceful; nevertheless he took a large military escort because he thought its sight would have a 'good effect'.[4] At this point, Gee's changing account of the reason behind the visit ('realize' versus 'arrange' payment of fine) and for taking a large military escort does not immediately emerge as significant but, as will become clear, it was an initial attempt at covering up the blunder at Maizar.

His opinion on the cause of the attack was that it 'was partly fanatical, but arranged by Maliks'.[5] The only thing in favour of the latter was that they saved the life of his assistant, Ghulam Muhammad Khan, by taking him down to a tower during the attack. The houses in Maizar and Sheranni were deserted as the tribes had fled to the mountains. However, Gee advocated that the houses or *kots* (hamlets, houses) should be razed to the ground to punish the tribes.

During this time, Sadda Khan, the chief of the Madda Khels, and some of the other Maliks sent a message to Gee asking whether they should come in. However, Gee reported to the GoI that the attack must have been planned beforehand and it was impossible that the Maliks could not have known about it. 'It is impossible to explain how such a well-directed fire broke out on all sides, if we suppose that the affair began accidentally.'[6]

Anderson, the Commissioner of Derajat and Gee's immediate superior, supported this view and reported that the outbreak was inspired by fanaticism. The Mullahs 'took advantage of Muharram to rouse fanatical feelings, and the unpalatable demand of the fine in Honda Ram's case gave them desired opportunity of stirring up resistance and bringing about fanatical outbreak.'[7] Further, he said that while it was mentioned to him by some local Maliks that the outbreak was unpremeditated and arose suddenly in consequence of irritation caused by fines due, he did not credit this and believed the attack to have been planned 24 hours beforehand.

> In any case the Maliks present at the time may have taken no active part, but they are guilty at least of connivance. It is impossible to believe that they were unacquainted with the attitude of their section or the preparations which must have necessarily been made beforehand. They gave no intimation whatever to the Political Officer, nor assisted in stopping the outbreak. It was an act of pure treachery, and is looked upon by every friendly person in the valley as opposed to the code of Afghan honor.[8]

Based on Gee and Anderson's urging, on 17 June the GoI sanctioned a military expedition that would advance to Maizar, destroy the kots there and occupy it for as long as necessary. The terms to be offered to the tribes were still not decided upon, and the GoI awaited a communication from the lieutenant governor of Punjab.

Meanwhile, new information started pouring in that gave a different slant to the causes of the Tochi attack and contradicted Gee's report. For example, A. J. Grant, political officer, Wana, in Southern Waziristan sent a report to the GoI in which he concluded:

> From all sources of information on this side (Mahsud and Darwesh Khel) the same report is received as to the cause of the Maizar outbreak. It is ascribed to irritation at Government putting a post in their country with an armed force to enforce payment of the fine for the murder of Honda Ram. All idea of fanaticism is eschewed. The Mahsuds and Wana Ahmadzais attach no importance whatever to Muharram and hardly know what the name means.[9]

He was referring to the fact that the religious festival of Muharram is celebrated by Shi'a Muslims and the Wazirs and Mahsuds are not Shi'a but Sunni Muslims. Grant's statement about 'armed force to enforce payment' directly contradicted Gee's account.

Further, Gee and Anderson's inquiry after talking to the local tribal levies and other people also pointed to a discontent over the fine. For example, the following account was given by Alam Shah, havildar of Sheranni levies:

> On the 8th June I and Sadda Khan and Alambe Khan left Datta Khel for Maizar to make arrangements for the Political Officer's visit. We stayed the night at Maizar with Sherin, Khoji Khel. Sadda Khan was with us. The same night Sadda Khan sent for Pyall, but he pleaded illness and did not come. Sadda Khan killed some sheep, and I with some other levies prepared food for the sepoys. On the 9th June I went to Drepilare Kot of Modoi to collect charpoys, but the villagers refused to give them. Modoi is the headman. He did not himself go to see Sadda Khan. After this Pyall came to see Sadda Khan and asked why the *fauj* was coming. Sadda Khan said, 'To realize the fine in Honda Ram's case.' Pyall said, 'It should be decided by Shariyat. If there is any one in my tribe or in the whole of Maizar who is guilty, we will pay our share of the fine, but not otherwise. The Muharrir was killed in Sheranna, and he was made over to you to protect. The relations of the murderer live in Sheranna and they should pay.' Sadda Khan said, 'This is a baradari matter. A large fine like this ought to be put on the whole baradari.' He said, 'I will kill you or

> be arrested by the Sarkar and transported, but I will not pay a fine without due cause.'[10]

Numerous other accounts were provided by other tribesmen that contradicted Gee and pointed to discontent over a large fine that was widely regarded as unjust. At the same time, Sadda Khan wrote letters and petitions to Gee and Anderson protesting his innocence and asking that he be allowed to see them and make his case. In a letter sent to Anderson on 28 June he said:

> If you will have kindness, you will withhold your hand and stop yourself from oppressing your subjects without proof of their guilt, so that the reputation of the Indian Government may not suffer. ... If the Government will in no case listen to our solicitations, it is proper that Government should not incur unnecessary expenses of an expedition and presence of troops, we shall on hearing from some reliable Government servant leave our country, and having entrusted it to Government will become exiles.[11]

However, the already sanctioned military expedition proceeded on the recommendation of the local officers, and the GoP, to punish the Madda Khels and destroy their villages. At the same time, the GoI decided that political control of the valley be taken over from the local officers Anderson and Gee and be handed over to the general officer who would be commanding the Tochi field force, Major-General G. Corrie Bird. Therefore, on 9 July Anderson handed over the political charge of the Tochi valley to General Bird.

Initially Gee was supposed to accompany General Bird as political officer attached to the expedition. However, Gee developed fever and was unable to continue his duties. Therefore, R. E. Younghusband, deputy commissioner of Bannu, was appointed as chief political officer with the expedition.

By this time Maizar and Sheranni were deserted as the villagers had fled to the hills and across the border. While maintaining distance, the tribes showed opposition to the advancing troops by firing at them and their camps. On 13 July, Bird issued a proclamation to the headmen of all sections of the Darwesh Khel living in Northern Waziristan. Stating the 'treacherous and cowardly' attack of the Madda Khels, he proclaimed to all concerned that:

> I am ordered by the Sarkar to proceed to Maizar with a force sufficiently strong to hold its own against all comers and to compel obedience to the orders of the Sarkar. And I inform you that it is my intention to destroy all the fortified kots in Maizar and Sheranni, whether resistance be shown or otherwise, and that I shall remain at Maizar or some convenient spot near to it, for so long as seems to me and the Government of India desirable. And I further inform you that I shall in due course announce the terms of punishment which the Sarkar may decide to inflict on all those who were in any way responsible for, or who took part in, the treacherous attack on the British troops; with whom alone it is my business to deal. And I warn all others who wish to live in peace with the Sarkar to refrain from obstructing my force, for, depend upon it, any further unfriendly acts will be severely dealt with (Kemball 1900: 12).

However, acts of resistance continued. The advancing British party was fired at, resulting in casualties. Telegraph wires were cut frequently. On 10 July, 100 yards of wire were carried off and several posts pulled up (ibid.: 13).

On 20 July, British troops under Brigadier-General Egerton arrived in Sheranni and a squadron went on to Maizar. Both places were found deserted though a collection of several hundred tribesmen was seen in a distance on the low hills to the south. The tribesmen kept their distance. A total of 4,660 troops were sent under Bird to punish the tribes (Kemball 1900). However, there was nobody to fight.

Over the next few days, the troops spent their time destroying the houses in Maizar and Sheranni. The destruction was completed on 5 August. The same day, General Bird issued notices to all sections of the Madda Khel to come in on 12 August and hear the further terms of punishment ordered by the GoI. The tribes refused to come in. On 17 August, Bird announced the terms of punishment to other sections of the Darwesh Khel as the Madda Khel were not present. The terms of the punishment were: (a) The Madda Khel tribe must come in and make submission, agreeing to surrender the Maliks which the GoI demanded. Seventeen Maliks were demanded, including Sadda Khan. (b) All stolen property must be returned or in default value determined by the GoI. (c) Payment of the fine of Rs 1,200 in Honda

Ram's case. (d) Payment of a fine of Rs 10,000 in cash or in arms, on account of the recent misconduct of the tribe (Kemball 1900: 16–17).

The Maliks present were sent to convey the message to the Madda Khel and the latter were given 10 days in which to come in and make submission. However, the Madda Khels did not appear. In the following days, several messages were sent to them to come in, but they refused to appear. On 2 September, the messengers brought back a letter from Sadda Khan. The translation of the letter was as follows:

> Maliks Din Muhammad, Imangul, Mani Khan, Nakkar Khan and Rezan Shah sent by you, reached here, and I was informed of the message that the Government wishes my presence. The reason for my non-attendance and distrust is that during the demarcation of the boundary between the Government of India and the King of Khorasan, the Amir (the pride of Islam), I applied for certain terms from Mr. Anderson, the Commissioner, for the satisfaction of my tribe; the tribe as well demanded the terms from the said officer. But the officers in charge of the Tochi Valley did not allow me to make those demands, and discredited me before my tribe. When the British troops came to Maizar for the realization of the fine in Honda Ram's case, I gave a notice to Mr. Gee and Ghulam Muhammad Khan that they should not go to Maizar as the Madda Khels would not pay the fine, because the Ali Khan Khel section only was charged with the offence; the murderer of the Hindu (muharrir) was also an Ali Khan Khel. The rest of the Madda Khel tribe would not in any case pay the fine, and a fight would surely ensue between the Government and the Madda Khels. Mr. Gee and Ghulam Muhammad Khan replied that they will see; and if the Madda Khels are true sons of their mothers, they will fight against Government for a moment. I took Ghulam Muhammad Khan's beard and begged him to grant six days' grace so that I may present the tribe at Datta Khel. Ghulam Muhammad Khan said that he intended to try the Madda Khels, and that, if they wished to fight against Government, he would give them a chance, and therefore a fine is to be realized from them without any proof. ... Therefore I have lost my hope and trust upon the Government officers as they trust each other's words and do not believe the words of a foreigner.[12]

A different story had started emerging that seemed to contradict the reports furnished by Gee and Anderson. In October, Bird was asked to send his report on the origin of the outbreak at Maizar and the extent to which Sadda Khan and Ghulam Muhammad Khan were aware of the attitude of the Maizarwals and the probability of their breaking out. He reported that Sadda Khan was the most influential Malik in Upper Tochi and was the main person whom the British had worked with since 1895, which is when they first started moving into the Tochi. Considering past record, he concluded that 'Sadda Khan was really sincere in his professions of loyalty to Government. He was, of course, actuated by self-interest; but he was wise enough to see that it was to his interest to support us, and he did so.'[13] Further, he ruled out 'deliberate treachery' on the part of the Maliks in the Maizar attack.

> If there had been deliberate intention to commit a treacherous attack on our troops, it is impossible to believe Sadda Khan and all his own immediate relations (to say nothing of the Khidder Khel Maliks and intelligent men like the Levy Havildar Alam Shah) would not have had some warning of it, and in that case would have conveyed a warning to the Political Officer; again in they had meant treachery, they could have easily shot down Mr. Gee and his escort of 6 cavalry sowars on the way to or from Dotoi; thirdly, the inhabitants of remote villages, instead of being ready on the spot to join in the fight, did not come up till they heard the sound of firing; fourthly, the women and children do not appear to have been sent away, as is the custom with Pathan tribes when a fight is coming off; mention is made in the evidence of Pyall's daughter, Mr. Gee speaks of the women joining in the fight and throwing stones, and four women are said to have been killed at Maizar, and nine women and children at Sheranni.[14]

Bird also raised the question that based on Ghulam Muhammad Khan's statements it seemed that he was not acquainted with the feelings prevailing among the tribe, which as assistant political officer was his job. Further, Sadda Khan in his petitions had accused the assistant political officer of not listening to his warnings that there would be trouble if the few days' grace in the payment of the fine was not granted. Bird advocated that an inquiry into both these matters be made from him. Bird's investigation threatened to reveal that Anderson had been misrepresenting to the GoI that things were functioning well and the policy was working. The opposite was true.

In the course of these developments, a rift started appearing between Bird and officers in the Punjab government. For example, Anderson criticised Bird's handling of the affairs and stated that the Maliks had not come in till now because of the want of confidence in the officers in the valley. He recommended that political control should be restored to the civil authorities and he be given a free hand to do whatever he can. The disagreement between Bird and the GoP would emerge again, and by now it was clearly evident that civil–military relations had become strained.

On 31 October Sadda Khan came in and surrendered to General Bird on assurance of his life and the promise of a fair trial. In August, Bird had recommended to the GoI the appointment of a special tribunal that would conduct the trial of the Maliks who had been accused of complicity in the Maizar attack. The GoI approved. Over the next few days, Sadda Khan gave his testimony to Bird and the other officers, the formal trial being scheduled for December. Anderson wrote to the GoP that he was opposed to a trial because then

> it will not be possible, as I brought to the notice of His Honour in a demi-official in July last, to establish against him [Sadda Khan] a charge of having organized the outbreak or taken an active part in the attack. This being so the result of Sadda Khan's trial conducted by a tribunal, such as is contemplated, will be that Sadda Khan will be pronounced not guilty of any serious criminal offence, and in view of the result of his formal trial will claim to be reinstated in his former position.[15]

Anderson again differed with the recommendations proposed by General Bird and seemed intent on getting Sadda Khan disposed of, rather than there being a trial which established the causes of the outbreak and who was responsible.

However, on 1 December 1897, a tribunal composed of three military officers and one political officer—General Bird, C. C. Egerton, J. A. H. Pollock and R. E. Younghusband—tried Sadda Khan and four others (Sheikh Nur, Ware Khan, Khanijan and Dande) who had been accused of complicity in the Maizar attack.[16] The tribunal recorded their testimony, cross-questioned them and also brought in various witnesses. Ghulam Muhammad Khan was brought in for further questioning. Gee did not appear but sent in his replies in writing.[17] Gee's conspicuous absence during the trial raises questions, especially when as the political officer in charge who was present during the attack he could have directly intervened and challenged the different accounts that essentially showed that he lied about the circumstances leading to the attack and what occurred at the time. His failure at cover-up is revealed through the answers he sent in writing as he could not refute the testimonies of Sadda Khan and others.

Sadda Khan's account of the outbreak shed a completely different light on the Maizar affair and was borne out by several witnesses. It also provided a counter-narrative of British actions in contrast to what the political officers had represented. First, when the British approached Sadda Khan about staying in Tochi in 1895, he had demanded certain conditions. Further, these conditions do not mention direct occupation but state that 'we agree to give a road through the Tochi'.[18] One of the conditions was that the tribes would not pay revenue:

> We agree to give a road through the Tochi, but ask that revenue may never be taken from us. We are poor people, and if revenue is ever taken from us, we ask that it may be fixed once for all and not liable to be increased from time to time; also that it may never be imposed during our own lifetime.[19]

Anderson accepted. Sadda Khan and the tribes wanted written *sanad*s (deeds of agreement) embodying these conditions, which were never granted. However, villages in the Dawar were assessed for revenue. People were dissatisfied and the inhabitants of one village named Spulga ran away to escape from the revenue. 'Ghulam Muhammad then had the doors of their houses broken open and the grain taken out to pay the revenue.'[20] He described many other instances of Ghulam Muhammad's bullying and oppressive behaviour towards him, and towards the tribesmen.

Sadda Khan's testimony established that the tribesmen had objected to the fine being placed on them for the murder of Honda Ram. Honda Ram had been murdered by Waris Khan who belonged to a section of the Madda Khels who did not live in Tochi. After the murder, Waris Khan had escaped across the border into the Amir's territory. Seven men were accused of being Waris Khan's accomplices.

They were produced before a tribal *jirga* (council of tribal elders) and were acquitted. But Gee and Ghulam Muhammad Khan demanded that the fine be paid. In February 1897, the fine was reduced from Rs 2,000 to Rs 1,200 as a result of the suspected men being exonerated. Then, according to Sadda Khan's statements, the following happened.

> Ghulam Muhammad then said, 'As these men have been acquitted, all the Ger Madda Khels must pay the fine.' The jirga said, 'the murderer has escaped, and the seven men have been absolved on oath. Why do you demand the fine from us now?' Ghulam Muhammad said, 'however that may be, you must pay.' The jirga again said they would not pay. Mr. Gee turned to me and said, 'you are a be-iman, and it is all owing to you that they make this objection.' I replied, 'I have not incited them to object. I cannot take it from them by force; they are hill-people. You should get it from them by some device and show them that they are bound to pay either by law or by custom.'[21]

The Maliks again sent their representatives to Ghulam Muhammad, saying they would not pay the fine and if the GoI wanted it, then they should take it from the Ali Khan Khels, Waris Khan's section. Again, in Sadda Khan's words, the following encounter occurred between him and Ghulam Muhammad Khan:

> The next day I said to Ghulam Muhammad, 'You oppose me, but I pray you not to act so tyrannically to the Madda Khels. They are stupid people.' Ghulam Muhammad said, 'you are making our trees to be men. Why cannot I realize the money from them? You stand aside, and I will take it from them.'[22]

On 8 June, Sadda Khan was in Datta Khel with other Maliks when Gee and Ghulam Muhammad told him to go and prepare food in Maizar for them and 400 or 500 troops who were coming to Maizar the next day to realise the fine. A short time later, Sadda Khan again went to Ghulam Muhammad to plead against their coming to realise the fine.

> I said, 'you intend taking troops to Maizar to realize the fine. The Madda Khels have no intention of paying. If you insist on demanding it and they refuse to pay, there will be a row.' He replied, 'you go and make arrangements for food. You are not responsible for the Madda Khels paying the fine.' I said, 'Well,

> then, don't go to Maizar, go to Sheranni, and I will call the Maliks there.' Ghulam Muhammad said, 'No. We will go to Maizar and test the sword of the Maizar people.'[23]

Sadda Khan had the food prepared, but the troops did not come on 9 June. A message was sent through a levy that Gee and 300 troops would arrive on 10 June so the food should be prepared for then. Again Sadda Khan had the food prepared. He said the people were engaged in their everyday business and were not completely sure why the troops were coming to Maizar. After the troops had eaten, Ghulam Muhammad told Sadda Khan, Alambe and Kotan to speak to the other Maliks and to 'realise' the fine. They did so, when Pyall retorted,

> 'I have asked Ghulam Muhammad not to press the fine; he should proceed either by law or by custom. If he insists, everybody is not here. Some are here and some are in the hills. He should wait five or six days. When people return from the hills, we will discuss the matter with them, and if they agree and Ghulam Muhammad Khan insists, we will pay.'[24]

Alambe and Kotan spoke to Ghulam Muhammad and he again would not listen to them. Sadda Khan, Alambe, Kotan with a few other Maliks present again attempted to convince Ghulam Muhammad Khan not to realise the fine. Finally, from Sadda Khan's testimony, the following occurred moments before the attack commenced:

> Kotan asked Ghulam Muhammad to allow five or six days for the payment of the fine. Ghulam Muhammad said, 'I won't give 2 1/2 days. I must have the money at once.' I then took hold of Ghulam Muhammad's beard and said, 'For God's sake give us six days' grace. Don't insist now. These people are stupid, and there will be a row. I will realize the fine in six days or bring the maliks to you. If you like, you can arrest the maliks and realize the fine without a row. If you want a surety, I will give Kotan as surety.' ... Ghulam Muhammad said, 'I will try them and see if they are men or not.'[25]

The people around heard this and started moving away, perhaps for fear that they would be arrested. This also fits in with Gee's statement that 'suddenly all the villagers cleared off'. Then, according to Sadda Khan, a shot was fired at him and at another Malik because the villagers were angry with him about the fine. Then the troops jumped up and began shooting. Sadda Khan insisted that no shots were fired at the troops except these two until the troops began to shoot. Then the cross-firing began. Sadda Khan along with Ghulam Muhammad Khan and other Maliks took cover and helped to save his life.

According to the tribunal, Ghulam Muhammad's evidence was given in 'a most unsatisfactory manner, and he pleaded ignorance of facts and of having forgotten material points which should have been indelibly stamped in his memory'.[26] He could not contradict Sadda Khan's story and all the evidence provided showed that what took place was coercion and not hospitality. It was established for a fact that a few days' grace was asked for and later admitted by Gee and Ghulam Muhammad, but they made contradictory statements as to what their response was. And the tribunal concluded that since Ghulam Muhammad Khan's evidence had been 'shaken in more than one particular',[27] the tribunal members were more inclined to believe Sadda Khan.

Gee's reports on the attack from the beginning were not consistent as to why he had gone to Maizar. The tribunal did not fail to notice this. On 10 June, in a telegram to the GoI, informing them of the attack, he said he had gone to Maizar for the '*realization* of fines' (emphasis in original). The next day, in a letter to the commissioner, he said, 'Sadda Khan and Alambe were sent on a day before to arrange for *payment* of fine' (emphasis in original). Again, in a report on 17 June, providing a full report on what had occurred at Maizar, he said that he paid a visit to Maizar to 'hurry on the *realization* of the fine in Honda Ram's case' (emphasis in original). It was later when he was ordered to look into the causes of the attack and the question of discontentment over the fine started being repeated that he said he had gone to 'discuss' the fine with the people of Maizar.[28] Let us not forget that for this 'discussion' he found it necessary to take a few hundred troops with him. Gee did not attend the trial and sent his written replies to the questions that the tribunal put to him, and instead of answering those questions fully, he objected to their line of questioning and provided inadequate answers. Gee's lies kept surfacing and by the time of the trial it was irrefutable that he had been making false claims.

The findings of the tribunal sat to try the Madda Khel prisoners and to determine the causes of the Maizar attack established the following points: (a) The Maizar attack was not a premeditated act of treachery. (b) The Madda Khels believed that the troops were going to *realise* the fine for Honda Ram's murder. (c) The Maliks asked for some days' grace and failed to obtain it. (d) There was a great deal of discontentment amongst the Madda Khels at the way the allowances had been distributed, the incessant fines placed on them, at Sadda Khan's being looked upon as the head malik by the GoI and finally the fine for Honda Ram's murder which they regarded as unjust. The tribunal also exonerated Sadda Khan of 'any guilty complicity or knowledge of the intentions of the tribe to attack our troops'.[29] However, they regarded that Sadda Khan had failed in his duty as the representative of the tribe. At the same time, they also were not slow to point out that Ghulam Muhammad Khan had failed in ascertaining the temper of the tribesmen. 'Ghulam Muhammad ought to have been able to gauge the feeling and temper of the tribe, and that he failed to do so, or if he did so, failed to inform Mr. Gee, shows that he was hardly fit for his position.'[30] Of course, this also raised the question of Gee's misrepresentations or incompetence. And while the tribunal was tactful in not being direct about this, its findings pointed to Gee having failed as political officer. The Foreign Secretary to the GoI, Sir W. Cuningham noted the following after reviewing the report of the tribunal:

> It must, I think, be admitted that in the political management of the Madda Khel, Mr. Gee was insufficiently informed by his assistant, Ghulam Muhammad Khan, and by Sadda Khan, the chief Malik. He seems not to have accurately known either the temper of the tribe and extent of dissatisfaction which existed at the time he went to Maizar, nor the actual facts as to what was taking place when he was there. The two men named, through whom he worked, were responsible for this; but it cannot be expected that a Political Officer will be well served by instruments such as they, unless they know that he is able to detect their shortcomings and to counteract any of their schemes for playing for their own hands.[31]

However, Gee was not accused directly or held accountable. Instead, local collaborators such as Sadda Khan and the other Maliks were called out as being responsible. The questions regarding his actions and competence, which were raised by the findings of the tribunal, were defended by Anderson and the new lieutenant governor of Punjab, Mackworth Young. According to Anderson, the reason why Gee and Ghulam Muhammad failed to be acquainted with the temper of the tribe was because the official staff in the Tochi was 'not equal to the requirements'.[32] Anderson said he could not understand how the tribunal had preferred the statements of Sadda Khan and Alambe to those of Gee and Ghulam Muhammad. Although he acknowledged that Sadda Khan and the others on trial had taken no active part in the attack, he still asserted that Sadda Khan 'was guilty of a gross breach of his duties'.[33] Apart from one of the accused, Anderson recommended that Sadda Khan and the other five should be detained as hostages 'during the pleasure of the Government',[34] as this would be the appropriate punishment. The lieutenant governor approved this recommendation. Even though Sadda Khan and the others had been exonerated, they were sentenced to jail for the duration of 'the pleasure of the Government'. This was not just for their 'offence' but also due to the tribe's non-compliance with the terms imposed on it by the GoI for the Maizar attack. Finally, Mackworth Young concurred with the tribunal that the attack was not premeditated. 'Women and children would not in that case have been left in the place.'[35] He also had to acknowledge the ruling of the tribunal that 'there was nothing in the conduct of any of the tribe which can be called treachery'.[36]

Therefore, the British established for themselves that the Maizar outrage was not a piece of 'treachery'. Yet Maizar remained intact in colonial historiography as an 'act of gross treachery, to which it would be difficult to find a parallel in frontier history'. As the following sections will demonstrate, the reasons for the Maizar attack, if brought in the open, threatened to reveal the failure of the policy in Waziristan.

MEN ON THE SPOT, INTERNAL EXPLANATIONS AND EXPANSION OF EMPIRE IN WAZIRISTAN

> Holding Wano is a game of bluff, which should never be played on a small scale.
>
> —Agent Governor-General in Baluchistan, 1892[37]

When the agent governor-general wrote the above to the foreign secretary in 1892, he might as well have been talking about all of Waziristan. He advocated permanent occupation, tribal allowances and posting political officers in the area. This is the policy that was undertaken in Waziristan, after much debate. In essence, it was a policy of interference and occupation, but the GoI did not want to admit this. So the policy was based on an emphatic refusal of the annexation of Waziristan. In January 1894, the GoI had written to Whitehall, 'We wish it to be clearly understood that nothing is further from our intentions than the annexation of tribal country on our frontier.'[38] But that was not all. While the British did not want to annex the Wazirs and their territory, at the same time they wanted to show them that they were 'our men'.[39] So the same telegram continued: 'We believe, however, that without annexation, and without interference in the internal affairs of the tribes, it will be possible to bring them further within our influence, and to induce them to regard themselves as owing allegiance to us.'[40] The government in London approved and the secretary of state sent the following reply:

> I trust that the tranquillity of the border, especially in the neighbourhood of the Gomal, will now be secured. I observe that your Government emphatically repudiates all intention of annexing tribal territory, but desires to bring the tribes whom this settlement concerns further within your influence. I approve generally of the policy thus described; but I trust that in carrying it into effect your Government will carefully abstain from taking any steps to extend your influence which may tend to bring about a collision with the tribesmen, or to the establishment of fresh posts beyond the frontier which may require armed protection.[41]

The cleverness with which the instructions of Whitehall and the declared policy in Waziristan were violated demonstrates the power of sub-imperialism and led to a series of events which culminated in the Tochi attack.

Early in 1894, a heated debate took place among the upper echelons of the British Government of India about their policy towards Waziristan. The question arose due to the agreement that the British had concluded with the Amir of Afghanistan in November

1893, which would demarcate the territories of British India and of Afghanistan. The settlement to demarcate, which the Amir had yielded to unwillingly, was in turn the result of a struggle for dominion between the British and the Amir. The essence of the problem was that the British realised, and admitted, that the territories in question were in no way theirs. But they did not want the Amir laying claim to them either. However, this problem was an imperial invention on the part of the British because tribal areas such as Waziristan may have at some time owed a nominal allegiance on their own terms to the Amir, but they were independent by the 1890s.

However, the undefined and constantly shifting nature of the tribes' relationship with the neighbouring powers was something that was unacceptable to the British imperial mind in India when imperialism had become a self-propagating machine. So in January 1894 Lord Lansdowne, the Viceroy of India, declared:

> I take it to be an axiom of frontier administration that a tribe, or group of tribes, situated between two comparatively powerful States must be under the influence of one or the other of those States. There may be moments when the tribe finds it convenient to face both ways and to keep up simultaneous relations with two rival Courts or Governments. We have had illustrations of this in the case of the Waziris themselves, who, while affairs were in suspense, held constant communications with Kabul on the one side, and with our Frontier officials on the other,... Such a condition of things is, however, fruitful of intrigue, and dangerous to all concerned. ... It is necessary that there should be a clear understanding with the Waziris, as well as with the Amir, that they are, to use a very convenient expression, 'our men,' and no one else's, or, as we should put it in an official paper, that they fall within our sphere of influence, and not within that of any other Power.[42]

Having decided without their wishes that they were 'our men', the British government then had to decide on what this policy meant and how best to implement it. So the debate on policy in Waziristan waged during much of 1894.

As a result of the agreement concluded between the British government and the Amir of Afghanistan, the latter was precluded from all interference in Waziristan except a small portion of it called Birmal. So the question arose what would be the state of affairs in the rest of Waziristan, which the British now claimed lay within their sphere of influence. The reason why it was 'absolutely necessary that this block of country should not be allowed to fall under Afghan influence'[43] lay in the fact that the military authorities had declared that in case of a Russian advance into Afghanistan, the best response for the British would be to advance to the Kabul–Ghazni–Kandahar line. And in order that this advance could be made with rapidity, it was necessary to control and be able to use the principal approaches leading from British India to that line. The local administration of the frontier regions was given to the GoP, which in turn was subordinate to the GoI. The question of Waziristan, under debate, was referred to the Punjab government for its observation as to the action that should be taken.

The first reports on the question were provided by three local officers—R. I. Bruce, commissioner and superintendent, Derajat; L. W. King, deputy commissioner, Dera Ismail Khan; and H. A. Anderson, deputy commissioner of Bannu (who appears as Gee's superior during the Maizar attack). Bruce, the senior-most of the three officers and one who for several years before had proposed a forward policy, made the following case. He stated that it was with remarkable equanimity that the tribes regarded the settlement concluded with the Amir, so far as they were acquainted with it. 'I do not for a moment say that the hill sections on the Tochi–Thall side are waiting to rush into our arms and say, "Mark out your boundary and our country; its routes and resources are open to you and we are your submissive subjects,"'[44] Bruce went on to say. But the tribes were willing to accept 'as reasonable terms for measures by which the country comprised within the new boundary would be pacified and opened up'.[45] The tribes would 'eagerly welcome' the establishment of military posts as they are 'alive to the fact that nothing can prosper amongst themselves, and that they will be constantly in hot water with the British Government and with the Amir unless they are constrained by some controlling authority to maintain peace towards one another'.[46] What this would mean in terms of resigning their independence, Bruce concluded that their idea of independence meant 'a title to be free of all wholesome controlling authority, with a general license to cut throats, maintaining a state of anarchy in the country, making it useless for all practical purposes and an actual source of danger and weakness in times of trouble'.[47] The objects of the government he assumed to be three, based on their past declarations:

> 1—To bring the tribes into line with ourselves by the establishment of intimate and friendly relations identifying their interests with ours, rendering the resources of the country available for our requirements, and thus making our border land and its tribesmen a factor of strength in the great scheme of imperial frontier defence, instead of a source of weakness as it is while left in the normal condition of anarchy. 2—The opening of the Tochi, Gumatti–Thall, and other routes, and the establishment of safe lateral communication between the Gomal and Kurram beyond the Mahsud hills. The latter may be said to be more particularly the local object and follows the first as a matter of course. 3—The amelioration of the condition of the frontier tribes by the extension of humanising influences over them, redeeming them from their semi-barbarous condition and putting them in the way of earning an honest livelihood.[48]

The actions and agendas of the men on the spot reveal different interests as stakes in this imperial debate.

In order to attain the above objects, he argued that the Sandeman policy[49] be applied to Waziristan. Essentially, the policy was to establish a military station in the area with an outpost and, more importantly, of giving the tribesmen and their leading headmen allowances. While King and Anderson concurred with the views of Bruce and proposed immediate demarcation of the boundary, they also pointed out that there was indication that the tribes were not wholly pleased with the agreement reached with the Amir which had 'sold' their territory without their consent to the Amir. The reference is to Birmal, which was considered joint country of all the Darwesh Khels and the tribe encamped there in the hot weather in order to graze their cattle. Anderson stated in his report:

> In the first place, until the Darwesh Khel have given us a mandate to align the boundaries of Waziristan, they not unnaturally question our right to fix their boundaries. Waziristan is a perfectly independent country according to their views, and

> they should be consulted before any portion of what they claim is assigned to a third party... It needs little argument to show that if the Waziris are dissatisfied with the boundary, they being headstrong hillmen, will not only be unwilling to assist in demarcating their boundary, but will do their best to throw difficulties in the way of the Commission appointed to do so.[50]

However, these problems could be addressed by bringing Waziristan under more direct control of the British government by giving them subsidies and raising levies from among them to keep the routes open. But both Anderson and King stated that it would be a mistake to proceed with the demarcation of the boundary without coming to some sort of arrangement with the tribes first. And finally all three officers, Bruce foremost among them, advocated the 'pacification' of Waziristan. The main reason for this was the tribal raiding and counter-raiding that might take place across the border, and would embroil the British in difficulties with the Afghan government.

Sir Dennis Fitzpatrick, the lieutenant governor of Punjab, differed from the view provided by Bruce and stated his case at length before the GoI. He viewed that agreement with the Amir did not necessarily impose on the British, or on the Amir, any obligation to establish an efficient system of control over the tribal territory falling respectively on the Indian and Afghan sides of the boundary line. He could conceive only one object of really great importance that would be served by establishing direct control over Waziristan—that of the imperial military defence of the Frontier against a foreign invader. Even if that were the case, Fitzpatrick argued for a policy of non-interference in the internal affairs of the tribes, in contrast to the scheme proposed by Bruce, Anderson and King, who recommended that the GoI establish internal peace and settle the disputes between the numerous divisions and sub-divisions of the Wazir tribes. Fitzpatrick's position was the following:

> All that is needed for our purpose is that we should have absolute and exclusive possession of the lines of communication to which we attach importance with a very narrow margin on each side; that we should be at liberty to construct proper roads, and eventually railways, along those lines, and guard them by posts, some of which would be garrisoned by our troops or police, and some tribal levies.

> I don't see why we should seek for anything beyond that; on the contrary, I see a very great deal against our doing so. If we once begin 'promenading' (as it is called in Assam) about the country off our lines of communication and interfering with the affairs of the tribes, undertaking to settle their disputes, and so on, we shall inevitably and beyond the slightest shadow of a doubt be gradually drawn on to interfere more and more, until we in the end practically take upon ourselves the government of the country....
>
> I don't see why we should not simply stick to our lines of communication and the posts on them, having nothing to do with the Waziris except in so far as we should engage their services for maintaining order on those lines, and leaving them outside of those lines to manage their own affairs, settle their own quarrels, fight their own battles, and enjoy in every way, and to as full an extent as they do now, that 'freedom of the wild ass' which they prize above all things in this world....
>
> I quite see that, in order to maintain this position of isolation in a country like Waziristan, we should have to put a strong curb on the benevolent aggressiveness of our frontier officers...[51]

Bruce was exactly one such 'benevolently aggressive' officer. Fitzpatrick realised that his scheme would entangle the government in the internal affairs of the tribes and therefore argued against the pacification of the Wazir country. Inside this policy debate and reflected within the different interests, the fundamental issue is about conceiving empire and how empire is constituted with different interests.

The case went to the GoI where it was discussed in the Governor-General's Council, the highest echelon of the state. The Council was composed of six members—the newly elected Viceroy Elgin, the Commander-in-Chief G. S. White, J. Westland, H. Brackenbury, C. B. Pritchard and A. P. MacDonnell. Elgin stated that it was necessary to tell the Wazirs that they now 'belonged to the British Government', but this should be done 'quietly', leaving it to Bruce and the local officers to make the necessary communications.[52] But generally it would be important to tell the tribes that

> we have come to terms with the Amir; that a certain line (giving the description of the convention) has been agreed upon; that the Commissioners of the two Governments will proceed in

> October to mark it off on the ground, and that in the meantime we call upon the tribes to respect it; that we have no desire to interfere with their affairs, but only to secure peace; and that in settling our arrangements for that end, we shall invite and welcome their co-operation.[53]

He reiterated the basic policy of the GoI: 'We are not to annex the country, i.e., the frontier of British India and the sphere of the local administration of British officials remain as before. On the other hand, we are to extend our influence over tribes beyond the frontier of British India.'[54] He added, 'I fail to attach any meaning to this, unless we are to control the intertribal relations, and especially anything that can affect the interests of Afghanistan.'[55] Finally, he advocated that some sort of tribute be taken from the tribes, not on fiscal grounds but for the reason that 'nothing would bring so home to the Waziris, that they are now "our men," as some payment, however small'.[56] Therefore, he concurred with the policy outlined by Bruce.

Brackenbury agreed with Elgin and proposed the establishment of a military post of considerable strength as the one way to control the Wazirs. White, the commander-in-chief, carried this argument further, stating that given that it was an 'absolute necessity' to establish one or more military posts in Waziristan, he could not see how this could be achieved without the military frontier being advanced. He argued:

> Posts thrown forward from the Derajat to Wano or possibly to Sheranni mean a military move to the front and consequently an advance of our military frontier. In this instance this advance has been forced on us by circumstances beyond our own control, and should be considered on its own merits and apart from any idea of unnecessary advance or aggression, which has of late years provoked, perhaps justly, adverse criticism from politicians both at home and abroad.[57]

He understood Bruce's proposal to mean an extension of British influence over Waziristan 'by a military occupation tempered by the presence of political officers'.[58] Without 'undue depreciation of his own cloth' he looked upon military occupation as an 'obligatory evil'.[59] Finally he proposed a strong force march through Waziristan because 'the impression made by a strong demonstration at first will be lasting, and will prevent any idea of successful opposition'.[60]

Thus, Elgin, Brackenbury and White endorsed Bruce's scheme. However, there was a contradiction at the heart of the scheme and indeed at the heart of the stated GoI policy. Whitehall had instructed the GoI that there was to be no annexation. The officials accepted such but argued that it was possible to bring the tribes under their 'influence' without annexing them. However, the proposals being argued by Bruce and the three figures in question advocated a kind of 'control' and 'influence' which essentially was annexation.

The other three members of the Council recognised and articulated this contradiction. Pritchard made the most forceful case:

> If we push forward our military posts beyond the Gomal, make roads through Waziri territory, levy tribute from the tribes, interfere in their quarrels, and undertake to prevent them from raiding into Afghanistan, we shall destroy the independence of the Waziris and be practically assuming the administrative control of their country, in whatever terms we may choose to describe our action. ... The cost of these operations will be enormous. In carrying them out we shall have to encounter and overcome much stubborn resistance; and, if the new line of posts along the Afghan border is laid, we shall find ourselves in contact with a fresh set of tribesmen who are likely to prove quite as troublesome neighbours to deal with in the future as the Waziris have proved in the past. A forward movement and a policy of the nature just described seems to me to transgress alike the declarations of policy made in our despatches to the Secretary of State, and the instructions of that authority.[61]

As to what the British position should be, he argued retaining their present frontier posts and strengthening their position by a limited scheme of tribal service as Fitzpatrick had suggested.

The others made the same point. Westland stated that even if it was necessary to fortify their position by use of a strong force while demarcating the frontier, then that must be done. But once demarcation was completed, he did not see any reason why the force could not be withdrawn.

> The Waziris are not pleasant neighbours, but they will be rather difficult and intractable subjects, and they will be extremely expensive ones. As to their mutual quarrels, these seem to me a strong argument for leaving them alone, for if they take a pleasure in cutting each other's throats, it is best for us to remain in a position in which we can look on with indifference, rather than voluntarily take up one where we are obliged to interfere.[62]

However, Westland, MacDonnell and Pritchard were brushed aside and the Council drafted a despatch to the secretary of state in England, proposing a policy along the lines of Bruce's scheme. While the details of how the policy was to be implemented were not completely clear, it was decided that: (a) it was necessary to establish a strong military post in the country; (b) a Demarcation Commission would proceed to mark out the boundary in October 1894, accompanied by troops; (c) at the same time, a political officer would be deputed to explain to the Wazirs the nature of the relations which the British government intended to establish with them as it was 'desirable that these negotiations should be carried on at a time when we are able to make a strong display of force';[63] (d) allowances would be given to the headmen and inferior men enlisted for service in levy posts. Brackenbury suggested a list of outrages committed in the Gomal to be attached to the despatch to make their case stronger. Westland, Pritchard and MacDonnell dissented from the despatch.

Fitzpatrick attempted till the last to provide a restraining hand. He said that Bruce, whether 'by hook or by crook', was attempting to draw the GoI on. He feared that the leading men of the tribes, whom Bruce wanted to subsidise and through whom the British worked, were ultimately 'too weak to control their people' in a country where the tribes were organised on an extremely democratic basis. 'This will, I fear be one of our greatest difficulties, if we undertake the pacification of Waziristan.'[64] In August 1894, Secretary of State Henry Fowler approved the policy with some reluctance and on the condition that interference with the tribes and the outlay of money in Waziristan would be kept within the narrowest limits that were practicable.

Sir Dennis Fitzpatrick's words would come back to haunt them in 1897. This layer of sub-imperialism shows the mechanics of imperial expansion in Waziristan. Imperial explanations aimed to get around the directives of the home government and therefore centre around a convoluted language that desisted from acknowledging actions that amounted to occupation. Therefore, the voices of Empire that were against expansion were marginalised.

CONTEXTUALISING THE MAIZAR ATTACK: IMPERIAL EXPANSION AND PUKHTUN RESISTANCE IN WAZIRISTAN

The demarcation having been sanctioned for October, it was decided that it would be unsafe for the delimitation to be attempted without a strong military escort. Here, one wonders that if the tribes were willing to welcome the British and come under their fold, as Bruce had suggested, then why proceed with a strong escort unless hostilities were anticipated. Owing, however, to the serious 'outrages' committed by the Mahsud Wazirs in the Gomal and Zhob valleys, it was considered best to take precautions. By this time, it had also been decided that the permanent military post under question would be established in Wana.

On 25 October, Bruce, having been appointed commissioner of the Delimitation Commission, arrived with a brigade of all arms in Wana. A few days before his arrival, he had received a letter from Mullah Powindah stating that troops should not be stationed at Wana, and that the British should abstain from interfering in the country as these areas were under Mahsud limits.[65] He also demanded the release of five prisoners that had been taken in 1893 for the murder of a British officer. Bruce sent back a reply to the Mullah, saying that he declined to have any communications with him except through the tribal Maliks.

Over the next few days, shots were fired into the camp at Wana and Bruce received 'alarming reports' that Mullah Powindah was gathering his followers with 'hostile intentions'.[66] On 2 November 1894, messengers from the Mullah arrived again to see Bruce, demanding assurance that the British government would not occupy Mahsud country and asking for the release of the prisoners. Again Bruce declined to have any communication with him and advised him to disperse his following and return home. British troops commanded by General Turner remained accoutred and alert.

On 3 November, Mullah Powindah and his followers, estimated at about 3,000, attacked the British camp at night. The British force, 'which was considered strong enough to suppress such opposition as any sections of the Waziris might be inclined to offer',[67] could not ward off the attack. At the break of daylight, the Wazirs retreated. The resulting loss to the British was 120 killed and wounded, including several officers. The GoI offered the tribes terms to make reparation which included (a) the surrender as hostages of 18 of the principal men engaged in the attack; (b) the banishment from the country of Mullah Powindah; (c) the surrender of every rifle, horse and the money stolen from the British camp. The Maliks were set the task of getting the Mahsuds to comply with the terms. They failed to do so.

Therefore, the GoI decided to sanction a punitive expedition against the Mahsuds. On 15 December 1894, political control was transferred from Bruce to Lieutenant General Sir W. S. A. Lockhart, and on 17 December 1894 he assumed command of the Waziristan Field Force. In order to punish the Mahsuds for the attack, the troops blew up their houses, carried off their forage and grain, and captured their flocks and herds. The Mahsuds had taken refuge in the higher valleys along with their families. The village of Marobi belonging to Mullah Powindah was completely destroyed with the exception of a mosque. The Lee-Metford rifle together with cordite was used for the first time in frontier warfare (Nevill 1912: 154). In February 1895, the Field Force also started the work of demarcating the boundary.

So far the Waziristan policy had not proved successful. It had become clear that the delimitation was resisted by the tribes, and they did not want the British in their country. The demarcation of the boundary was undertaken with military force and coercion. Following these events, Bruce wrote a report to the GoI, attempting to explain the situation. He stated that since the opening of the Gomal Pass in 1889, 'a uniform and consistent policy' had been pursued in regard to the Wazirs.

> The foundation on which this entire policy rests, which is the same as that which has so successfully been pursued in Beluchistan, is support and encouragement to leading headmen

> who throw in their lot with and range themselves on the side of Government, the controlling through them of the marauding factions and bad characters, and the consequent maintenance of peace and order.[68]

He stated that it would be 'an unfortunate mistake' to conclude from this punitive expedition that this policy had been a failure. To prove that the policy had not failed, he pointed to the 'friendly attitude' of the Maliks who wanted the British in their country. The fact that there was a large proportion of 'marauding factions' who wanted otherwise made it difficult to bring the policy to successful issue; 'but if persevered in and reasonable support is afforded by the Government, there is no obstacle that cannot be overcome'.[69] Therefore, he again advocated the permanent occupation of Wana. Military failures are glossed over and imperial explanations are in favour of expansion.

OCCUPATION OF TOCHI AND ORIGINS OF THE MAIZAR ATTACK

It was at this time that the British entered Tochi and began their dealings with the Madda Khel, which led to a series of events that culminated in the Maizar outbreak over two years later. In December 1894, one of the columns attached to the Field Force had marched through northern Waziristan to reach its destination of Razmak. In February 1895, the troops entered Tochi with the purpose of demarcating the northern portion of the boundary. It was at this time that Anderson, the deputy commissioner of Bannu, summoned the Madda Khel and the Dawar in order to explain to them the objects of the GoI. Lockhart, in his report, thanked Anderson for he made it possible for the troops to march through the Darwesh Khel country and 'succeeded in overcoming all objections on the part of the inhabitants to my advance up the Tochi valley'.[70] Sadda Khan was one of the main Maliks whom Anderson dealt with. The Tochi Maliks met with Anderson in Bannu and said they did not wish the British to enter Tochi as they were afraid that their country would be occupied. Anderson assured Sadda Khan and other Maliks that the purpose of the government was just to delimit the boundary and it did not wish to occupy Tochi. Sadda Khan arranged for supplies and sent men to escort the troops during the delimitation. Men on the spot created misrepresentations: (a) to mislead the tribesmen, and (b) to deliberately disguise the conditions that the military would be entering into. In the face of blatant failure during the coming Maizar attack, they would be found out, otherwise the details of these lower levels of Empire's operations would remain hidden. This is a concrete example of sub-imperialism.

At this time Anderson and Bruce communicated to the GoI that the Maliks of Tochi were friendly and expressed their willingness that the occupation of Tochi by the British should continue:

> The Darwesh Khels of the Tochi, the Tori Khel, Mohmit Khel and Madda Khel, have shown conclusively by the friendly way in which they welcomed us that they are exceedingly well disposed to us, and that they do not in any way resent our coming into the valley. All sections have expressed their willingness that our occupation should continue. They are quite ready to accept allowances and to observe the conditions in return for which they are granted.[71]

Anderson presented a scheme for the permanent occupation of Tochi that included the distribution of allowances and the establishment of military posts.

Why did the men on the spot misrepresent or, in this case, lie about what was taking place? What is apparent immediately is that Anderson and Bruce before him were the architects of the policy in Waziristan. The policy was a total failure. As to the intentions and temper of the Darwesh Khel, in his testimony Sadda Khan provided the following account of what occurred after the delimitation in the area had been completed. The Tochi Maliks were gathered in Miran Shah and had agreed that the British troops should be asked to return. At this point, Anderson and Ghulam Muhammad Khan, the deputy assistant of police at Bannu, sent for Sadda Khan alone and said, 'We intend to take over the Tochi (i.e., all within the boundary pillars). Why do you not agree? If you say you agree, the other maliks will follow you.'[72] Sadda Khan said he would agree if they accepted certain conditions and recognised him as 'the biggest man in Tochi'.[73] Further, he said that the British would have to give the tribes money so they could be persuaded to agree to British presence. Anderson promised to this effect. Sadda Khan as 'collaborator' represents a complex position. He can be seen negotiating the forces of Empire rather tenuously, perhaps for his own interests, and to some extent balancing what seemed like an inevitable imperial intrusion.

On 13 May 1895, the troops moved up to Boya, a cooler part of the valley. On the same day, a British officer of the 6th Punjab Infantry, Limond, a sepoy and a *syce* (stable attendant) were attacked by four men. Limond and the syce were killed; the sepoy recovered. Three of the assailants were bayoneted or shot by the British troops and the fourth ran away. He was discovered soon after and shot two days later. The houses of all four were blown up. However, to inflict the utmost severity for this attack, the bodies of the first three assailants were burnt. This was an act of defilement that the tribes regard as being worse than mutilation. If a body of a person is burnt and not buried, in accordance with Muslim custom, then the person is denied paradise. The burning of bodies created much bitterness in Tochi. A few days later, the Maliks of the Tochi valley sent the following written petition to Anderson:

> The bodies of the three persons of Khare Killa Amzoni who attacked a British officer on the 13th near camp Boya were burnt which was quite contrary to our religious ordinances. No such action was ever taken during Pushtu times, and this has been greatly disapproved of both by the Darwesh Khel and the Dauris of the Tochi valley. It has brought shame on us. We request therefore that the Government should suitably compensate us for this shame which we endured, as the burning of dead bodies is objectionable and prohibited according to the Muhammadan Law.[74]

Anderson decided against compensation but reported that the burning of the bodies had 'created so great a stir throughout the Tochi Valley'[75] that such an action should not be repeated in future. Bruce also remarked that 'the Muhammadans regard the burning of bodies as hitting below the belt and I must say I have some sympathy with the feeling and not think that, assassination being amongst their methods, is sufficient reason for our resorting to such measures'.[76] As to the attack itself, Bruce hastened to assure the GoI that he would not conclude 'from the acts of a few individual fanatics that the general feeling and wish of the people for our occupation of the Tochi, so frequently expressed, had changed, and should recommend that they should have no effect on the Government policy'.[77] Anderson also dismissed the attack as one inspired by 'pure fanaticism'[78] by a gang of bravos and assassins. Once again discontent and resistance are covered up and imperial explanations function for a continuation of a failed policy.

However, Pukhtun resistance to the occupation of Tochi continued in the form of ongoing attacks. A few days later, on 18 May, another attack occurred in Miran Shah where a Pathan lance-naik of the 2nd Punjab Infantry was killed by Wazir herdsmen. One of the herdsmen was killed in retaliation and 10 people found in the vicinity of the attack were taken prisoners and their flocks detained. Reports also started coming in that a change had come over the people of Tochi, they had become strongly hostile towards the British taking possession of their country. There were reports that the troops harassed the people in Tochi: 'The camels graze on and injure their trees and nobody takes the matter into consideration. They say Shaftala (grass), &c., are not paid for at all. The sepoys take fruit from the gardens by force.'[79] There were also reports that the tribes were looking to Mullah Powindah for leadership to help them oppose the British. The Mullah was attempting to effect peace between the Mahsuds and the Darwesh Khels so that they could resist the British. An interesting point to note here is that there were other men on the spot (officers and local informants) who did not share the same stake in concealing the tribes' response to the occupation as did Anderson and Bruce.

Anderson and Bruce discounted these reports. Bruce claimed that 'popular feelings could be accurately gauged by Sadda Khan'[80] and other leading Maliks, who approved of the British presence. Anderson stated that the feeling of discontent was due to the fact that allowances had not been granted as yet. Once the allowances were distributed, the feeling of dissatisfaction would disappear.

The GoI went along with their assessment. Anderson submitted a scheme of 13 posts to be established in the Tochi. Meanwhile, several difficulties arose over the question of how best to distribute the allowances. Anderson proposed handing over the allowances to the tribes and letting them decide how to make the distribution among individuals and different sub-sections. Bruce pointed out that their entire policy was aimed at singling out certain Maliks and strengthening their position, so that they would be able to control their tribes in the interest of the British:

> I would also point out that in my opinion the granting of small allowances to a great number of big and little Maliks on the basis of tribal distribution will not of itself secure an efficient hold on any tribe. At any time when the tribe's relation with the Government become strained in any way, the individual Maliks having only small interests in the allowances will not as a rule mind risking them, while we cannot safely reckon in working on the tribe as a whole merely through these allowances. It is therefore most desirable that the self interests of the men of note and leading in the country should be bound up with ours, so that in times of trouble or difficulty we may be able confidently to reckon on their ranging themselves on the side of Government.[81]

Meanwhile, shots continued to be fired into the British camp and a few days after the attack in Miran Shah, another attack occurred there inside the post when two sepoys were stabbed. Anderson explained to the GoI that

> it is impossible to expect that in a highly fanatical country like Dawar fanatical outrages will not occur, and in the same way we cannot expect savage young Waziris to become at once orderly and obedient subjects. It is likely enough, too, that intriguers will make foolish efforts to organize against us the unruly elements in the tribes of the valley and their brethren, not with the object of driving us out of the country, but with the view of increasing the allowance.[82]

However, Anderson was getting lists made of the 'more turbulent characters' and a careful watch would be maintained on them.[83] The higher authorities went along with the views of Bruce and Anderson. The chief secretary to the GoP wrote to Bruce in reply to his reports:

> It may of course be that whatever feeling there is against us in the Tochi at this moment worth speaking of is due merely to the

> delay in granting the allowances, and some of those untoward incidents which must, in spite of all care and vigilance, occur from time to time when a military force is in camp in a strange country, but we must be on the lookout for and carefully study any symptoms going to indicate more deep-lying and permanent causes of ill-will against us.[84]

The military occupation of Tochi continued and posts continued to be built. The GoI had accepted the views of the 'men on the spot' that in order to open up the Tochi route, it was necessary to establish permanent military posts there. The policy in Tochi was based on strengthening the hands of Maliks such as Sadda Khan, who approved of British presence in their country. And the 'men on the spot' Bruce and Anderson also indicated to the GoI that except for a few 'turbulent spirits' the inhabitants of Tochi approved of the British being there. The allowances were finally distributed to the tribes in November and December 1895. How the policy was functioning is clearly evident in the events that followed.

In February and March 1896, 'tribal agitation and demonstrations'[85] occurred in Tochi. On 9 February, there was a 'riotous demonstration'[86] in the Sheranni post by the Madda Khels. About a hundred members of the tribe had gathered there to discuss the allowances. Several 'minor Maliks' had gathered there who had not been given any allowances. According to Anderson, 'excitement followed the discussions, and some of the more turbulent spirits threatened to turn the Munshi out of the temporary Sheranni post and also threatened some of the levies'.[87] The mob also threatened the posts. Piyal and Nur Muhammad were leaders in the discussions that preceded the riot, but they restrained the mob and assisted the Munshi. The gathering dispersed.

On 14 February, Anderson reported that an 'extremely aggressive'[88] letter was sent to the political officer, Casson. He did not discuss the contents of the letter but attributed it to a 'fanatical writer'.[89] Anderson reported that the Maliks represented to him that 'a certain amount of agitation prevailed', and that Sadda Khan ascribed the agitations to 'insufficient and incorrectly distributed allowances'.[90] Further, Sadda Khan 'persistently represented that the agitation had grown beyond his control, and he asked that troops should be sent up the valley to assist him in suppressing it'.[91] On 16 March, during the religious festival of Id, another demonstration occurred. A large number of people had assembled at the ancestral tombs of Sadda Khan's family, as was the custom. The gathering turned into an agitation when the Mullahs charged the Maliks with bringing British troops into their country. Once again the precarious role of Sadda Khan as a collaborator is highlighted. Far from being able to control the tribes, instead as Malik he is constantly challenged amidst the growing resistance. The people dispersed, but various 'alarmist reports'[92] were received by the muharrirs of the posts. Anderson discredited these reports because he felt that the muharrirs 'were being utilized by the intriguing Maliks for their own ends'.[93] He felt that the Maliks, including Sadda Khan, were responsible for the agitation, the main reason for which was the desire of the Maliks and tribesmen to put pressure on the GoI to make a substantial increase in the allowances. He believed that Sadda Khan had instigated the agitation. Anderson stated that this belief was shared by 'that shrewd and well-informed observer, Gholam Muhammad Khan, Assistant District Superintendent, Police'.[94] But he concluded that he did not doubt Sadda Khan and the other leading Maliks' 'loyalty as a body and individually to their promises made to Government'.[95] 'I do not doubt that Sadda Khan in asking for troops really wishes the support of troops to strengthen his authority over his section.'[96] Casson did not agree with Anderson and Ghulam Muhammad Khan that Sadda Khan was responsible for the agitation. On the last day of March, Anderson met with many of the Maliks, when they demanded certain conditions:

> The Maliks, however, unanimously pressed me to obtain for them some written assurance for the satisfaction of their tribesmen that the government will not take revenue from them; they will be exempt from Court Fees; their jungle and grazing grounds will not be interfered with; that their mines will remain their own; that cases regarding women will be decided according to their own customs and offenders will be confined in jails in the Tochi.[97]

The event that occurred next is the one that was most immediately connected to the Maizar outbreak. On 9 June 1896, Honda Ram, the muharrir of the Sheranni post, was murdered by Waris Khan, who belonged to the Ali Khan Khel section of the Madda Khels. At this point, Gee had taken over the position of political officer of Tochi Valley, Anderson having been promoted to Bruce's former position, commissioner and superintendent, Derajat. Waris Khan escaped soon after into Birmal, which was now Afghan territory. The British could have demanded his surrender from the Afghan authorities. However, Anderson decided that if such a demand were made, the Afghan authorities would be entitled to make a reciprocal demand on the British 'which may be inconvenient'.[98] This showed that the object of British policy of delimiting the boundary and occupying Tochi with a view to facilitating the solving of raids and 'outrages' across the border was unsuccessful. So instead of pursuing the known murderer, Gee called upon the Maliks (none of whom were present in Sheranni on the day of the murder) to surrender several people who had 'incited' Waris Khan to commit the murder even though he was alone at the time. These people were supposed to be religious students of Mullah Ghain-ud-din who, according to Anderson, had been regularly preaching against British occupation and 'promising paradise to any one who should kill a servant of Government'.[99] The Maliks expressed their inability to Gee to bring in the people whose surrender he demanded.

Anderson, at this point, submitted a report on the general situation in the Tochi. He stated that it had become unsafe for the levies and the men of the Border Military Police to move around the area. Further, he stated:

> Intrigues against the Maliks and their authority are at work, and in fact the control of the Maliks over the turbulent characters of their sections has been relaxed. Offences have been committed in which the offenders have not been brought to justice, such as the looting of the contractor's fir poles near Dre Vasta, the destruction of bricks at the Muhammad Khel Post, the murder of two coolies of the Muhammad Khel Post, the theft of the Kanirogha Muharrir's property, the killing of a levy sowar's horse, the attack on the dak sowar near Pakki Killa, and the theft of his horse. The Maliks find themselves growing weaker and unable to control the bad characters.[100]

Despite trying to downplay the resistance, now it was becoming difficult to keep up the pretence that the policy based on strengthening the Maliks by bribing them had proved successful. Besides, Anderson's constant urgings that the inhabitants of Tochi approved of British presence, if true, were working in a strange way—unless the majority of the inhabitants had turned into 'turbulent spirits'.

Anderson and Gee submitted to the GoI that the only way to remedy things was to advance troops into the Upper Tochi to strengthen the hands of the Maliks. Further, Gee proposed that two fines be inflicted on the Madda Khels: one of Rs 2,000 to punish them for the murder of Honda Ram and another fine of Rs 1,000 for the agitation that had occurred in February 1896. The reason why Gee added the latter fine, even though it had not been inflicted at the time of the agitation, was that by now the muharrirs of other posts, all of them Hindu, had resigned and refused to serve. Gee and Anderson's logic was that the muharrirs having withdrawn, they had no employee in that tract for whose safety they were responsible. So they could now 'realize fines by putting additional pressure on the tribe, and this is a reason for imposing fines now which did not exist before'.[101] Of course the infliction of fines would not mean the exemption of suspected persons from arrest.

In February 1897, the suspected men including Mullah Ghain-ud-din were produced before Gee and tried. They were exonerated from the murder of Honda Ram and released. Gee reported that the Mullah appeared to be 'a quiet retiring man with more learning than the ordinary run of Mullahs usually possess, and I regard his coming in and taking the oath as most satisfactory'.[102] At this time, Gee reduced the fine from Rs 2,000 to Rs 1,200. After this point, we have two versions of what happened—already discussed above. Gee's account, presented after the Maizar outbreak, varies, though later, as there was some dispute about the distribution of this fine, he told the Maliks that he would visit Maizar to 'discuss' rather than 'realise' the fine. Sadda Khan presented another story which was backed up by other testimonies. The tribunal accepted Sadda Khan's story.

Following Gee and Anderson's recommendation, after the murder of Honda Ram, troops were moved into Tochi at Datta Khel. However, Anderson reported that something more was needed.

> ...[W]e cannot expect to get the Darwesh Khels well in hand for our purposes unless we undertake to establish peace and order in their country, and this can not be effected without interfering in their internal disputes. Admitting then that we must interfere in the settlement of internal disputes, the question arises whether we are in any way bound not to interfere in their internal concerns. At the time we concluded our settlement with the Darwesh Khels in 1895 we told them that we did not want to take possession of their country, nor to interfere in their internal affairs, and so long as they behaved themselves and did not force us to do so, we should not interfere, nor take possession of their country.[103]

Asked by the lieutenant governor 'whether this interference in the internal disputes of the Darwesh Khels is not a breach of faith with the tribe', Anderson responded that even if they had led the tribe to believe that they would not interfere in their internal disputes, 'their subsequent conduct has been such as to absolve us from any obligation to abstain from doing so'.[104] He considered that the best means to carry out this interference were: (a) the early construction of a fortified position in Datta Khel; (b) the early construction of a road via Idak; and (c) 'the assignment of a sufficiently large Military escort to the Political Officer with full discretion to move about within a certain defined area'.[105] These would greatly strengthen British position. However, soon after there was another 'outrage' when some camel *sowars* were fired upon, and one of them was killed. Other 'offences' continued and are presented, as compiled by Gee, in Table 3.1.

The next 'outrage' to occur was the Maizar attack. When the attack occurred, Gee and Anderson reported that it was fanatical. This fit in with what had by now become an entrenched trope within the pattern of their past explanations that whenever an 'outrage' was committed, it was the work of 'fanatical' and 'turbulent spirits' and did not represent the majority of the people. Thus, imperial explanations do not just serve the pattern of having to justify empire externally but, as we see here, especially in the face of continuous failure, they have to explain it internally too, especially in order to legitimise expansion. But in the case of Maizar, it could not be argued that it did not represent the feelings of the people as almost all the inhabitants had taken part.

Table 3.1: 'Outrages' committed by Madda Khels, as compiled by H. W. Gee

No.	*Parties*	*Nature of Offence*	*Brief Account of Settlement and Final Order*
1	Empress *versus* Maliks Khiddar Khel, Momit Khels and Madda Khels of Ger and Kazha	Rioting in February 1896	Tribal fine of Rs 1,000 imposed on account of the agitation at Sherennai
2	Khitab Gul, &c., of Kohat *versus* Manzar Khels and Pai Khels	Robbery of property worth Rs 147.80 near Pai Khel on 29 January 1897	The offence was committed in the Pai Khel limits, but the Manzar Khels were suspected to be the offenders. Hence, both the tribes have been fined Rs 100, which will be paid as compensation, the loss being exaggerated—25 February 1897.
3	Davi Ditta, Contractor, *versus* Dauris and Manzar Khels	Murder of two coolies on 15 June 1896 at Muhammad Khel	Two coolies were murdered while the Muhammad Khel post was being built. Suspicion fell on the Manzar Khel. Both the tribes were fined Rs 600 out of which Rs 200 will be paid to the brother of the deceased.
4	Empress *versus* Manzar Khels and Pai Khels	Murder of two coolies on 21 October 1896	The offence was committed in the Pai Khel limits, but the Dauris are willing to take oath that Gulbadshah, Dauri, is one of the real offenders. Gulbadshah is the hamsaya of Momirogha Manzar Khels, and the Maliks state they cannot produce him. A fine of Rs 600 has been imposed in equal shares upon Manzar Khels of Momirogha, Pai Khels and the Malakh villages. Out of this Rs 200 will be paid to the heirs of the deceased—25 February 1897.

(contd)

Table 3.1 (contd)

No.	*Parties*	*Nature of Offence*	*Brief Account of Settlement and Final Order*
5	Aya Ram of Idak *versus* Pai Khel and Manzar Khel	Robbery of Rs 200 cash and clothes on 6 February 1897	A joint fine of Rs 100 has been imposed on the two tribes, which will be paid to the complainant as compensation. The loss was exaggerated.
6	Ibrahim, &c., of Pai Khel *versus* Manzar Khels of Pakki Killa	Wounding four donkeys and robbery of clothes on 7 February 1897	The Pakki Killa village has been fined Rs 15 as compensation—25 February 1897.
7	Empress *versus* Manzar Khels	Firing shots into Datta Khel Camp on the night of 3 February 1897	The offence was committed in the Khiddar Khel limits, but Manzar Khels and Macha (Madda Khels) are suspected to be the offenders. A joint fine of Rs 30 has been imposed on the three sections—25 February 1897.
8	Sobhat of Bannu *versus* Manzar Khel and Khiddar Khels	Robbery of clothes and car-rings between Drewasta and Pakki Killa on 13 February 1897	Tribal responsibility was enforced, and both the sections have been fined Rs 12 in equal shares—25 February 1897.
9	Empress *versus* Pakki Killa...	Firing shots into Datta Khel Camp on the night of February 7h/8, 1897	Some thieves crept into the camp bazaar at night. One of them, named Mir Gul, Manzar Khel, was shot dead by a sentry. A shot was also fired towards camp when Captain Burne was investigating the case. The Pakki Killa (village) has been fined Rs 30 for firing the shots, and the case of theft is still pending—25 February 1897.

(contd)

Table 3.1 (contd)

No.	*Parties*	*Nature of Offence*	*Brief Account of Settlement and Final Order*
10	Empress *versus* Manzar Khel, Macha and Kiddar Khel	Firing shots into Datta Khel, Camp on the night of 13/14 October 1896	A joint fine Rs 30 has been imposed on the tribes—25 February 1897.
11	Ahmad Din, &c., camp Datta Khel, *versus* Pakki Killa, Manzar Khels, Khiddar Khels	Theft of a bag containing shoes on the night of 21 January 1897	Manzar Khels and Khiddar Khels have been fined Rs 30 in equal shares. This will be paid to the complainant as compensation—25 February 1897.
12	Gokal Chand of Datta Khel camp *versus* Pakki Killa, Manzar Khels and Khiddar Khels	Theft of clothes on the night of 30/31 Janurary 1897	The tribes have been fined Rs 50 as compensation—25 February 1897.
13	Empress *versus* Pakki Killa, Manzar Khels and Khiddar Khels	Theft of a sack cloth of Commissariat Department. Camp Datta Khel, on the night of 2/3 February 1897	The tribes have been fined Rs 45—25 February 1897.
14	Empress through Khani and Zahir Shah, levies, *versus* Macha Madda Khels	Attacking a Dauri Beher and firing shots on the levies near Tor Kaura	Khangai and Machas are suspected of the offence and fired at the levies who went in pursuit. The Macha Madda Khels have been fined Rs 50—25 February 1897.
15	Shahab-ud-Din, Kharoti, *versus* Pai Khels and Manzar Khels	Theft of Rs 15 on 9 November 1896	Both the tribes have been fined Rs 10 as compensation—25 February 1897.

(contd)

Table 3.1 (contd)

No.	*Parties*	*Nature of Offence*	*Brief Account of Settlement and Final Order*
16	Harsa Ram of Hangu *versus* Manzar Khels and Khiddar Khels	Robbery of Rs 94 Nandrami and Rs 27 Kaldar and clothes on 16 February 1897	The Manzar Khel and Khiddar Khels have been fined Rs 50 as compensation—25 February 1897.
17	Empress *versus* Madda Khels of Kazha	Intrigue against Government in Kazha on 5 March 1897	The Madda Khels were fined Rs 30—5 April 1897.
18	Landak, Madda Khel, *versus* Karim Khan and Pir Muhammad, Sheranna levies	Robbery of property Rs 8-8-0 on 18 March 1897	The accused fined Rs 8-8-0 as compensation—5 April 1897.
19	Empress *versus* Madda Khels	Murder of Honda Ram, Muharrir of Sheranni, on 9 June 1896	The tribe fined Rs 1,200.

Source: 'From—H. W. Gee, Esquire, C.S., Political Officer, Tochi Valley, To—The Commissioner and Superintendent, Derajat Division, d. 23rd Feb 1897', Proceedings of the Government of India, Foreign Frontier, National Archives of India, May 1897.

The rulings of the tribunal itself established beyond doubt that the attack was not treacherous. Further, the series of events in North Waziristan since 1895 establish that the attack was anything but 'sudden'. Since the beginning of British presence in Tochi, there had been a consistent pattern of resistance to British occupation which Maizar was a part of. Table 3.1, which Gee compiled as showing 'outrages' and 'offences', clearly documents this resistance. But the attack occurred immediately because of the fine—the tribes regarded the fine as being unjust and resisted what they saw as an attempt by troops to collect it by force. Pukhtun oral tradition also points to the same set of reasons and confirms that the attack was not planned.[106]

The following account of the Maizar attack was provided by Malik Ghula Khan Khalifa, who witnessed the attack as a young boy of about seven years (see Figure 13).[107] It is presented in his own words with minor grammatical changes:

> The fight at Maizar began in this way. One of the members from the family of Khandaan brought a man who was going to teach. His name was Honde, he was a Hindu. A man killed him. Then the British fined the people 1200. Then Sadda Khan told the British that you should bring an army with you. When they brought the army everyone had to pay. The tribe told Sadda Khan, 'You brought him here, why should we pay? You wanted him to teach, we will not pay.' That is why the dispute started.
>
> Our leaders said Sadda Khan has brought Honde and the army to our area. Since he is responsible, he should pay. Why should the entire tribe pay? Then the people said, 'Let's attack them.' That is how we attacked them. People came in a cheegah to the spot where the British were gathered.[108] Women, men everyone attacked them. Sadda Khan ran away and the Khan Bahadur ran with him. Six hundred and sixty British were killed at Maizar. Eighty-three of our Madda Khels were killed as well.
>
> After the attack, our people went away from our village into the mountains for three years. Then the British army came.

Figure 13: Malik Ghula Khan Khalifa

> They destroyed our lands, our kots, trees—anything they found. Sadda Khan is the one who brought about the settlement with the English. The English said that the tribe should give Yargamal [hostages] and say sorry. But it was Sadda Khan who paid the money to the English.

The following account of the Maizar outbreak was provided by Malik Abdul Wadud, Madda Khel, the great grandson of Sadda Khan (see Figure 14).[109] It was the most comprehensive of the oral accounts collected and is presented in his own words:

> Nearly a 100 years have passed since the Maizar war. That was the time of swords and shields. There was a Hindu Munshi

Figure 14: Malik Abdul Wadud, Madda Khel

named Honda Ram. Our people killed him. The man who killed him was called Waris Khan. Waris Khan's tribe is Ali Khun Khel. There was an agreement amongst the Madda Khels that we will not let the English come to our land. Honda Ram was brought by Sadda Khan and the people questioned Sadda Khan as to why had he brought him to Sherrani. However, it was the English who had sent Honda Ram.

The tribe viewed Honda Ram as the man of the English. They killed him because they said that the 'Munshi is the hand of the Government which wants to touch us'. They said to each other, 'Today it is the Munshi, tomorrow it will be the Tehsildar and the day after the Khan Bahadur and then the Political Agent.' It is a ruse to occupy our land. This land is not even enough for us. It is a narrow land.

The Munshi's presence in Tochi was pretence. He pretended that he was there to teach children, but the real purpose behind his presence was that the British wanted to occupy the land. There was also a Bangi, who was the Munshi's assistant. The Bangi would order the people to carry cowdung in gornai [jute sacks]. Our people said: Have things gone so far that now we have to carry cowdung?

Waris Khan ran away. Gee wanted to fine us Rs 1200. The people held a maraqqa and the jirga decided that we couldn't pay. The tribe said they couldn't pay because they didn't have the money.

There was no preparation for the attack beforehand. People were cutting crops. It was the hot season. The British came to Maizar with three brigades. People said they have come here and want to collect all the money. We don't have it.

There was a woman called Bashara. She told the people of Maizar that the Sikhs and the English are dancing in Khivi [a spot in Maizar where the jirgas meet] and you are just sitting here. She said that there was no other way out—they had to fight. Bashara caused the attack. The leader of the people who attacked was called Pyall.

The British sounded a bugle, but the Madda Khels did not know this thing. The fight started with the sound of Rapal. About 67–68 of our Madda Khels died in this fight. Many English died, including their officers. Afterwards our people crossed over into Afghanistan. Sadda Khan gave himself up to the British and

> spent seven years in prison—four years in Dera Ismail Khan and three years in Miran Shah. He wanted to save the tribe—they were poor and fed up.
>
> We lost our villages. In the Maizar war our lands and our kotas were destroyed. The land became barren, no crops were grown. The British set fire to the wood of the houses that they had destroyed next to the graveyard. They shot houses with canon even though nobody was there. The British stayed in Maizar about six months. Then they got fed up. They couldn't manage being there, they became ill and their faces became swollen. Then they went back.
>
> Sadda Khan was the leader of the tribe. He saved the tribe by giving himself up. He tried to keep both the government and the tribe happy. He also tried to keep the two apart so they wouldn't fight.
>
> The English came and wanted to occupy our land. They were aggressors and they were cruel. We would not allow them to occupy our land and that is why we fought them. That is why we sacrificed ourselves and killed them also. 'They wanted to take our own land from us, so what do you expect.'

All the Madda Khel elders mention this same basic narrative—the attack was not pre-planned and occurred due to the Madda Khels resisting an attempt by British troops to collect a fine by force, a fine that they regarded as unjust. But underlying that is the fact that they put up a continual resistance to what they saw as an attempt on the part of the British to occupy their land. This continual resistance is extensively recorded in British documents as 'outrages'.

In the end, the political officers blamed the Maliks, Sadda Khan foremost, for the attack. We have to remember that these are the same Maliks on whom their entire policy in Waziristan had rested. The attack in Maizar demonstrated a complete failure of this policy. It also demonstrated that the political officers had failed in their main job of gauging the temper of the tribesmen and keeping the higher authorities informed of such. The evidence presented here shows that Gee's actions did not stem from incompetence but rather from a deliberate attempt to misrepresent the situation at Maizar. Gee was all too familiar with the dissatisfaction of the Maliks, the tribal discontent over the fine and the ongoing opposition of the tribes to

British occupation of Tochi. Gee's actions were an attempt at coercion and it is likely that he thought the display of force would bring them to order. Is that not why he had taken such a large military force to Maizar, because it would have a 'good effect'?

Finally judging from the objects declared by both the GoI and the local officers, the policy was a miserable failure. The GoI had stated that they had no desire to interfere in the affairs of the tribes, but only to secure peace. The government in London had approved this policy on the condition that the government in India would abstain from extending their influence, which 'may tend to bring about a collision with the tribesmen, or to the establishment of fresh posts beyond the frontier which may require armed protection'.[110] The very things that the GoI had set out to avoid were achieved. If the general aim was to bring the tribes into 'friendly relations' with the British, the opposite had been achieved. The tribes were so alienated that instead of aiding the British in any scheme of imperial defence, they had attacked the British. Further, this imperial scheme itself was showed up. The posts established and the troops placed in Tochi could not defend themselves against the tribes. It is unlikely that they would have performed well against an advancing Russian army, especially without the support of the tribes. The specific reason why Tochi itself had been considered important in this scheme of imperial defence lay in its strategic location as a route to the Kabul–Ghazni–Kandahar line. However, the military authorities in Tochi, after the conclusion of the operations of the Tochi Field Force, declared it useless as a line of communication:

> The Tochi Valley is an essentially bad military position, being a long narrow *cul de sac*, both flanks being hemmed in by tribesmen only waiting an opportunity to be openly hostile, and who in peace-time even are ever ready to raid convoys and travellers, thus necessitating numerous posts along the line of communications. It was at one time considered to be the easiest and most direct route to Ghazni, but the upper portions of the river are narrow and liable to dangerous floods, and even when the limit of British influence (Dotoi) is reached, there still remain ten marches through a difficult and hostile country between that place and Ghazni.[111]

The ultimate imperial object, which necessitated the forward move into Tochi and its subsequent military occupation, was rendered useless.

NOTES

1. 'From—Political Officer, To—Simla and Punjab', 10 June 1897, PGoI, FF, NAI, June 1897.

2. Ibid.

3. In colonial literature, it is referred to as both 'Sheranna' and 'Sheranni'. Here I use Sheranni. It is also spelt as 'Shirani'.

4. 'From—Gee, To—Commissioner & Superintendent, Derajat Division', 19 June 1897, PGoI, FF, NAI, July 1897.

5. Ibid.

6. Ibid.

7. 'From—Commissioner, Derajat, To—Simla & Punjab', 16 June 1897, PGoI, FF, NAI, June 1897.

8. Ibid.

9. 'Extract from Wana Diary for 21st to 24th June 1897', PGoI, FF, DoA, Peshawar, July 1897.

10. 'Enquiry into the Causes of the Maizar Outbreak & Conduct of Maliks, &c.', PGoI, FF, NAI, July 1897.

11. 'Translation of a Letter Dated 26th Muharram 1315 Hijra, Corresponding to 28th June 1897, from Sadda Khan and Other Madda Khel Maliks, to H. A. Anderson, Esquire, C. S. I., Commissioner and Superintendent, Derajat Division', PGoI, FF, DoA, June 1897.

12. 'Translation of a Letter from Malik Sadda Khan, Madda Khel, dated 4th Rabi-us-Sani 1315 H. Corresponding to the 2nd September 1897', PGoI, Sec F, NAI, October 1897.

13. 'From—Major-General G. Corrie Bird, C. B., Commanding Tochi Field Force, To—The Secretary to GoI, Foreign Department, d. 25th September 1897', PGoI, FF, NAI, October 1897.

14. 'From—Major-General Corrie Bird, To—GoI, d. 13th October 1897', PGoI, FF, NAI, October 1897.

15. 'From—The Commissioner and Superintendent Derajat Division, To—The Officiating Chief Secretary to the Government of Punjab', PGoI, Sec F, NAI, September 1898.

16. The GoI had demanded the surrender of seventeen people, but only these five surrendered. When the trial commenced, one more came in—Alambe. He was not tried, but his opinion was recorded by the tribunal.

17. See Appendix A to this volume.

18. 'Statement of Sadda Khan to General Bird on 1st November 1897', PGoI, Sec F, NAI, September 1898.

19. Ibid.

20. 'Statement of Sadda Khan to General Bird on 2nd November 1897', PGoI, Sec F, DoA, September 1898.

21. Ibid.

22. Ibid.

23. Ibid.

24. Ibid.

25. Ibid.

26. 'From—Major-General G. Corrie Bird, Commanding Tochi Field Force, To—The Secretary to the GoI, Foreign Department, d. 28th December 1897', PGoI, Sec F, NAI, September 1898.

27. Ibid.

28. Ibid.

29. 'Memorandum by Major-General G. C. Bird, President. Trial on Madda Khel Prisoners, 27th December 1897', PGoI, Sec F, NAI, September 1898.

30. 'Opinion on Trial of Sadda Khan and other Madda Khel Maliks for Complicity in the Maizar Outbreak', 18 December 1897, PGoI, Sec F, DoA, September 1898.

31. 'Note by W. J. Cuningham', 17 January 1898, PGoI, Sec F, NAI, September 1898.

32. 'From—H. A. Anderson, To—The Offg. Chief Secretary to Government, Punjab, d. 27th Feb 1898', PGoI, Sec F, NAI, September 1898.

33. Ibid.

34. Ibid.

35. 'Note by Sir W. Mackworth Young, Lt. Governor, Punjab', 2nd March 1898, PGoI, Sec F, NAI, September 1898.

36. Ibid.

37. From—Agent Governor-General in Baluchistan, Quetta, To—Foreign Secretary, Simla, PGoI, FF, NAI, 9 September 1892.

38. 'From—GoI, To—The Secretary of State, 3rd Jan 1894', PGoI, Sec F, Keep With (K.W.), NAI, April 1894.

39. Ibid.

40. Ibid.

41. 'From—Secretary of State, To—GoI, 2nd February 1894', PGoI, Sec F, NAI, April 1894.

42. 'Arrangements for the Demarcation of the Amir's Frontier from the Vicinity of Wakhan to the Persian Border by Joint British and Afghan

Commissions in Accordance with the Agreement Concluded with His Highness in November 1893', PGoI, Sec F, K.W., NAI, April 1894.

43. Ibid.

44. 'From—R. I. Bruce, Esq., C. I. E., Commissioner and Superintendent, Derajat Division, To—The Officiating Chief Secretary to the Government of Punjab, 28th Feb 1894', PGoI, Sec F, NAI, April 1894.

45. Ibid.

46. Ibid.

47. Ibid.

48. Ibid.

49. Bruce was a disciple of Sandeman and believed his methods in Baluchistan for pacifying the tribes would work well in the Pukhtun areas as well. The policy was one of working with headmen. However, critics pointed out that there were no headmen among Pukhtuns and the policy would not work.

50. 'From—H. A. Anderson, Esq., Deputy Commissioner of Bannu, To—The Commissioner and Superintendent, Derajat Division, 25th Feb 1894', PGoI, Sec F, NAI, April 1894.

51. Dennis Fitzpatrick, 'Note by His Honor the Lieutenant-Governor of the Punjab on the Demarcation of the Waziri Boundary', 14 March 1894, PGoI, Sec F, K.W., NAI, 1894.

52. Elgin, PGoI, Sec F, K.W. NAI, 1894.

53. Ibid.

54. Ibid.

55. Ibid.

56. Ibid.

57. Private papers of Sir George White as Commander in Chief India, 29 May 1894, PGoI, Sec F, K.W., IOR/BL, London, 1894.

58. Ibid.

59. Ibid.

60. Ibid.

61. C. B. Pritchard, 6 June 1894, PGoI, Sec F, K.W., NAI, 1894.

62. J. Westland, 31 May 1894, PGoI, Sec F, K.W., NAI, 1894.

63. 'From—The GoI, To—The Secretary of State for India', PGoI, Sec F, NAI, July 1894.

64. 'Extract from a Letter from Sir D. Fitzpatrick, K.C.S.I., Lt.-Governor of the Punjab, to the Viceroy, dated Camp Thal, 20th March 1894', PGoI, Sec F, NAI, July 1894.

65. Mullah Powindah had emerged as a leader of the Mahsud Wazirs in 1889, when the British first started encroaching in Waziristan. He set himself

up and was seen as a leader in opposition to the Maliks who the British had been subsidising and whose influence they sought to strengthen. By 1894, Mullah Powindah had gathered a formidable following which included those Maliks as well who did not support the British. He used the banner of religion to rally support to his movement. However, his goals were political—to resist the British in order to preserve the independence of Waziristan. He emerged as a charismatic political-religious leader which made it even more difficult for the Maliks, subsidised by the British, to oppose him.

66. 'From—R. I. Bruce, Esquire, C.I.E., Commissioner and Superintendent, Derajat Division, and British Commissioner, Waziristan Delimitation Commission, To—Lieutenant-General Sir William Lockhart, K.C.B., C.S.I., Commanding Waziristan Field Force, 19th March 1895', PGoI, FF, NAI, June 1895.

67. Ibid.

68. 'From—Bruce, To—Lockhart, 19th March 1895', PGoI, FF, NAI, June 1895.

69. Ibid.

70. 'From—Lieutenant-General Sir W.S.A. Lockhart, K.C.B., C.S.I., Commanding the Waziristan Field Force, To—The Adjutant-General in India, d. 30th March 1895', PGoI, FF, NAI, June 1895.

71. 'From—H. A. Anderson, Esq., Deputy Commissioner, on Special Duty, Waziristan Delimitation Commission, To—The Commissioner and Superintendent, Derajat Division, 21st April 1895', PGoI, FF, NAI, November 1895.

72. 'Statement of Sadda Khan to General Bird on 31st October 1897', PGoI, Sec F, NAI, September 1898.

73. Ibid.

74. 'Translation of a Petition Presented by the Darwesh Khel and the Daur Maliks of the Tochi Valley, to H. A. Anderson, Esq., Political Officer, Tochi Valley, Dated the 17th May 1895', PGoI, Sec F, DoA, August 1895.

75. 'From—H. A. Anderson, Esquire, Deputy Commissioner, on Special Duty, Waziristan Delimitation Commission, To—The Commissioner and Superintendent, Derajat Division, d. 17th May 1895', PGoI, FF, NAI, June 1895.

76. 'From—R. I. Bruce, C. I. E., Commissioner and Superintendent, Derajat Division, To—The Chief Secretary to Government, Punjab, d. 20th May 1895', PGoI, Sec F, NAI, June 1895.

77. Ibid.

78. 'From—Anderson, To—Commissioner, 17th May 1895', PGoI, Sec F, NAI, June 1895.

79. 'Extract from Waziristan Diary for the Week Ending 4th June 1895', PGoI, FF, DoA, August 1895.

80. 'From—Bruce, To—The Chief Secretary, d. 20th May 1895', PGoI, FF, NAI, June 1895.

81. 'From—R. I. Bruce, Esq., C.I.E., Commissioner and Superintendent, Derajat Division, and Chief Political Officer, Waziristan, To—H. A. Anderson, Esq., Deputy Commissioner, on Special Duty, Waziristan Delimitation Commission, d. 18th July 1895', PGoI, FF, NAI, November 1895.

82. 'From—H. A. Anderson, Esq., Deputy Commissioner on Special Duty, Waziristan Delimitation Commission, To—R. I. Bruce, Esq., C. I. E., Commissioner and Superintendent, Derajat Division, d. 8th June 1895', PGoI, FF, NAI, August 1895.

83. Ibid.

84. 'From—H. C. Fanshawe, Esq., Officiating Chief Secretary, to the Government of the Punjab, To—The Commissioner and Superintendent, Derajat Division, d. 28th May 1895', PGoI, FF, NAI, August 1895.

85. 'From—H. A. Anderson, Esquire, Political Officer, Superintendent, Derajat Division, To—GoP, d. 10th April 1896', PGoI, FF, NAI, June 1896.

86. Ibid.

87. Ibid.

88. Ibid.

89. Ibid.

90. Ibid.

91. Ibid.

92. Ibid.

93. Ibid.

94. Ibid.

95. Ibid.

96. Ibid.

97. Ibid.

98. 'From—Commissioner, Derajat, To—Simla & Punjab, d. 13th June 1896', PGoI, Sec F, NAI, October 1896.

99. 'From—H. W. Gee, Esquire, B.C.S., Political Officer, Tochi Valley, To—The Commissioner and Superintendent, Derajat Division, d. 25th June 1896', PGoI, Sec F, NAI, October 1896.

100. 'From—H. A. Anderson, Esquire, Commissioner and Superintendent, Derajat Division, To—The Chief Secretary to Government, Punjab, d. 4th July 1896', PGoI, Sec F, NAI, October 1896.

101. Ibid.

102. 'From—H. W. Gee, Esquire, C.S., Political Officer, Tochi Valley, To—The Commissioner and Superintendent, Derajat Division, d. 23rd Feb 1897', PGoI, FF, NAI, May 1897.

103. 'From—H. A. Anderson, Esquire, Commissioner and Superintendent, Derajat Division, To—The Chief Secretary to Government, Punjab, d. 11th Jan 1897', PGoI, FF, NAI, March 1897.

104. Ibid.

105. Ibid.

106. Interviews in Waziristan were conducted in May 1995. At the time Waziristan was off-limits to outsiders. The authority of the political agent, as representative of the GoI, was confined to the compounds of his office and home at Miran Shah and he only travelled under the protection of machine-gun-armed levies. It was lucky and unusual for me to be able to travel to Waziristan and conduct field research there—being able to examine local archives in the Political Agency of North Waziristan and being able to conduct interviews with Madda Khel elders who recalled the Maizar attack as if it occurred yesterday. Two (an elder, Malik Ghula Khan Khalifa who was a small boy in 1897, and Sadda Khan's great-grandson, Malik Abdul Wadud) in particular provided a clear and comprehensive historical narrative that aligns with the sub-imperial account that emerges from British confidential documents.

107. During the interview in May 1995, Malik Ghula Khan Khalifa claimed that he was about 7 years old at the time of the attack. It is difficult in this area to determine the exact age, but in his own words he was of the age when his 'milk teeth were falling out'; therefore, he was too young to participate in the attack. At the time of the interview, he was over a 100 years old. Interestingly, the translator of these interviews, Babri Gul Wazir, remarked many times that Khalifa used words that have not been used in several decades, which further confirmed his involvement in this war. While it is beyond the scope of this study to do justice to the many startling historical details provided in the oral testimonies, it is important to mention that the families of Malik Ghula Khan Khalifa and Sadda Khan come from opposing factions. Khalifa's uncle Pyall, who was killed in the attack, consistently opposed British presence and blamed Sadda Khan for his role in the British occupation of Tochi. Khandaan, as mentioned in his narrative, was Sadda Khan's son. Khandaan's son was Zangi Khan who was Malik Abdul Wadud's father.

108. Cheegah means that when something serious is happening, people stop what they are doing and rush to that spot spontaneously.

109. This interview was conducted in 1995.

110. From—Secretary of State, To—GoI, 2nd February 1894, PGoI, Sec F, K.W., NAI, April 1894.

111. C. C. Egerton, Brigadier-General, Commanding 1st Brigade, Tochi Field Force, 'Memorandum on Future Distribution of Troops in the Tochi Valley, d. 20th August 1897', PGoI, Sec F, NAI, September 1898.

4

THE UPRISING IN SWAT

Local Politics and Imperial Entanglements

Sub-imperial evidence in the case of Swat reveals a similar pattern as the Maizar attack. The 'sudden' and 'fanatical' nature of the attacks is emphasised to cover up the unpreparedness of the military garrisons in Malakand and Chakdara to cope with the attacks, leaving them beleaguered until relieved with reinforcements. Misrepresentations by the man on the spot attempt to conceal the discontent and resistance in Swat which had its origins in the occupation of Swat in 1895. Here middlemen such as the Khans of Nawagai and Dir were actively bribed and used to break Pukhtun resistance to the occupation of Swat. Interestingly, in England, the question erupted in a parliament debate where many argued that it was the violation of agreement with the tribes to honour their independence that had led to the revolt. Internal imperial explanations come into play that highlight technologies of Empire in the Frontier as a consequence. What made the revolt in Swat somewhat unusual was the appearance of the figure of the 'Mad Mullah' which helped preserve the argument of 'sudden' and 'fanatical' nature of the attack. Since he did not emerge out of the tradition of mullahs in the Frontier, this led to him being viewed as part of a phenomenon of spontaneous millenarianism to be found in other parts of the colonial world. Pukhtun oral tradition corroborates sub-imperial evidence and clearly helps us better understand the role of Sartor Fakir within the revolt.

SUB-IMPERIAL POLITICS AND THE ATTACKS IN MALAKAND AND CHAKDARA

Major H. A. Deane, Political Agent for Dir, Swat and Chitral, was the government's man on the spot. It was his job to keep the government informed of affairs in the aforementioned areas. A few weeks prior to the attacks on Malakand and Chakdara, he sent reports to the GoI on the general situation in Swat. In the beginning of July 1897, he had interviewed several jirgas from the Upper Swat and said that these jirgas 'accept the fact of their being under Government influence in a good spirit' and had made up their minds to '"lay hold of the skirt" of Government for good and all'.[1] He also stated that Muhammad Sharif Khan, the Khan of Dir, had invaded or 'gained possession'[2] of Upper Swat. The Khan of Dir was one of the leading men that the British had supported since 1895. He received allowances from them and in Deane's words 'owes his position'[3] to the GoI. On 3 July 1897, Deane conferred on him the title of Nawab on behalf of His Excellency the Viceroy. However, Deane mentioned in his report that the Nawab established guards in Upper Swat who 'habitually bully and harass the people'.[4] The Nawab in his movement against Swat was opposed by the Mian Guls who represented to Deane that they were aggrieved that the government had allowed the Nawab of Dir to occupy Upper Swat.[5] They also sent letters to Deane alluding to a former promise of the government made to the Akhund that they would never interfere in Swat. The important point Deane emphasised about this situation was that 'the power of the Mianguls, trading on the old Akhund's name is broken'.[6] In conclusion, he remarked that

> an advantage in the Nawab Dir's action lies in his having, as a Muhammadan, dealt a blow to fanatical working in the country, and it has also proved useful from another point of view, viz., that the men of Upper Swat are impressed with the fact that any opposition to Government on their part would be hopeless.[7]

From the British point of view, things in Swat were fairly satisfactory. Deane had informed the GoI as such just five days before Malakand and Chakdara were attacked.

When the posts were attacked, naturally the government looked to their man on the spot to inform them what had happened and why. The government wanted all the information about the '"Mad Mulla" who has raised the country against us in Swat; and any other indications of the reason for this sudden outbreak'.[8] The GoP also speculated: 'Was this a sporadic fanatical outburst or [sic] the result of preconcerted tribal action?'[9] Further, they could not find anything on the Mad Fakir in their files.

Deane's first full report gave the following account of the rising in Swat. He said that on 18 July 1897, he had received information that a fakir had suddenly appeared in Swat, professing that 'one small pot of rice, which he had with him, was sufficient to feed multitudes; also professing to multiply to the vision of people a few small flags that he had with him'.[10] However, upon enquiry, all Deane could elicit about the Fakir was that he was a mad man. He was said to be the brother of a man called Zardad from Buner who, some 15 years ago, had accidentally killed the Fakir's son and since that time the Fakir had been a 'lunatic'. However, Deane said that according to Rahim Shah, his chief agent who knew 'the whole of this country', this story was not creditable and the Fakir was a stranger to those parts. A couple of days later, the Fakir started claiming that he had heavenly hosts with him and it was his mission to turn the British out of Malakand and out of Peshawar. The Fakir also stated that he had been visited by deceased fakirs who had told him that the mouth of British guns and rifles 'would be closed, and that our bullets would be turned to water'.[11] Further, he had no need of human assistance, for the heavenly hosts with him were sufficient. Up to 25 July, according to Deane, the people merely regarded him as 'a mad man'. However, the next day, the Fakir moved towards Malakand with some boys aged 13–14 years. As he kept moving, a British officer spotted him being joined by about 400 men, for the most part unarmed. The next thing to occur was the attack on Malakand by a party of about 1,000 men led by the Fakir. After the relief of Chakdara, the Fakir retired to Landaki and was trying to 'stir up a further disturbance'. He also talked of further disturbances elsewhere. Finally, Deane reported that the whole rising was 'an astounding business, and the people seem to have lost their heads and all view of their own interests in a blind belief that we should be turned out of the country'.[12] As to the causes of this outbreak, he thought it was due to 'the steady and continual working of the Amir and his agents',[13] something that had been going on since Swat was occupied in 1895. That it occurred now was directly due to 'the chance of the right man being found to start the business'.[14]

In the meantime, higher officials in the GoI speculated on what could have caused this outbreak. E. H. S. Clarke, the assistant secretary to the GoI, Foreign Department, noted the following:

> With the vague information before us regarding the very sudden outbreak, it is only possible to conjecture what has caused it. For my part, however, I have no doubt that the real origin of the disturbance is the Khan of Dir's 'invasion of Swat.' What was the object of this invasion? 'To assert himself against the fanatical party lying on his flank in Upper Swat.' The fanatical party included the Adda Mulla, the Palam Mulla, the Mian Guls, &c., instigated from Kabul. The effect of the Khan of Dir's movement was—I am again quoting Major Deane—'to be the tearing away of the "purdah" which the Mian Guls have thrown over Upper Swat, and to minimise the chances of necessity arising later for action on the part of the Government of India to break up a hostile fanatical combination.' ... Well, the Khan invaded Swat by strategem, and if any credence is to be attached to the Mian Gul's letter to the Lieutenant-Governor and the statement of his emissary, he plundered the people ruthlessly. Major Deane says no levies were employed in the invasion: the emissary said the levies were employed. Mian Gul asked if the Government had authorized the attack: if not, 'let the Sarkar stand aside, let me fight the Khan of Dir, and see what occurs.' Early in June, the Upper Swatis began sending in messages to Major Deane to save them from the Khan of Dir. Major Deane replied that, until they came in and established friendly relations with Government, he saw no reason for troubling himself about them.[15]

The Secretary was demonstrating this point by using evidence provided in Deane's earlier reports and the quotes in his note are taken from the same. All this, according to him, pointed to the fact that the Khan of Dir was regarded as the servant of the British; therefore, his occupation of Upper Swat was regarded by the people as practically the British occupation of Swat and the mullahs could say that the people gained nothing by going to see Deane. Finally, even though Clarke could not find any reference to the mad fakir in the list of mullahs kept in files, he concluded that 'with such material to work on, it did not require a very prominent man to start the trouble'.[16] Viceroy Elgin's response to Clarke's reasoning was: 'All this is guess work. Mr. Clarke may be right, but if so, Major Deane has been utterly at fault. I reserve my judgement.'[17] Deane's failings as a political officer and especially in using a brutal and oppressive middle-man to suppress the people in Swat start to surface and are recognised as such. However, once again, we sense the unease in acknowledging this outright and thus Empire avoiding accountability.

Meanwhile, reports came in from other parts of the Frontier where attempts had been made to gather native opinion as to why the outbreak had occurred. For example, the Confidential Diary of the district superintendent of police in Kohat stated that the Malakand outbreak was much talked about in Kohat and other areas and it came about for the following reason:

> *Rahim Shah*, Kaka Khel, who, for services rendered to Government, has been amply rewarded, has partly on this account and partly owing to his immoral character made himself most obnoxious to the Swatis. Their grievances and complaints against Rahim Shah were prevented from being brought to the ears of the Political Officer, Malakand, through the instrumentality of Mian Ahmad, Extra Assistant Commissioner, Assistant Political Officer, who is himself a Kaka Khel, again. The Swatis of Upper Swat are not satisfied with the appointment of Muhammad Sharif Khan of Dir, who is said to be hankering after their country and to have had consulted *Rahim Shah*. The latter is said to have replied to him that, as it was foreign territory, he could do as he liked and the British would not interfere. The Swatis being confident that the British would allow no interference or permit their country to be taken over by Sharif Khan. Sharif Khan having accomplished his purpose with regard to 2/3rds of Swat, the grandson of the old Akhund has been left the remainder and called upon the Bonerwals and Amazais to assist him in expelling Sharif Khan. They excused themselves at first on various pretexts, but finally agreed to assist him and determined to attack Sharif Khan. However, on

> reflection they agreed it was useless seeing that Government would put another man in his place, so they finally decided to combine and attack the troops at Malakand.[18]

All the different native accounts received by the GoI gave the above version as the cause of the attack. Officials in India acknowledged that these reports also threw doubt on Deane's theory that the rising was brought about due to the Amir's instigation. Native opinion gathered from various sources stated that the idea of the attack having been instigated from Kabul was 'merely a conjectural inference drawn from recent events'.[19]

However, the GoI sent the Amir of Afghanistan a letter informing him of the reports that they had received, specifically that certain Afghans had crossed over and fought in the risings. According to the British Agent at Kabul, the Amir held a darbar and professed that he had always maintained friendly relations with the British. The British Agent wrote to the government that he believed the Amir was sincere and was not behind the disturbances. The Amir himself sent a long letter to the Viceroy, in which he again professed his friendship to the British and said that no tribesman from his territory would openly have joined the attack. But it was possible that some of them could have crossed over in the night by unfrequented roads: 'How is it possible to keep watch on thieves during nights along such an extensive frontier?'[20] In response to the Viceroy stating that guards should be appointed along the Kabul river and other roads so that no one could cross over to the other side, the Amir wrote:

> My kind friend, such an arrangement could only be possible by posting about ten thousand soldiers on all the mountain tops and at all fords in the district. Then they will be able to execute properly such an arrangement, otherwise how would it be possible to stop the people who are familiar with the country?[21]

But he had instructed local officials on his side to watch any open movements of the tribesmen. The Amir, however, wrote of what he had been able to gather on the causes of the disturbances. He stated:

> I saw some of these people, and asked them by way of advice why they were disobeying the illustrious British Government, and exposing themselves to slaughter and loss. They said that

> their proceedings were undertaken owing to the hopeless circumstances in which they were involved, and they gave particulars as stated below, i.e., that during former years a firm promise was given, on behalf of the illustrious British Government, to the frontier tribesmen that they would always be exempted from the restrictions of Government laws, and would remain independent in their own country; that when they received such orders from the great Government, they lived with perfect assurance of mind and never paid any taxes to any one; that subsequently the frontier British officials, disregarding the orders of the Government of India issued to them (tribesmen), began to make roads in their country and subsequently asked them for revenue and inflicted fines, etc., upon them and generally treated them in the same way as the old inhabitants of India were treated. That the people inhabiting hilly tracts are generally poor and possess no property; that they have therefore, exposed themselves to destruction, and they desire that the frontier officials should act in accordance with the promise which the Government of India had given them. ... Apparently the complaints of these people are against the local frontier officers of India. It is possible that Your Excellency may have received similar accounts.[22]

Further correspondence passed between the Amir and the GoI, and the latter decided to accept the Amir's repudiations as honest. Deane himself later decided not to pursue the idea of the Amir's complicity in regard to the Mamunds.

Reports also came in giving further information on the 'Mad Mullah'. For example, a native political officer in Khyber sent the following particulars.[23] The Swat fakir was a native of Buner. He had fought in the Ambeyla campaign along with his brother who was known as 'Phalwan'. He travelled for many years in the Middle East and Central Asia and, three years before appeared in Kabul, interviewed the Amir and expressed himself as a 'ghazi'. The Amir thought him 'mad' and dismissed him with the charity of a few rupees. After that he went to Mullah Najm-ud-din, also known as Mullah Adda, and then went on to Buner where he became custodian of the shrine of a saint. He was an old man, could read and write, and in Buner was known as Sartor (bare-headed) Fakir.

Another account of the mad fakir was sent by the deputy commissioner of Peshawar. The fakir's name was Saidulla and he was a native of Rega, a village in Buner. About 12 years ago, Saidulla gave up worldly affairs and took up residence in Pir Baba Ziarat. After he had been a fakir for two years, he began to talk of 'ghaza', but he also started preaching doctrines that were contrary to 'Shariat' and this set the mullahs against him. In the last two years he travelled and lived in Mecca and Medina. During his absence some of his relatives murdered one of his sons due to a family quarrel. 'On his return from Mecca, Saidulla called up his son's murderers and told them that he had given up Afghan ways as well as all worldly affairs, and that therefore, instead of avenging his son's death, he forgave them: this magnanimous conduct on his part brought him into discredit.'[24]

The GoP was also trying to piece together the various fragments of information. The chief secretary, in a note to the lieutenant governor, commented that 'the rapidity with which even more distant tribes joined seems to indicate that there must have been some previous concert as to the plan of action to be adopted'.[25] Further, 'it is clear from the numbers implicated that eventually it became a tribal attack and not a mere fanatical outbreak'.[26] Considering the nature and tactics of the attack on Malakand and Chakdara, he was not inclined to view it as blind fanaticism:

> As a surprise was evidently intended, the first attack would naturally have been by a smaller force, and when that failed an attack in strength followed. The Kotal is the key of the position, and consequently that and not the north camp which might probably have been easily rushed, was selected for the first attack to cut our line of communications and Chakdarra and the north camp were left practically undisturbed on 26th–27th. There was a good deal of method in the madness of the Diwana Baba, and I am personally of opinion that the circumstances indicate a maturity of design and plan which is quite inconsistent with the theory of a blind head-long fanatical outburst which would have been directed against the first object on which it could vent its fury.[27]

A few weeks later Deane sent in another report to the government in continuation of his earlier one. He claimed that from what he had been able to gather he could not accept the Khan of Dir's invasion of Swat as being a cause of the rising. 'There are many grounds on which my opinion on this point is framed, the main one being that this was not a tribal but a religious disturbance.'[28] He continued: 'I have made every effort to ascertain in other ways what these causes really were, and the results of my investigation have confirmed me in my opinion that a widespread and deep fanatical feeling is at the bottom of the matter.'[29] Despite overwhelming evidence to the contrary, Deane insists on denying native accounts and representing the attack as 'fanatical' or 'religious'. These also help discount the history of oppression in Swat backed by Deane and local efforts to seek redress which he denied as well. Once again clinging to 'fanaticism' deflects the failure and misrepresentations of the political officer.

On 1 September 1897, the GoI sent a long letter to the secretary of state for India in London, describing the 'sudden disturbances' that had broken out. As to why these disturbances had occurred, the letter read:

> The cause of the original outbreak at the Malakand is by no means clear. Major Deane is of the opinion that the success of the rising was due to the bold advance of the mad Fakir, who was at first almost alone, and to the hold that he had obtained over the people by his pretended miraculous powers. Major Deane is emphatic on the point that the rising was fanatical and not due to tribal discontent or movements.[30]

A year later Deane obtained some correspondence which indicated that the 'late disturbances are the outcome of the working started in 1895, and that this working was due to Government having moved troops into Swat in contravention of an alleged promise made after Ambeyla in 1863 to the Akhund that Government would not interfere in Swat'.[31]

Deane in all but his last report, written a year after the revolt in Swat, insisted that the cause for the attacks on Malakand and Chakdara lay in a sudden wave of fanaticism that swept over the country. A 'mad fakir' appeared, claiming miraculous powers, and the people 'lost their heads'. This was the view that was made public and one that was presented by colonial historiography as well. However, this view is not borne out by the next layer of sub-imperial evidence comprising British confidential documents.

Prior to the outbreak, Deane informed the GoI that the state of affairs in Swat was satisfactory, the people 'accept the fact of their being under Government influence in a good spirit' and made up their minds to '"lay hold of the skirt" of Government for good and all'. However, around 18 July 1897, Deane had received reports of a fakir who suddenly appeared in the country, claiming he could 'feed multitudes' with 'one small pot of rice'. The Fakir also started giving out that he had heavenly hosts with him and 'his mission was to turn the British off the Malakand and out of Peshawar'. The main purpose of having a political officer in the Frontier was that he would keep the government informed of events that were important in safeguarding their position. Deane clearly failed to do this. His report, a few days before the revolt, was off the mark. Further, he did receive information of events that led to the outbreak. Why did he not take action, and why were the garrisons not prepared? This crucial question, while largely ignored in historiography, did not escape notice by the authorities in India. E. H. S. Clarke, the assistant secretary to the GoI, noted how the 'best Political Officers may be deceived when dealing with frontier tribes'.[32] He continued:

> Here we have Major Deane writing, just five days before the outbreak of the biggest fanatical disturbance we've had for years, as follows:- 'In conclusion I would remark that an advantage in the Nawab of Dir's action [i.e., by the invasion of Upper Swat] lies in his having, as a Muhammadan, dealt a blow to fanatical working in the country, and it has also proved useful from another point of view, *viz.*, that the men of Upper Swat are impressed with the fact that any opposition to Government on their part would be hopeless.' The events of the last five days have proved these conclusions to be utterly wrong. There was no such powerful fanatical combination against us at present throughout the Chitral campaign, and on that occasion the country-side was up against us as invaders; again, the men of Upper Swat not only do not seem impressed with the fact that opposition to Government would be useless, but they have learnt *that the forces on the Malakand and Chakdarra are not strong enough for*

> *move out against them, and that for days we could only act on the defensive.*[33]

W. J. Cuningham, secretary to the GoI, also remarked that it was difficult to reconcile 'the apparent friendliness, at the beginning of the month, of the Upper Swat jirgas with the unanimity of Upper and Lower Swat in rising to the call of the nameless and apparently hitherto unknown "mad Fakir"'.[34]

Clarke, as we saw above, was inclined to believe that the origin of the disturbance lay in the Nawab of Dir's invasion of Upper Swat and his oppression of the people. The people regarded Nawab of Dir as a man of the British. Various native reports pointed to this being the main reason for the outbreak. However, Deane was never pressed on these points. He refused to accept this version for the reason that this was not a 'tribal but a religious disturbance' and a 'deep and fanatical feeling is at the bottom of the matter'. But Deane does not explain 'fanaticism'. In fact, the information that he does provide contradicts his statements. For example, he forwarded translations of correspondence between the mullahs that he had obtained.[35] In his opinion, these letters were important evidence 'of concerted working on the part of the different religious leaders'.[36] In another place he stated that the Fakir had started the disturbance in Swat prematurely and his utterances hinted at disturbances elsewhere. This, according to Deane, demonstrated that the 'whole business has been a carefully thought out and badly executed plot'.[37] This is hardly consistent with the theory of the Fakir being a madman and the outbreak being a case of sudden fanaticism. As we saw, the GoP was also sceptical of the theory of 'blind fanaticism'. For the lieutenant governor of Punjab, the attacks demonstrated a 'maturity of design and plan' and also showed a 'method in the madness' of the Fakir.

In the face of all information that indicated the contrary, why did Deane continue to emphasise 'fanaticism'? Clearly, if Deane supported the other information, it would reveal that he had failed in his duty as political officer on two counts: first, in not being able to gauge the situation, which was his paramount duty; second, in supporting the Nawab of Dir's invasion of Upper Swat, if that precipitated the revolt. Further, was this failure simply a case of his incompetence? The confidential documents point to something different—that there was a reason behind his actions. These inner workings of Empire show how another layer of knowledge and representation functioned in Frontier imperialism.

Prior to the attacks on Malakand and Chakdara, the Khan of Dir invaded Upper Swat. Deane received reports that the Khan 'plundered the people ruthlessly'[38] and the Upper Swatis had sent Deane messages in early June to save them from the Khan. But Deane supported this move of the Khan, who was recognised as a man of the British since 1895 when the British first entered Swat. His reason was that this was advantageous to the British because it dealt a blow to the fanatical elements in the country and of impressing upon the Upper Swatis that any opposition to the government was hopeless. By fanatical elements, Deane essentially meant the people who were opposed to the British—the mullahs and the Mian Guls. He reminded the government that in 1895 the Upper Swatis had collected under the Mian Guls to oppose the advance of British troops through their country.[39] This 'fanatical party also assumed a hostile attitude towards the Nawab of Dir for throwing in his lot with the British Government'.[40] Although Deane admitted that 'the Nawab of Dir's views naturally incline towards self-aggrandisement, to be attained by turning to his own uses the strength he owes to Government',[41] the important point was that the power of the Mian Guls was broken. In supporting this move Deane believed that he was breaking the back of the opposition to British presence.

The GoI received information from multiple sources, including native informants, which pointed to a different set of causes than the ones provided by Deane. As we saw, officials in both the GoI and the GoP were sceptical of the idea of 'fanaticism' being the main reason for the outbreak. Further, they also recognised the contradictions in Deane's explanations. However, the GoI officially accepted Deane's position and reported his view to the secretary of state in London. They described the Khan of Dir's invasion of Upper Swat as an action which no doubt caused 'considerable local excitement'.[42] But Deane essentially sanctioned this move and the GoI approved it because they thought it would bring the fanatical party under control. The GoI described the outbreak in Swat as 'an outburst of fanaticism, as serious as it was sudden',[43] but in conclusion state that the cause of the outbreak was not clear. However, they do state that Deane as their political officer on the spot was emphatic that the outbreak was fanatical and not due to tribal discontent.

With a vast intelligence network at their disposal, the numerous political officers, the native agents, it is difficult to accept that the government could not determine, or at least offer, likely reasons for this revolt against them apart from a vague 'fanaticism' that Deane insisted on. Further, if all native reports pointed to the Nawab of Dir's action, why did the GoI refuse to attach credence to it? The first point that emerges in answer to this question is that if that was the case, Deane was as much to blame as the Nawab. The second point is that if the outbreak was not a case of 'sudden fanaticism', then the British should have been able to cope with it better. In fact, Deane did have information of 'trouble brewing' a few days prior to the revolt.

Once again the military preparations and readiness in responding to that attack are called into question. The beleaguered garrisons were incapable of action until reinforced. In fact, the commander-in-chief, George White, telegraphed Colonel Meiklejohn soon after the attack commenced, asking, 'Can you not hold fort on Malakand with small force having stores and wounded in it and take offensive with rest of your available force?'[44] Meiklejohn responded that there was not enough time to get stores into fort.[45] Just prior to the outbreak Deane had warned Colonel Meiklejohn that it might be advisable to move out the moveable column, but in his report later Deane said that he was loath to do this for the following reason:

> The column could only take five days' supplies with them, of which the men would have had to carry two—the movement would at once have caused a gathering to assemble about the Fakir—and the best and in fact only chance of the man being quietly removed was in the people themselves removing him. Further there would have been no troops left to guard the north and Kotal camps, both with a large amount of valuable stores which could not have been removed for safety into the fort under a week, and in event of a disturbance arising and the people taking to the hills above the Malakand, the water-supply of the fort would have been cut off, and it was certain we should

> have to return and fight our way back to the Kotal camp and recapture the Kotal.[46]

As it turned out the north camp was abandoned anyway where a large quantity of ammunition, guns and transport was located. The commander-in-chief telegraphed the following on learning this news: 'Regret to hear your abandonment of tents. Could you not have removed them, or at the worst burnt them to prevent them becoming a trophy?'[47] The tribes, after capturing the stores, burnt the tents. Deane's reason for abandoning the camp was that it was necessary for the defence of the Kotal and to save the transport 'which, in event of serious attack on the north camp, could not be protected by the troops in the camp'.[48] Deane added that 'the difficulty of our position was that our men were getting worn out with continual fighting, and the number was not sufficient without reinforcements to enable a counter-move to be made'.[49] In fact, attempts were made to go on the offensive. The day after the attack started, troops were sent in pursuit of the attacking party, but they were ordered to retire, when they spotted large numbers of tribesmen on the surrounding hills (*Frontier and Overseas Expeditions from India*, 1: 370). Again on 1 August, in response to Chakdara's 'despairing appeal for help' and the fact that the men there were 'worn out' and the garrison was running short of provisions, it was decided to send troops to help them. According to Deane:

> this morning it looked as if the gatherings had mostly withdrawn, and I feared that they had done so to throw their whole strength on to Chakdara. A cavalry reconnaissance was sent out to try and push through, but they were attacked in the most plucky manner on the bad ground over which they had to go and had to retire.[50]

In fact reinforcements did arrive while the attacks were occurring, but their arrival did not help the situation much. On 27 July, the Guides Cavalry, 160 sabres and the Guides Infantry, 250 rifles arrived at Malakand (*Frontier and Overseas Expeditions from India*, 1: 371). On 29 July, one squadron of the 11th Bengal Lancers marched into Malakand. Later that day the 38th Dogras and 35th Sikhs and details of the Guides arrived at Dargai under Colonel A. J. Reid. Dargai, situated at the foot of the Malakand Pass, was marked by a mud fort which during the operations expanded into an entrenched camp surrounded by an entanglement of barbed wires. Out of the 21 men of the 35th Sikhs who died from heat apoplexy, 18 were left dead en route.[51] Therefore, the regiments were ordered to rest and they did not arrive in the Malakand camp until 31 July. On 30 July, 200 rifles of the 31st Punjab Infantry, who had formed the garrison of Dargai, were also sent up to the Malakand camp. On the arrival of the reinforcements Deane discussed with Colonel Reid whether a forward move could be made. 'We have discussed whether we should not make a forward move, but there is the unanswerable reply given that the men are exhausted—further an offensive move is of little use unless it can be continued and we can advance.'[52]

Finally Deane concluded with the admission that the attacks had 'shown up the weak points'[53] at both Malakand and Chakdara. The lieutenant governor of the GoP, on learning of the abandonment of north Malakand and the retirement of the Guides Cavalry, remarked: 'I may mention that Deane got snubbed for pointing out in 1895 that the North Malakand Camp was quite unsafe and was told that His Excellency the Commander-in-Chief had personally selected it. The result has proved Deane to be right.'[54] Once again civil–military tensions are alluded to.

The attacks demonstrated a failure of British military arrangements—a point that is never mentioned in colonial historiography, and something that officials in both the GoP and GoI were aware of. It showed that they could not hold their own in event of a serious attack by the tribes. The revolt also demonstrated the failure of their political policy. The tribes had clearly not accepted British presence in Swat in 'good spirit'. The Khan of Dir's invasion of Swat had not achieved the result intended—breaking up opposition to the British, an opposition that Deane described as the 'fanatical element'. If Deane had been pressed on the contradictions in his reports, it would have pointed not to his incompetence but ultimately to the failure of British policy in the area. By clinging to the idea that the outbreak was an outburst of 'sudden fanaticism', these questions are submerged.

MISSING VOICES OF EMPIRE

The revolt in Swat was neither sudden nor fanatical, if by fanatical it was meant that it was a 'religious disturbance'. The roots of this revolt went back to 1895 when the British first entered and then occupied Swat. A year after the revolt, Deane himself forwarded further correspondence among the leaders of the revolt. He said that he had been informed that the disturbances were the outcome of the workings that had started in 1895, and the reason behind it was that the government had occupied Swat in contravention of a promise made to the Akhund that they would never interfere in Swat. All the information that Deane obtained pointed to this. Deane's own opinion, in conclusion, was the following:

> After the lapse now of a year and after persistent enquiry, I hold the opinion that it was the chance arrival of the Sartor Fakir, the extraordinary influence he gained as a possible 'buzurg,' and especially the confidence he showed in starting almost alone that precipitated the outbreak which, notwithstanding the working which had been going on, not only surprised us but the people themselves, for neither women nor children nor property were removed from the villages, nor were there any jirga meetings. But for his arrival and the manner in which he made his move, the outbreak might have been delayed for want of opportunity, but that it would have occurred ere long I entertain no more doubts than the tribesmen themselves, who in their own words say 'it had to be some day'.[55]

The questions that are missing in colonial historiography, and are implied but not fully explored in British confidential documents, exploded in a heated debate in both the houses of Parliament in February and March 1898. The Earl of Northbrook stated in the House of Lords:

> It seems an extraordinary thing that we should have had 4,000 troops, or more than a brigade, on the Malakand and at Chakdara, and that a force which ought to have been able to hold its own against any attack from the tribesmen, would have been exposed to disaster if it had not been for immediate reinforcements from the Punjaub.[56]

The debate was particularly bitter in the House of Commons when the Liberal party brought the charge of 'breach of faith' against the ruling Conservative government and alleged that an explanation for the revolt was to be found 'in a policy chargeable, and properly chargeable against Her Majesty's Government'.[57] Referring to the government's explanation for the war, another member declared:

> What is the official view—the view of the official mind—on this serious, this disastrous transaction? Why, that it is neither more nor less than a 'spontaneous outbreak of fanaticism', 'a bolt from the blue', which no one could foresee, for which no one is to blame, and which we are to accept as one of those inscrutable calamities with which Providence at times afflicts mankind. Our opinion is, that it is not necessary to resort to the hypothesis of miracle or accident. We believe, and it is the purpose of this Amendment to ask this House to declare, that I will not say the only—but that a large contributory factor in bringing about this state of affairs is the policy deliberately adopted by Her Majesty's present advisers, in the teeth of the decision of their predecessors, that that policy is the source of a large part of the mischief that has now overtaken us.[58]

The policy being referred to by Mr Asquith, who spoke these words, was the Conservative government's decision to retain Chitral, thus reversing the decision of the Liberal government. In 1895, in conclusion of the Chitral expedition, the Liberal government had decided to evacuate Chitral for two reasons, which the opposition reiterated now. First, because Chitral had been considered important as a point of observation, but the treaty with Russia made Russian aggression impossible without a 'violation of international compact'.[59] But more importantly, Chitral was 'useless unless connected by a main road to Peshawar'.[60] The difficulty was that if this road was to be built it had to pass through 150 miles of independent tribal territory. Another member pointed that the government was aware of the hostility of the intervening tribes and had therefore appealed to the people of Swat and Bajaur in 1895 by issuing a proclamation which 'intimated the intention of a British force to secure a passage and retirement, and only a passage and retirement, and that after it left there should be no annexation of the country, and that there should be no permanent occupation of the soil'.[61] However, during the Chitral expedition, at various points along the road including the Malakand, the tribes offered the most obstinate resistance to the progress of British troops. Mr Walton concluded: 'The country had risen, and after the retirement of the expedition it was clear, and the Indian Government perceived, that no road through these valleys could be made or maintained without encountering a resistance similar to that which had already been encountered.'[62] Therefore, on 13 June 1895, the Liberal government issued the decision to withdraw from Chitral. A few days later, the Conservative government took office and decided to retain Chitral and to build a fortified road that would pass through Swat. This, the Liberal opposition charged, was a 'breach of faith' and the tribes viewed the road and the military posts as an encroachment of their country and therefore broke out in rebellion in 1897. A member of the opposition in the House of Lords quoted from a translation of a letter from the Mullah of Adda to other mullahs and elders saying, '"The Kaffirs" [that means the English] have taken possession of all Mussulman countries, and owing to the lack of spirit on the part of the people, are conquering every region. They have now reached those countries of Bajaur and Swat.'[63] 'Those are the countries,' he went on to say,

> through which you made the road, and this is the action on our part which is selected by this Mullah as proof that you are invading the independence of the tribes. ... The tribes, who naturally cherished their independence, seeing the fortified post established on their territory at Malakand, came to the conclusion that it was part of the policy to gradually extend our administration and power over the whole of the tribes.[64]

The opposition also attacked the assertion by the government that 'the tribes were delighted, and that there was nothing they desired so much as to be incorporated under British rule'.[65] They stated that the documents that pointed to the tribes regarding British influence favourably essentially showed that the tribes wanted British troops so that they could defend themselves: 'To defend them against what? Against the tribes that were around them, who were hostile to them, because they were supposed to be friendly to our rule. That shows exactly the point. It showed that a vast quantity of the tribes were still hostile to us.'[66] The Liberals carried the argument further and stated that whatever agreements were entered into with the tribes were done at a time when there was a force of 15,000 British troops in their country on its way back from the Chitral relief expedition. 'Well, Sir,' Mr Walton declared, 'the consent of the tribes, obtained under military pressure of this kind, was a somewhat hollow and unsatisfactory agreement.'[67] Further, the opposite party claimed that not one of them was signed with any tribe or chief who had not been paid off by the British. The Conservatives could not deny these charges directly. One member stated that according to the terms of the Proclamation the government would have left the tribes alone if they had left the government alone. But they fought the troops 'in thousands half the way to Chitral'.[68] Therefore, the British were not tied to what the Proclamation had promised. Further, the Conservatives resorted to the fact that many of these issues were superseded by the most important one, that of imperial defence. They claimed it was important to retain Chitral as a post of observation in the scheme of imperial defence and in order to do so the road was a necessity. However, they could not really reply with any force to the specific arguments brought forth by the Liberals that the tribes had broken out because they resisted British encroachment on their independence. Major Deane in a note of a rather rare nature commented candidly as the 'man on the spot' on the controversy in the House of Commons. Two points that he made were particularly relevant, and if the Liberals had seen the note it would have made their case inarguable. First:

> Is it really imagined that the disposition of Pathan tribes is such that they are capable of entering into an agreement with Government for the maintenance of a road through their country, unless they feel themselves powerless to resist the request for it, as in the case of the Afridis after the Afghan war, and with these people after the Chitral Expediton? *They agreed because they had seen our force.*[69]

Second, he argued that the only way the government could maintain order in Swat and the adjoining areas was by annexation. He asked: 'Is Chitral of sufficient strategical value to justify the commencement of annexation of this tract of country?'[70] Deane answered his own question:

> If Government could easily afford men and money for taking over this country I would say, do it. If we could annex Swat and go no further, I would also say do it. We cannot, and it would be useless to pretend that we can. As matter stand it must be fully considered whether Chitral is of such importance as to justify the first move being made. For many reasons in my own opinion, it is not. The line is a minor one of defence, not serious invasion could take place by it, the country itself would oppose any invasion, the road leads to our ultimate border, the Pamirs, and offers no possibility for an offensive movement on our part beyond it.[71]

Oddly enough, Deane seems to be confirming the argument of the Liberals and once again, contradicting all his earlier assertions that the tribes had accepted British influence happily. Clearly the official view also offered by colonial historiography does not hold up, especially since much of it relied on Deane's earlier statements which, apart from not being supported by evidence, fall apart in the light of his last report and this note.

MILITARY OCCUPATION AND ORIGINS OF THE SWAT UPRISING

Deane's last report and the arguments of the opposition point to a missing recent history that makes clear the causes of the revolt in Swat. They show that the outbreak was neither 'sudden' nor 'fanatical' but had its roots in a discontent that went back to 1895 when the British first entered Swat in order to save a besieged garrison in Chitral. The state of Chitral is situated about 150 miles north of Swat and is surrounded by ranges of mountains often exceeding 20,000 feet. The British government decided that Chitral was important strategically and since 1878 sought to control its external affairs in a direction 'friendly to our interests', and 'to secure an effective guardianship over its northern passes' (*Frontier and Overseas Expeditions from India*, 1: 42). However, in 1895 the British decided to interfere in an internal dynastic quarrel and sent troops to Chitral. This resulted in the British force being beleaguered in Chitral fort on 3 March 1895. On 14 March, the GoI ordered the mobilisation of a division in order to relieve the besieged garrison. However, there was another reason for sending the troops to Chitral. This was to break the power of Umra Khan, the chief of Jandul state, which bordered Chitral on the south. Umra Khan is viewed by the Pukhtuns as one of their greatest heroes. By 1893, Umra Khan had succeeded in establishing his authority over Dir, the greater part of Bajaur and a portion of Swat. In 1894 Umra Khan entered into an alliance with the Khan of Nawagai. His control now extended from the Dir–Chitral border in the north to the Swat river in the south. In 1895 Umra Khan appeared to be gaining a strong presence in Chitral. He was also the son-in-law of the late Mehtar and now moved to Chitral and joined hands with Sher Afzul, one of the claimants to the throne. The majority of the Chitralis also went over to the side of Sher Afzul. Sher Afzul sent a message to the British promising to be friends with the government on the same terms as the previous Mehtars, but on the condition that no British officer should reside in the country. The British regarded the alliance between Umra Khan and Sher Afzul as being hostile to their interests. Therefore, Surgeon-Major Robertson, the British agent at neighbouring Gilgit, arrived in Chitral with troops and formally recognised Shuja-ul-Mulk, a 10-year-old boy, as the Mehtar of Chitral. This led to fighting between the Chitralis and the British troops which led to the latter shutting themselves in the fort on 3 March 1895.

On 26 March 1895, 15,000 troops, over 30,000 followers and 30,669 animals were concentrated in Nowshera to proceed to Jandul and Chitral (*Frontier and Overseas Expeditions from India*, 1: 523). As this march necessitated passing through Swat, the British had a few days earlier, on 17 March, issued a proclamation that was sent to all the tribes concerned:

> To all the people of Swat and the people in Bajaur who do not side with Umra Khan
>
> Be it known to you, and any other persons concerned, that:-
>
> Umra Khan, the Chief of Jandol, in spite of his often-repeated assurances of friendship to the British Government, and regardless of frequent warnings to refrain from interfering with the affairs of Chitral, which is a protected State under the suzerainty of Kashmir, has forcibly entered the Chitral valley and attacked the Chitrali people.

> The Government of India have now given Umra Khan full warning that, unless he retires from Chitral by the 1st of April, corresponding with the 5th day of Shawal 1302 H., they will use force to compel him to do so. In order to carry out this purpose, they have arranged to assemble on the Peshawar border a force of sufficient strength to overcome all resistance, and to march this force through Umra Khan's territory towards Chitral.
>
> The sole object of the Government of India is to put an end to the present, and prevent any future, unlawful aggression on Chitral territory, and, as soon as this object has been attained, the force will be withdrawn.
>
> The Government of India have no intention of permanently occupying any territory through which Umra Khan's misconduct may now force them to pass, or of interfering with the independence of the tribes; and they will scrupulously, avoid any acts of hostility towards the tribesmen so long as they on their part refrain from attacking or impending in any way the march of the troops. Supplies and transport will be paid for, and all persons are at liberty to pursue their ordinary avocations in perfect security (*Frontier and Overseas Expeditions from India*, 1: 524–25).

Notwithstanding this proclamation, thousands of tribesmen gathered to oppose the advance of the troops and the latter had to fight several battles in order to get through.[72] A rare instance when the British speak admiringly of the tribes can be found in Younghusband's account of the battles fought in Swat. He wrote the following:

> Of the enemy's bravery it is difficult to speak too highly, and individual cases were conspicuous. One leader, carrying a large red and white banner, called on his men to charge the Scottish Borderers when they were half way up the hill. The charge was made, but all his followers gradually fell, till the leader alone was left. Nothing daunted he held steadily on, now and again falling, heavily hit, but up and on again without a moment's delay, till at last he was shot dead close to the British line. More desperate courage than this is difficult to imagine.[73]

At this time the British also paid off Safdar Khan, the Khan of Nawagai. For a yearly subsidy of Rs 12,000 and a present of 1,000 rifles, the Khan agreed to use his influence over the Tarkanri tribesmen so that they would not offer opposition and to furnish supplies and render assistance to the troops. He failed to do this to the satisfaction of the British, and at best maintained a neutral attitude. The political officer with the expedition, Major H. A. Deane interviewed Muhammad Sharif Khan, the deposed Khan of Dir, who offered to assist the British force in return for arms and money. By the end of April 1895 the besieged garrison in Chitral had been relieved. The Khan of Dir captured Sher Afzul and brought him, along with a number of leading men of Chitral, into the British camp on 27 April. The prisoners, including women and children, numbered about 900. Sher Afzul, his daughter and a few leading men were sent to India as prisoners. The others were subsequently sent back to Chitral. Umra Khan was sent a message to surrender unconditionally to the government. He fled across the border into Afghanistan. The object of the Chitral relief expedition had been accomplished.

The GoI recommended to the secretary of state the retention of a British force in Chitral and the maintenance of a road that would pass through the intervening territories. In June the secretary of state informed India that in view of the large number of troops required to ensure the security of the road and the burden which would consequently be thrown on Indian revenues, this proposal was unacceptable. However, before the evacuation of the troops could occur, the government changed in England and the new secretary of state informed India that they would reconsider the question. On 10 August, formal assent was given to the proposal to retain Chitral and arrangements proceeded to construct fortified posts in Malakand and Chakdara.

Two months later, the GoI wrote to the secretary of state that there was no reason to suppose that the tribes regarded the occupation of the Malakand as an infringement of the proclamation issued on the despatch of the Chitral Relief Force: 'On the contrary, the Ranizais and Swatis and others from the Peshawar border to the Panjkora river have petitioned for the retention of troops in their country, to protect them and help them in protecting the road, and to maintain internal peace.'[74] The petitions were filed by people who had been paid off by the British and who feared that in light of the assistance they had furnished they were likely to suffer injury at the hands of tribesmen if British troops were withdrawn.[75] As one member in Parliament had pointed out, this demonstrated that the majority of the people were still hostile towards the British. In fact, until the Chitral Relief Force was withdrawn, people continued to resist their presence by firing into camps, cutting and carrying away telegraph wires, and wounding and killing camp followers. Further, people made no effort to cultivate their fields. The British responded by executing 19 men, making arrests and imposing fines payable in grain or cattle. The Khan of Dir was reinstated to his former position and was given most of Umra Khan's possessions, in addition to an agreement whereby he would receive money and arms from the British.

The Khan of Dir in general was regarded as oppressive. General Stedman wrote from Camp Laram in July:

> In sober truth the country-side is almost entirely in favour of the Umra Khan family. The villagers say—'Stay here yourselves if you like, if you give us back a strong Khan: but what is the use of the Khan of Dir? We believe that the revenue he is now wringing out of us is remitted to safe-keeping in India, and that he will run away at the first sound of danger as *he did before*. What we want is a *man*, be he good, bad or indifferent, who will protect us in return for his taxation.'[76]

He concluded by saying that it was a pity that their 'only friend in these parts should prove such a very weak reed to rely on'.[77] It was their money and arms that had bolstered his position but the people were 'by no means happy under him'.[78] By forcing upon the tribes the Khan of Dir and Mian Rahim Shah, who was again 'amply rewarded for his services' and became Deane's native agent subsequently, the British had interfered in the internal affairs of these areas, something that the GoI kept assuring the secretary of state that it was not their desire to do. They claimed that they desired only to maintain their line of communication with Chitral.

Until 1895, the British had recognised the independence of the Swat tribes. Even after sanctioning the construction of military posts in their country, the British claimed that the last thing they wanted was to interfere with the tribes or to annex their territory. However, that is essentially what they did. Prior to the outbreak, the Mian Guls brought this up with Major Deane when the Khan of Dir invaded

Upper Swat, an action that was approved by Deane, and referred to the promise made by the British to the Akhund after the Ambeyla campaign that they would never interfere in Swat. Deane did not reply to them but stated the following to a jirga of tribesmen:

> I informed them that as, when Government wanted a road through this country to relieve its own men besieged in Chitral fort, they, instead of giving the road, or of remaining aloof, had chosen to associate themselves directly with the enemies of Government in opposing our advance, and that having assumed an attitude of hostility, which they had further maintained by not sending in their jirgas, during the past two years to make peace, they themselves had cancelled whatever promise was made, and according to their own Pakhtun Wali, Government would have been justified in invading their country to punish them. Fortunately they did not ask me whether we were really the aggressors, or I should have had to explain that necessity knows no law.[79]

These sub-imperial workings point to the fact that resistance to the British had started in 1895, and continued till the full-blown revolt broke out in 1897. In 1896 also there was some 'unrest' and the mullahs attempted to incite the tribes to revolt, or 'stir the fanaticism of the people' as the British put it, but no serious outbreak occurred at that time. Clearly, at no point is the assertion borne out that the tribes had accepted British influence in 'good spirit' and that the revolt was a 'bolt from the blue'. However, if this resistance was continual, why did it turn into a major revolt in 1897? Pukhtun accounts of this war provide us with an idea of how it happened.

ORAL TRADITION IN SWAT: SARTOR FAKIR AND PUKHTUN RESISTANCE

The Pukhtuns do not view 1897 as an isolated event. For them, it was part of a continuous struggle against the British. The revolt is almost always related or compared to other battles (the Pukhtuns use the words *fight*, *war* and *jehad* interchangeably) fought with the British. It was a struggle in which religious leaders played a pivotal role, when other chiefs like the Khan of Dir were bought off by the British and others like the Mian Guls were not able to play a dominant role, even if they did oppose British occupation. The year 1897 is linked immediately to 1895 when the tribes first fought the British, but they were defeated. For the Pukhtuns a major reason for that defeat was the fact that the Khan of Dir went over to the side of the British. Faridun Khan, a village elder from Swat, recited the following *tapa* that was composed in 1895:

> Something strange has happened
> The English have come
> So hurry and show up at Malakand
> The women of Ranizais have become deveiled (bepardah)
> The oppression on them is increasing
> The brave men are dead and their young women are widows
> The families of these men may now be considered mirat
> People are deserting us and going towards Sharif Khan who leads them
> People are dishonoured as Sharif Khan leads the deserters
> The British now have a cantonment
> They have appeared at Aladand
> This news has reached Kashkar [Chitral][80]

The British reached Kashkar and stayed there. Even after the people failed to stop the British from crossing Swat, they used to come out to fight the British. Faridun Khan narrated how the Bajauris used to attack the British:

> The Bajauris would attack the camps at night. There would be mules, horses and cows so the bullet was bound to hit something. But in the morning they would be pushed back and would run back to the mountains. When the Bajauris continued to do this, the British felt trapped, so they asked the Khan of Nawagai to save them from the Bajauris. He replied, 'I fear them myself—how can I help you?'[81]

However, the Khan of Nawagai was also regarded as an ally of the British. There is a tapa about him as well:

> Now that the British have established cantonments
> God have mercy on the Shamozais, all of them martyred
> My heart aches for the 3000 Andalzais lying dead on the battlefield
> Damn the Akazais of Manki

> They have become cowards
> They take a bundle of money from the British
> Condemned forever, those who take money from the British
> The Khan of Nawagai does not even accept the Holy Prophet's faith
> Of course he will die a degraded man.[82]

In the case of Swat, the dynamics of middle-men within imperialism are widely recognised.

The people of Swat viewed the British presence in Swat as occupation. According to them, the British captured Malakand and Chakdara in 1895: 'The country was overrun and Malakand and Chakdara were kalaband [bound, encircled].'[83] From Bajaur to Dir, people regard the Malakand as their area. Whatever happened there was taken as collective responsibility of all the adjoining tribes. Deane himself mentioned this in one place after the attacks: 'The Malakand is regarded as being what it really is—the key of the whole country—and the feeling that has been instilled in the people is that, so long as we possess it, we hold the whole country.'[84] Here we see directly both sub-imperial accounts and Pukhtun oral tradition corroborating each other.

While the people continuously opposed British presence and attempted to resist it by cutting telegraph wires, firing into camps, and so on, it was the religious leaders who played a key role in the major revolts. However, it is important to point out that their role and motivation are primarily political resistance to imperial occupation. The revolt of 1897 is seen as Sartor Fakir's war. He is an intriguing figure for the people of Swat and Buner. The people of Buner still wonder at how an ordinary man from their village became so revered and dared to wage war against the British. Most of them recount the following about him. When the people of Buner heard that war was being waged in Malakand by a *pir* called Sartor Fakir, they went to Malakand to join in and to see who this great man was. When they arrived, somebody recognised him and said, 'Is he not Sadullah Bai.'[85]

Sartor Fakir belonged to the Abazai tribe and came from the village of Rega in Buner. His real name was Sadullah. He was an old man, a 'white-beard' when he fought in Malakand in 1897. Not much is known about his life before he fought in Malakand. What can be gathered is that some years prior to the revolt he left Buner. The people from Buner say that he was illiterate and came from a poor family. Others say that it seems that he travelled for a few years, after he left Buner and before he appeared at Malakand, and gained knowledge in the Middle East, Kabul and India. However, since he did not preach about religious matters, the impression gained that he might be illiterate. However, the old men of Swat recount Sartor Fakir's role in the 1897 war clearly. The oldest of these men, Haji Nawab Khan, participated in the revolt himself as a young boy (see Figure 15). The following account was provided by him:

> Sartor Fakir, also known as Mullah Mastan or Fakir Baba, stands as an unusual figure among the religious leaders. It is well known that he belonged to the Abazai tribe and came from the village of Rega in Buner. But not much is known about his adult life until he became known as a saint and started waging war in Swat. When he fought in 1897 he was already an old man, a 'white-beard'. Some people in Buner say that he came from a poor family and was illiterate. However, others say that it seems that he had acquired religious knowledge from travels in Kabul, India and the Middle East. But since he did not preach about purely religious matters people thought that he was not versed in them. (His grandson said, 'Would he have gathered thousands of supporters if he was illiterate?') Everybody agrees that his main purpose was jehad. Waged war against the British. Called it that because thought it would mobilise people. Went from house to house and asked people to join him in the fight against the British. People did not join him first. When children and young boys joined him then others followed. Would not accept invitation to dinner. Would collect bread from house to house and would only eat that. Also fought against people of Dir. He did not attach himself to anything material. He lived like a Sufi, married four times. Was not really a warrior, didn't like violence. He was called Mulla Mastan because of the way he preached/ powerful charismatic and aggressive. God had put the enmity of the British in his heart. The British were powerful; no one wanted to make enemies of them. When the people had been defeated in Malakand in 1895 they had become afraid. Then God sent Sartor Fakir and he opposed the British. Little boys joined him first; carried flags and went from village to village.

Figure 15: Haji Nawab Khan, the oldest living witness to the 1897 revolt, in 1995

> Collected bread from house to house with his followers and would eat with them. He used to simply say do Ghaza against the British. God had given him such charisma that he managed to scare the British.[86]

Pukhtun accounts provide a different narrative of this war, but one that overlaps with what we can construct from British confidential documents. While part of a continuous opposition, the revolt in 1897 had its roots going back to the occupation of Swat in 1895 when the British first entered Malakand. The struggle against the occupation of Swat was renewed in 1897. Pukhtuns in Swat and Buner give Sartor Fakir credit for mobilising them to resist the British (see Figure 16). However, they do not ascribe religious motives to his actions and Pukhtun oral tradition does not view him as a 'mad-man': 'All of Swat was with Sartor Fakir. If he was mad, people would not have sided with him.'[87] When asked whether he was able to perform miracles, the answer was: 'His miracle was that he dared to fight the British.'[88]

The case of Sartor Fakir presents an unusual case because he defies both traditional models of leadership within the Frontier, such as the mullahs, as well as the features present in millenarian

Figure 16: Sartor Fakir's grave

movements. Pukhtun oral tradition does not anywhere support the idea that magic or miracles were a factor in his being able to mobilise people to oppose the British. However, despite his quiet non-violent persona, it is likely from the preceding evidence that he stepped into a vacuum in leadership that grew out of a complex interplay of factors such as the growing power of middlemen, especially the Khan of Dir, as well as local politics around the role of the Mian Guls.

As in the case of Maizar, the revolt in Swat demonstrates military unpreparedness and failure. Sub-imperial evidence points to the attacks having their origins in the occupation of Swat in 1895 and being exacerbated due to the oppressive nature of how this occupation was experienced on the ground. Again, like Gee, Deane's misrepresentations of realities on the ground were discovered, but he was not held accountable. And again, like Maizar, this history of Empire does not enter either official accounts or the enduring historiographical narrative of the revolt in Swat as a spontaneous, fanatical outburst.

NOTES

1. 'Extract from Diary of the Political Agent for Dir, Swat and Chitral for the Week Ending 4th July 1897', PGoI, FF, NAI, September 1897.
2. 'From—Major H. A. Deane, C.S.I., Political Agent for Dir, Swat and Chitral, To—The Secretary to the GoI, Foreign Department', 21 July 1897, PGoI, FF, NAI, September 1897.
3. 'Extract from Diary for the Week Ending 4th July 1897'.
4. 'From—Major Deane, To—The Secretary to the GoI', 21 July 1897.
5. Mian Guls were the two grandsons of the late Akhund of Swat. The Akhund of Swat was a deeply revered figure among the Frontier tribes who looked to him as a spiritual guide. Even though he opposed the British during the famous Ambeyla Campaign of 1863, he is described in official accounts with reverence. They described his position towards the tribes by comparing it with that of the Pope of Rome. The Akhund died in 1877. While the Akhund had for the most part kept aloof from 'worldly affairs', he opposed the British because his main goal was to preserve the independence of Swat. The Mian Guls were the successors of the Akhund and the people of Swat collected under them to oppose the advance of British troops in 1895.

This party was also hostile to the Nawab of Dir for 'throwing in his lot with the British Government' and again for invading their territory with British consent. The Mian Guls were also supported by certain important mullahs like the Adda Mullah. This combination and their position is described by Deane as 'fanatical working' ('From—Major Deane, To—The Secretary to the GoI', 21 July 1897).

6. 'Extract from Diary for the Week Ending 4th July 1897'.

7. 'From—Major Deane, To—The Secretary to the GoI', 21 July 1897.

8. Note by W. J. Cuningham, 28 July 1897, PGoI, K.W., NAI, September 1897.

9. 'Note or Precis: Disturbances in the Malakand', PGoP, K.W., DoA, Peshawar, September 1897.

10. 'From—Major H. A. Deane, C.S.I., Political Agent for Dir, Swat and Chitral, To—The Secretary to the GoI, Foreign Department', 8 August 1897, PGoI, FF (250–973), NAI, September 1897.

11. Ibid.

12. Ibid.

13. Ibid.

14. Ibid.

15. Note by E. H. S. Clarke, 28 July 1897, PGoI, K.W., NAI, September 1897.

16. Ibid.

17. Note by Elgin, 28 July 1897, PGoI, K.W., NAI, September 1897.

18. 'Extract from the Confidential Diary No. II of the District Superintendent of Police, Kohat, for the Week Ending 31st July 1897', PGoI, K.W., DoA, September 1897.

19. Note by E. H. S. Clarke, 20 August 1897, PGoI, K.W., NAI, September 1897.

20. 'Translation of a Letter from His Highness the Amir of Afghanistan and Its Dependencies, to the Address of His Excellency the Viceroy, dated the 12th Rabi-us-Sani 1315-H., Corresponding to the 10th September 1897', PGoI, Sec F, NAI, November 1897.

21. Ibid.

22. Ibid.

23. 'From—Lieutenant-Colonel Muhammad Aslam Khan, C.I.E., Political Officer, Khyber, To—The Commissioner and Superintendent, Peshawar Division', 4 August 1897, PGoI, K.W., DoA, 1897.

24. 'From—The Deputy Commissioner of Peshawar, To—The Commissioner and Superintendent, Peshawar Division', 8 August 1897, PGoI, K.W., DoA, 1897.

25. 'Note or Precis: Political Situation as Regards the Bonerwals and the Peshawar Border Generally', PGoP, K.W., Punjab Government Archives, Civil Secretariat, Lahore, September 1897.

26. Ibid.

27. Ibid.

28. 'From—Major H. A. Deane, C.S.I., Political Agent for Dir, Swat and Chitral, To—The Secretary to the GoI, Foreign Department', 31 August 1897, PGoI, FF, K.W., NAI, November 1897.

29. Ibid.

30. 'To—The Right Hon'ble Lord George F. Hamilton, Her Majesty's Secretary of State for India, From—Elgin, G. S. White, J. Westland, J. Woodburn, M. D. Chalmers, E. H. H. Collen, A. C. Trevor', 1 September 1897, PGoI, Sec F, NAI, 1897.

31. 'From—Deane, To—The GoI', PGoI, Sec F, NAI, 1898.

32. Note by E. H. S. Clarke, 30 July 1897, PGoI, K.W., NAI, September 1897.

33. Ibid.; emphasis added.

34. Note by W. J. Cuningham, 28 July 1897.

35. See Appendix B to this volume.

36. 'From—Major H. A. Deane, C.S.I., Political Agent for Dir, Swat, and Chitral, To—The Secretary to the Government of India, Foreign Department', 24 September 1897, PGoI, Sec F, NAI, November 1897.

37. 'Diary of the Political Agent for Dir, Swat, and Chitral for the Week Ending 26th September 1897', PGoI, NAI, 1897.

38. Note by E. H. S. Clarke, 28 July 1897.

39. 'From—Major H. A. Deane, C.S.I., Political Agent for Dir, Swat and Chitral, To—The Secretary to the Government of India, Foreign Department', 21 July 1897, PGoI, FF, NAI, September 1897.

40. Ibid.

41. Ibid.

42. 'To—Hamilton, From—Elgin &c.', 1 September 1897.

43. Ibid.

44. 'Telegraphic Conversation, His Excellency the Commander-in-Chief and Colonel Meiklejohn', 27 July 1897, PGoI, FF, K.W., NAI, September 1897.

45. Ibid.

46. 'From—Deane, To—The Secretary to the GoI', 8 August 1897.

47. 'Telegraphic Conversation', 27 July 1897.

48. 'From—Deane, To—The Secretary to the GoI', 8 August 1897.

49. Ibid.

50. 'Diary of the Political Agent for Dir, Swat and Chitral from the 30th July to the 11th August 1897', 12 August 1897, PGoI, FF, NAI, September 1897.

51. 'Despatches from Brigadier-General Meiklejohn and Major-General Sir Bindon Blood, K.C.B., on the Operations of the Malakand Brigade and the Malakand Field Force up to 26th August 1897', Military Department Records, Serial No. 33, NAI.

52. 'Diary of Political Agent from 30th July to 11th August 1897'.

53. Ibid.

54. 'Note or Precis: Disturbances in the Malakand', PGoP, K.W., DoA, September 1897.

55. 'From—Deane, To—The GoI', PGoI, Sec F, 1898.

56. The Earl of Northbrook, 7 March 1898, *Parliamentary Debates*, Lords, India Office Records and Private Papers/British Library (IOR/BL), London.

57. Mr John Lawson Walton, 14 February 1898, *Parliamentary Debates*, Commons, IOR/BL.

58. Mr Asquith, 15 February 1898, *Parliamentary Debates*, Commons, IOR/BL.

59. Walton, 14 February 1898.

60. Ibid.

61. Ibid.

62. Ibid.

63. The Earl of Kimberly, 8 February 1898, *Parliamentary Debates*, Lords, IOR/BL.

64. Ibid.

65. Sir W. Harcourt, 8 February 1898, *Parliamentary Debates*, Commons, IOR/BL.

66. Ibid.

67. Walton, 14 February 1898.

68. Sir Lewis McIver, 15 February 1898, *Parliamentary Debates*, Commons, IOR/BL.

69. 'Note by Deane on the House of Commons Debate', 17 April 1898, PGoI, K.W., 1898 NAI; emphasis added.

70. Ibid.

71. Ibid.

72. A detailed account of the fighting can be found in Younghusband and Younghusband (1895).

73. Ibid.: 91–92.

74. 'To—The Right Hon'ble Lord George F. Hamilton, Her Majesty's Secretary of State for India, From—Elgin, G. S. White, A. E. Miller, H. Brackenbury, J. Westland, A. Mackenzie, A. C. Trevor', 9 October 1895, PGoI, Sec F, NAI, 1895.

75. See Appendix C to this volume.

76. 'From—General E. Stedman, To—The Hon'ble Lieutenant-General Sir Henry Brackenbury, K.C.B.', 26 July 1895, PGoI, K.W., NAI, 1895; emphasis in original.

77. Ibid.

78. Ibid.

79. 'Extract from Diary for the Week Ending 4th July 1897'.

80. Faridun Khan, Mohammad Khel, interview by author, May 1995, Swat. A *tapa* is a form of Pukhtun folk poetry. *Mirat* referred to a family left without male heirs; such a family was considered to have lost status and its property was redistributed.

81. Ibid.

82. Ibid.

83. Hermuz Khan, interview by author, May 1995, Buner.

84. 'Diary of Political Agent for the Week Ending 26th September 1897'.

85. They had expected to meet a famous saint and were disappointed at first to recognise an ordinary man from their village. Interviews by author conducted in April, May 1995, Swat and Buner.

86. Haji Nawab Khan participated in the attack on Malakand in 1897. He was a young boy at the time and carried a flag, like many other young boys, for Sartor Fakir when he was mobilising people. In his own words, he was of the age when 'hair on his face had started to grow'. He was between 110 and 115 years old at the time of the interview in 1995. Haji Nawab Khan, interview by author, 28 April 1995, Swat.

87. Haji Nawab Khan, interview by author, 28 April 1995, Swat.

88. Ibid.

5

THE DELIBERATE CREATION OF THE 'BLACKEST DAY'

Sub-imperial Politics and Imperial Defence

The loss of the Khyber presents the most spectacular military failure within the revolt and perhaps within the history of the colonial encounter in the North-West Frontier.[1] Why was it not defended and how could it fall is a question that has remained unanswered in historiography. The attack was not sudden. It was publicly known that Afridis were planning an attack upon military positions in the Khyber as they had communicated their grievances to the officials several weeks before the attack. Therefore, imperial explanations here take on a different significance as they are directly tied to imperial defence and cannot claim 'fanaticism' or 'treachery' to account for military unpreparedness and the resulting failures. The usual tropes do not suffice as explanations and therefore are, unsurprisingly, not invoked. Also, in contrast to the previous attacks, the fall of the Khyber takes on the tone of a scandal (in the press and in the houses of parliament) because of the Khyber's central role within imperial defence. Here imperial explanations are directly tied to imperial defence and the form of sub-imperial evidence illustrates the inner workings of imperialism, both at the lower levels as well as the higher levels of decision-making, which led to the deliberate loss of the Khyber, perhaps the climax of sub-imperialism.

THE SITUATION IN KHYBER PRIOR TO THE ATTACK

Early in August 1897, British officials began hearing of the possibility of an Afridi attack on Jamrud and the posts held by garrisons of the Khyber Rifles in the Khyber Pass.[2] These reports were communicated to the commissioner of Peshawar, Sir Richard Udny, and to Captain Barton, commandant of the Khyber Rifles. As a result, Captain Barton, in consultation with Colonel Aslam Khan, political officer, Khyber, at once took steps to provision these posts and to strengthen the garrisons. The garrisons normally consisting of 349 men were raised to 554 men. As Landi Kotal was the most advanced post, dominating practically the whole of the Khyber, its strength was increased from 200 to 354 Rifles and reserve ammunition there was increased to over 50,000 rounds. Captain Barton further made provisions for ration and supply of water.[3] In Captain Barton's words:

> I made the chaukidars of the 'Ulus' well work extra hours raising water. On the 17th August there was 9 feet of water in the covered masonry tank in the fort; the daily waste for drinking, washing and garden irrigation, etc., with over 400 souls living in the fort, was only 3 inches. From this it will be seen that with care there would have been an ample supply for a garrison of a thousand men, for at least twelve days, and if limited to drinking purposes, would have lasted for a much longer period.[4]

The military situation at the time was as follows[5]:

On 17 of August, there were two columns in the Peshawar District:

The Shabkadar Column.

1 Field Battery.
1 Native cavalry regiment.
1 British infantry regiment.
1 Native infantry regiment.
6 Companies Native infantry.
1 Company Sappers and Miners.

The Peshawar Column.

1 Battery, Royal Horse Artillery.
1 Mountain Battery.
1 British cavalry regiment.
2 Wings British infantry.
1 Battalion Native infantry.

Troops were being moved up from various stations in India, and on 17 August two reserve brigades arrived at Rawalpindi, bringing up the total of the reserve brigades to 7,800 men.

On 18 August the concentration statement was as follows[6]:

Peshawar Garrison.

1 Battery Royal Horse Artillery.
1 Field Battery Royal Artillery.
1 Company Royal Artillery (to arrive on 21 August)
2 Squadrons British cavalry.
1 Regiment Native cavalry.
3 Wings British infantry.
2 Companies British infantry.
4 Battalions Native infantry (1 Battalion to arrive on 21 August).
1 Wing Native infantry.

Jamrud Column.

1 Battery Royal Horse Artillery.
1 Mountain Battery Royal Artillery.
1 Regiment British cavalry.
1 Wing British infantry.
1 Wing Native infantry.
7 Companies Native infantry.

Bara Garrison.

50 Sabres Native cavalry.
1 Company Native infantry.

Force at Shabkadar.

1 Field Battery Royal Artillery (6 guns).
1 Regiment Native cavalry.
1 Wing British infantry.
1 Battalion Native infantry.
5 Companies Native infantry.
1 Company Sappers and Miners.

Michni Garrison.

50 Sabres Native cavalry.
1 Company Native infantry.

On 17 August, Captain Barton received information that a force of Shinwaris[7] was advancing to attack Landi Kotal, their object being to loot the caravan serai.[8] The serai was at a distance of about 800 yards from the fort, out of sight, and had only a small guard. Realising it was quite indefensible as it was commanded on three sides at close range, Barton moved a company out on the low hills that commanded the caravan serai and the approaches to it. He sent a picket of local Shinwaris to hold Michni Kandao, 2 miles from Landi Kotal, and directed them to check the enemy by firing and give warning of their approach.

The same day Barton received information of a large Afridi gathering advancing to attack the Khyber posts. He wrote to the commissioner, asking for a small reinforcement of regular troops.[9] That night Barton received a telegram from Colonel Aslam Khan, political officer, Khyber, saying that troops were on their way. The next day, on 18 August, Barton despatched a demi-official letter to the commissioner in which he stated that his reasons for asking for troops were:

> 1) The possibility of a large Afridi force attacking (Subadar Mursil states that all the clans of the Tirah Afridis have joined the movement) and their being helped by a flank attack from Dakka.
> 2) The fort is a big place to hold with the men I have got against a large force, and though I have much confidence in them and they seem most anxious to have a row even with their own people, still if they were surrounded by their own tribesmen it might be hard for them, especially as this business seems to be purely fanatical.
> 3) The bazar and Kafila serai could not possibly be defended with the numbers I have, from a large tribal force, being so badly placed, and so far from the fort.
> 4) The possibility of an Afghan attack. Subadar Mursil states that the Afridis received a letter from the Afghan Commandant of Kai saying that if they wished help in the attack on the Khaibar he would give it them.
> 5) Even if the Afridi lashkar fizzles away into a small force, the Kafila guards will have to be much strengthened, and without help I could not well spare the men.
> 6) The presence of a few troops here will keep the Khaibar Zakha Khel from doing anything foolish.[10]

He concluded by saying that there was a danger of a possible *coup de main* from Afghanistan, a force of guns coming in while the British were busy with the Afridis. And finally he said: 'I hope if I have said anything presumptuous you will forgive me, but I thought it right, being on the spot, to say all I knew and thought of the situation.'[11]

A few hours later Barton received a telegram from the commissioner that contained peremptory orders for him to withdraw from Landi Kotal to Jamrud, leaving his garrison behind.[12] According to Barton's own account later, he was much distressed at this order.[13] He called all the native officers and men, told them what had occurred, handed over the fort to them, saying that he had asked the commissioner for help, which of course would be granted and he would return with reinforcements.

As mentioned earlier, Udny had been receiving news since early August of the possibility of an Afridi-Orakzai combination to rise against the British. GoI had also received information to this effect. On 15 August 1897, the foreign secretary asked the commissioner whether he believed these reports.[14] The commissioner replied on the same date that this information should be treated with great caution. On 15 August, another report was sent by Mr Donald, political officer, Fort Lockhart, Samana, stating that the Afridis were prepared to attack Jamrud.[15] The commissioner again telegraphed the foreign secretary that everything was quiet. On 16 August, the chief secretary to the GoP wrote to the Foreign Department that the lieutenant governor thought 'it would be a matter of surprise if there were no disturbance on the Peshawar–Kohat frontier, and we should be prepared for all possibilities'.[16] He also advised that a force should be ready to move from Peshawar in the event of an attack made by the tribes to the west and south-west of that district.

On 17 August, Udny telegraphed the foreign secretary that he was watching events in the Afridi and Orakzai country very carefully. His reports from reliable sources said that so far there was no serious or general movement either among the Orakzais or Afridis.[17] Later that day, Udny again sent a telegram to the foreign secretary saying that Malik Amin Khan (an important Malik working for the British) had brought the news that an Afridi lashkar 10,000 strong had left Tirah on 16 August to attack the Khyber road and posts.[18] The lashkar was expected to reach Bazar Valley on 17 August and the Khyber on 18 August.

Upon receiving this news, Udny discussed the situation with General Elles, commanding the Peshawar district, and with Aslam Khan. General Elles, in Udny's own words, considered that as 'a point of military honour' Captain Barton must remain at Landi Kotal 'at all hazards'.[19] Udny, for the moment, accepted this view. They agreed therefore that measures should be taken to prepare against an attack. Elles decided that he would telegraph for reinforcements and that the following troops would move at daybreak from Peshawar to strengthen Jamrud and 'to act as a demonstration against the Pass itself':[20]

	Men
3 guns 'K' Battery, Royal Horse Artillery	123
4th Dragoon Guards	462
4 guns No. 3 Mountain Battery, Royal Artillery	109
Wing, Gordon Highlanders	386
21st Gurkhas	732
Wing, 26th Punjab Infantry	280
Total	2,092

General Elles then left Udny and Aslam Khan. A few hours later, inspite of Elles' and Aslam Khan's opinion, Udny decided to withdraw Captain Barton from his post at once, and sent him orders. It was the commissioner's decision.

The British had expected the tribes to attack the Khyber on 18 August. The attack did not take place till 23 August. By this time many reinforcements had arrived in Peshawar. Troops were stationed at Jamrud waiting to move out immediately. Barton said later that he hoped everyday that troops would be sent out. However, no troops were sent. It had been decided to let the Khyber go.

Initially, when information about the attack was still scant, the authorities tried to make out that the garrisons had not put up a fight and had deserted over to the attacking lashkar. This would certainly have helped in justifying the decision to leave the garrisons to their fate. However, Aslam Khan and Captain Barton soon contradicted this notion with detailed reports of what occurred. The following account of the attack on the Khyber posts and the fighting that occurred is drawn from these reports.

On the morning of 23 August, the Afridi Lashkar numbering a few thousand reached Ali Masjid. Here, it divided into two portions, one remaining at Ali Masjid and the other proceeding towards Fort Maude. The tribes burnt the two towers lying towards the south-west of Ali Masjid. They were held by two sepoys each and were immediately evacuated on the approach of the lashkar. The tribes then burnt the house of the Naik of the Khyber Rifles. Then the lashkar proceeded towards Fort Maude, which was held by 42 men of the Khyber Rifles of various clans and about 100 Kuki Khel tribesmen under Malik Kambar.

General Elles sent a battery of the Royal Horse Artillery with the Dragoon Guards and four companies of British Infantry towards Fort Maude. Seeing the battery and thinking they were going to be relieved, the garrison opened a heavy fire on the lashkar. The battery, however, only advanced to within 2 or 3 miles of the fort and then retired to Jamrud. 'On the retirement of the battery and cavalry to Jamrud, feeling themselves left to their fate and outnumbered, a hundred to one, with no water and very little ammunition left, they evacuated.'[21] Of the Fort Maude garrison, 11 Zakha Khels deserted to the attackers with their rifles. This was the only case of desertion. With regard to the conduct of the garrison, Aslam Khan wrote:

> I do not think they are in the slightest degree to blame for evacuating their posts. They were outnumbered, as I said a hundred to one, they had run out of water, had little ammunition, the enemy were in many cases their near relations, and they rightly conjectured they were not to be helped but left to their fate, and this with a large British force encamped in full view within five miles of them.[22]

Of the Kuki Khel tribesmen, one was shot dead and another was severely wounded. The loss of the lashkar was estimated to be 18 killed.

The lashkar then commenced attack on Ali Masjid. The fort was held by 57 men of the Khyber Rifles, and about 40 Kuki Khel tribesmen under Malik Amin Khan. The garrison held out till 7 pm when the men, finding themselves outnumbered and seeing Fort Maude in flames, evacuated the fort, which was then burnt down by the lashkar. The garrison had one Khyber Rifle killed and two wounded, and one of the Kuki Khel tribesmen was killed. The British were not sure of the lashkar's losses. The estimates given were from 12 to 20.

Landi Kotal, being the most advanced, was the most important post in the Khyber. It was garrisoned by 504 men (along with Fort Tytler and Gurgurra, two minor posts) of whom 21 men, being native officers, buglers and munshis, had no rifles. The tribes began their attack on Landi Kotal at 8 am on 24 August. They advanced along the road from the Khyber and were fired on by the garrison. Losing three men, they moved behind the low hills to the south of the fort. They occupied the crest of these hills and the block house and fired into the caravan serai. An hour later, they had surrounded the fort and continued firing into it all day and night. The defending garrison returned the fire. Next morning Ain Khan (a nephew of Malik Khwas Khan) came into the open, waving a cloth, saying he had a message from the Aka Khel Mullah. He was let into the fort. He said he was authorised to make terms. He asked the garrison to surrender the fort, stating that the British had left Jamrud and it was doubtful if they could hold on to Peshawar. 'The native officers knowing that Forts Maude and Ali Masjid had been burnt, and that no attempt had been made to relieve either of these places decided to make terms.'[23] They asked that the Aka Khel Mullah move his force and by the evening they would evacuate the fort with their baggage and retire to British territory. Ain Khan agreed and informed the Mullah who immediately ordered the different clans to retire to a mile away from the post. The lashkar started moving off and Subadar-Major Mir Akbar told the men to come down from the walls and collect their baggage. As the men holding the bastion in the north-east corner started to do so, some tribesmen (Zakha Khel and Shinwaris), who were hiding in a *nullah* close by, climbed over and began looting the officers' quarters. Subadar Mursil brought a few men of No. 4 Company, Peshawaris, to clear them out, killing five men and a woman who had come with them. However, in this engagement Subadar Mursil was shot through the head and killed. By this time, most of the lashkar had moved off, but some of them, seeing that the walls had been left, rushed to them and started climbing over. At this point, other retiring tribesmen also ran back and joined in. The sepoys returned to man the walls and fired at the tribesmen at the foot of the walls. It was at this point, according to Aslam Khan, that the tribes suffered their heaviest loss.

At this point, the jamadar of the post, after consultation with Subadar-Major Mir Akbar, called out for the standard of their clan (the Malikdin Khel) to come close outside the gate, which was then opened. It was the son of Subadar Mursil (who had just been killed) who bore the standard of the Malikdin Khel. The lashkar rushed in through the gate and the garrison, to save their lives, went and stood under the standards of their respective tribes, except for the men of the British territory who were robbed by the Afridis of their rifles and belts. Part of the garrison (No. 6 Company) climbed down the northern wall and escaped. The Afridis captured the post, looted the building and then set it on fire. The losses of the garrison were 10 men and one native officer killed, and one native officer and one man wounded. The number of attacking tribesmen claimed to have been killed was about 200.

Finally, Aslam Khan reported that given the circumstances, the conduct of the garrison was very good.

> Subadar Mursil, Malikdin Khel, fought with the greatest bravery, and until he was killed on the second day he thwarted the designs of Subadar-Major Mir Akbar, who wished to hand over the fort. Subadar Jawas, Shinwari, also behaved with great gallantry. He was shot through the shoulders early on the 25th, but continued at his post until the fort was taken and then did what he could to save men and Government property.[24]

After burning the post, the Afridi lashkar carried off their dead and wounded and left the Khyber.

The Khyber remained closed for four months, and the British made no attempt to retake it. The loss of the Khyber was regarded as a disaster. There was much criticism about it in the press and in the British parliament. It was described by a high-ranking official as a day of 'shame and humiliation' for the British. Lord Roberts in a speech in Parliament talked of the 'incomprehensible manner' in which the Khyber Rifles had been deprived of the support of their British officer at the time 'when that support was most needed'.[25] A *Pioneer* correspondent remarked scathingly that no one, least of all Captain Barton, could have conjectured that the Government would leave the Khyber Rifles entirely to their fate and that 'a policy of scuttle would have been pursued' (*The Risings on the North-West Frontier* 1898: 111).

The Government and the opposition in England asked the secretary of state for an explanation.

SUB-IMPERIAL DECISION-MAKING AND THE LOSS OF THE KHYBER

Seemingly, the British lost the Khyber due to Udny's decision. As mentioned earlier, Udny sent Barton peremptory orders to withdraw from Landi Kotal—inspite of Elles' and Aslam Khan's wishes and much to Captain Barton's indignation. Why did he do so?

Let us follow Udny's line of action in making that decision and his reasons for doing so. On 17 August when Udny sent Captain Barton orders to withdraw to Jamrud, he stated: 'If your garrison could be relied upon, I would never recall you. As it is, the men on such an occasion are absolutely untrustworthy, and I consider it my duty to order you to come down to Jamrud at once, and it is your duty to obey this order.'[26]

If the men of the Khyber Rifles were considered untrustworthy and unreliable, then obviously they could not be expected to defend and hold the Khyber, especially against their own kith and kin, and even more so when they were to be left without their commandant. Then why did Udny not order them up too and make an attempt to send in regular troops to hold the Khyber?

However, two days later, Udny changed this argument. On 20 August, he wrote to the chief secretary of the Punjab government saying that he, along with General Elles and Aslam Khan, was opposed to calling in the Khyber Rifles even if matters were as bad as represented in his earlier telegram, for it would be immediately supposed that the British had 'abandoned the Pass' and the posts would be looted. He stated:

> Although in withdrawing Captain Barton I said that his garrison could not be relied upon, we are all of the opinion that we must trust Khyber Rifles under their own native officers to the end, and that even if they eventually failed us and bolted with their arms and ammunition, this would not be so bad as showing distrust of them by calling them into Jamrud before they had been fairly tested.[27]

Further, he stated that he was disinclined to send in troops 'merely for protection of Khyber posts and road'.[28] He thought that the Maliks should be required to act up to their agreement(s) without extraneous assistance. And if troops were sent in, the question of their supply would be 'an awkward one'.[29]

First Udny recalled Captain Barton, saying that his garrison could not be trusted. Then he stated that the authorities should not show their distrust of the Khyber Rifles by recalling them and that the Maliks should act up to their agreements. The question of the defence of the Khyber seems to be irrelevant and is not considered; rather what Udny is preoccupied with is whether the Khyber Rifles will stand 'their test'. The test, by any reasoning, is completely absurd. How could a garrison of a few hundred men defend and fight against 10,000 well-armed men (the estimated number of the lashkar that left Tirah for the attack on the Khyber)? The question of the Maliks being asked to act up to their agreement was raised as a big issue and will be discussed later in the chapter. As to supplies for the troops, Captain Barton had already arranged for that, but Udny later claimed ignorance of this fact. What is surprising at this point is that Udny shows no concern about the fact that their posts were under threat and that the British might lose the Khyber, which they considered to be very important, strategically and for their prestige.

Between 17 August and 23 August, Udny had several days to reinforce the Khyber. A strong force had by now collected in Peshawar and Jamrud. Captain Barton had, until he was recalled, been making preparations for strengthening the posts and arranging supplies for the troops. There was no doubt that the existing garrisons in the Khyber could not have defended it against a force of several thousand. Yet, neither Udny nor the authorities made an attempt to send reinforcements to defend the Pass. The fundamental question as to why has remained unanswered. In fact, its defence did not seem to be much of an issue.

Udny later gave the following explanation as to why he decided to withdraw Captain Barton and not send in troops:

> The first question for immediate decision (as the Afridi 'lashkar' was expected to make its appearance in the Khaibar next day) was whether Captain Barton should be recalled from Landi Kotal

and the defence of that post left to its garrison of Khaibar Rifles under the command of their own native officers, or whether he should remain there to conduct its defence in person. No force of troops, it appeared, could be spared from Peshawar of sufficient strength to be pushed up the Khaibar for the support or relief of Landi Kotal, and I think we were all three agreed that, if it were only possible to withdraw Captain Barton, the least objectionable course under the circumstances would be to do so, and to leave the garrisons of the Khaibar Rifles in all their posts to make the best defence they could make (or might be inclined to make) without assistance. It is difficult to remember the exact tenor of our conversation, and I can only speak for myself; but my own view—though I cannot be quite sure how fully I stated this to General Elles—was that by recalling Captain Barton we should be removing what would otherwise be a very great incentive to a fanatical gathering to attack Landi Kotal, *viz.*, the desire to capture a post commanded by a British officer, and that, if he were withdrawn, the Afridi 'lashkar' might hesitate to make any attack in earnest upon this or other posts held only by their own tribesmen if the latter proved true to their salt and showed that they were prepared to defend them. Moreover, even if the posts were attacked and the garrisons in spite of their resistance were overpowered by numbers, there was no reason, I thought, to fear that men who had assembled in the name of a *jehad* would harm Muhammadan fellow-tribesmen after any actual fighting was over, so that there could be no question of 'leaving the Khaibar Rifles to their fate' or of abandoning them to 'whole-sale massacre'; and in this respect subsequent events have shown that I judged correctly. Although therefore under clause 5 of the Khaibar Agreement there was nothing to prevent us from sending troops to re-occupy the Pass if they had been available, it seemed to me that it would be a mistake, on this the first occasion that the Khaibar arrangements had ever been seriously strained or tested, to relieve Maliks of their responsibilities under clauses (2), (5), (6) and (12)—for which it must be remembered that they had been very highly paid during a long course of years—by withdrawing their agents the Khaibar Rifles simply because we were not in a position to support them by military force.[30]

Udny says that the 'first question' upon receiving news that a big force was going to attack the Khyber was whether Captain Barton should be withdrawn or not. It is rather startling that the defence of the Pass—if it was, as the British claimed, an important strategic post—is not a concern. If the Russians were to appear near the Khyber, would the question be its defence or to assess how a handful of levies would behave against an overwhelming army. Second, Udny was not a military man and not in charge of the military situation. His claim that troops could not be spared was not borne out by the number of troops stationed in Peshawar and in Jamrud. Further, he overrode the local military commander, Captain Barton, and the Lt-General Commanding the Forces, Punjab, who in the circumstances was the responsible military adviser.

The following clause from the agreement that was entered into with the Afridis in 1881 was what Udny referred to, and it also became the justification for withdrawing Barton and not sending in troops:

> Our responsibility for the security of the road is independent of aid from Government in the form of troops; it lies within the discretion of the Government to maintain its troops in the Pass, or withdraw them, and re-occupy at pleasure; we will provide such number of men as the Government may direct to carry out the duties, and to enable us to render the road secure.[31]

According to this clause, the Government was not called upon to support the tribesmen. However, it seems from the phrase 'render the road secure' that this agreement was directed at keeping the road (which was the trading route) open and protecting caravans from raids and attacks, which was the concern during ordinary times. The present situation was one where British military posts were threatened, and it was impossible for the Khyber Rifles to have defended them without aid. If it was in British interests to keep the Pass open, then, as Udny himself remarked, 'under clause 5 of the Khaibar Agreement there was nothing to prevent [them] from sending troops to re-occupy the Pass'.

Given that the British army prided itself on its organisation and its soldiers, it would be unthinkable that an officer from a British regiment could be withdrawn at a time when they were threatened by attack and the regiment left to itself. However, in stressing the above agreement, it seemed that the British were exempted from supporting the Khyber Rifles because they were a local levy of tribes and not a regular regiment, even if it was in their own interest that they support them. But the Rifles were, more or less, a native regiment officered by a British officer, a fact that was acknowledged by Udny himself. He stated in a memorandum:

> As to the Khyber Rifles, it seems advisable for me to note that they are the present form of the Jezailchi Corps, which originally consisted for the most part of men provided by the Maliks under clause (6) of the 1881 Agreement and subject to their control, who were paid R7 a month if they carried matchlocks or R8 if they brought rifles. Gradually this corps became more and more 'regularised,' the men were supplied with Sniders, the property of Government, while they were withdrawn by degrees from the control of the Maliks, and a very material addition was made to the Government posts in their charge by the erection in 1888–89 of the fortified serai at Landi Kotal. From time to time the tribal Maliks still continued to assert their right of control, but these claims were steadily resisted by the Political Officer in charge of the Khyber, and before the Afridi rising occurred last summer this control had practically disappeared, so that the Khyber Rifles were very similar in organisation to a regiment of the Native army, though until Captain Barton was appointed in 1896 the important element of British officers was entirely wanting.[32]

William John Cuningham, foreign secretary to the GoI, put it more directly:

> ... if we have a body of men recruited, paid, armed, drilled and commanded by officers of the Indian Government (and except for appearance sake it does not matter whether these officers be British or Native, if they are Government officers) it is better, I believe, to acknowledge at once that the body is a British Militia regiment and no longer keep up what has become not much less than pretence, that it is a levy of tribes supplied and maintained under tribal responsibility.[33]

Thus, the claim that the British were not called upon to support the Khyber Rifles, and that the Maliks were responsible under the circumstances, once again does not hold.

The reasons given by Udny for recalling Captain Barton and for not reinforcing the Khyber Pass with troops are not convincing. Many officials at the time were not convinced and thought his actions strange. Captain Barton was indignant and protested strongly. Aslam Khan in a confidential handwritten letter claimed:

> For want of troops we were unable to protect the Pass—which was left to itself and when once occupied by the enemy, it was not safe to move up troops—without running the risk of some serious loss. Though had the Pass been occupied by even a small force in the first instance, as a reinforcement to the Khyber Rifles, it would have never been lost.[34]

The reaction of the Punjab government was the same. They could not comprehend Udny's policies. Since early August, when news of an Afridi attack had been coming in from various sources and Udny seemed eager to disregard it, Dane, chief secretary, Punjab, remarked:

> Though Commissioner doubts that there will be trouble, the information given by Donald, who is a reliable man, is very detailed, and I think we should ask that Kohat should now be strengthened. It will take troops at least three days to get there. Udny's rather deliberate movements are hardly suited to the present crisis. While he is making up his mind the affair comes off.[35]

In preparing a report on the loss of the Khyber, Dane again stated how Udny was ready to discredit information warning him about the Afridi uprising, and went on to say:

> Indeed there is reason to fear that his distrust of his information may have rendered him less anxious about the safety of the posts and consequently less disposed to comply with Colonel Aslam's and Captain Barton's suggestions that the garrison of Khaibar Rifles should be stiffened by the despatch of a military force, when on 20th August this apparently could have been done with safety. The garrisons so strengthened would probably have been able to hold out in Ali Masjid and Landi Kotal until more troops could be hurried up, and the whole position would have been saved.[36]

It is clear that Udny's decisions led to the loss of the Khyber. It is also evident that many officials at the time were not in favour of his policies and thought his actions incomprehensible. Udny's explanations are not convincing. Further, was it possible that Udny could have taken such a crucial decision on his own and without consulting the GoI? In fact, until 17 August, Udny was in constant communication with the GoI about information concerning the impending attack on the Khyber. Then why did he let the Khyber go? Was it just a case of misjudgement on his part that in the face of one of the largest revolts faced by the British on the Frontier he was: (a) utterly dismissive of reports of an Afridi attack—a tribe regarded by the British as one of the most formidable on the Frontier; (b) completely ignorant of the question of supply, something that he based his decision on partly; (c) recalled the local commandant without explaining his reasons to him; (d) seemed more concerned with how a handful of levies would perform rather than saving a position that the British regarded as being of extreme importance? If this is true, then Udny's actions point to sheer incompetence, which resulted in a policy of blunder. However, as the evidence in the next section shows, Udny did continue communications in secret after 17 August, and it is these confidential telegrams that contain the key to understanding why the Khyber was not reinforced and the reasons for its subsequent fall.

TENSIONS AND POLITICS OF SUB-IMPERIALISM

Secret communications between officers in the Punjab government and the GoI from 18 August to 26 August are illustrative of the inner workings of imperialism that reveal the direct decision-making that led to the loss of the Khyber. However, the political authorities in India were neither involved in nor aware of this communication.[37] These telegrams passed between three officers and the Army Headquarters.

On 18 August, after Udny had sent Barton orders to withdraw, he sent a telegram to the Army Headquarters in Simla saying:

> Now, however, that no officer remains in the Khaibar whom it would be necessary to succour or relieve, I entirely agree with General Elles that if Landi Kotal or other posts are attacked or the road molested the right course is not to attempt to force our way up the Khaibar, but to leave them alone in the Pass from this side and to threaten Tirah...[38]

The same day Elles sent a telegram to the Army Headquarters where he mentions 'the scheme' in the Intelligence Branch, of which two printed copies existed and which had the approval of General Sir William Lockhart. He says:

> To hammer our heads at Khyber is to play their game and there is nothing to be gained at present; the Serai must go and no efforts could save it. The scheme attacks them at their tenderest point. I would ask for orders as there may be political complications I am unaware of.[39]

The scheme Elles referred to was a document that laid out an invasion of Tirah. Commander-in-chief George White was an advocate of this invasion and indeed for an annexation of Tirah. When the Tirah expedition had been sanctioned, there was a heated debate in the governor general's council.[40] The other members ruled against any idea of annexation. White dissented.[41] He was overruled as there was no support from the secretary of state and the Home Government.

These telegrams demonstrate that days before the attack occurred, Elles and Udny were not concerned with any attempt to save the Khyber Pass, but were already using its fall as a possible move into Tirah. At this point, one is led to ask: Whose idea was it to let the Khyber go, so that it would provide the justification for an invasion and possibly an annexation of Tirah? Udny made the decision on the spot to let the Khyber go, and Elles supported him, but it does not make sense that two local officers could have been entirely responsible for this crucial decision.

In cases of local disturbance, the responsible military adviser was the lieutenant-general of the command who was under the commander-in-chief. The General Officer Commanding, General Elles, was under the lieutenant-general commanding. The Lieutenant-General Commanding, Sir George Wolseley, was not consulted by Udny and Elles, or by Udny when he decided to recall Barton. The lieutenant-general commanding strongly urged on the Army Headquarters the importance of supporting the Khyber Rifles and of sending in regular troops to defend the Khyber. On 18 August, he wrote to the Army Headquarters, soon after he discovered that Udny had recalled Barton:

> ... unless it is absolutely necessary it appears to me very inexpedient to abandon Landi Kotal and leave the Khyber Rifles to make what terms they can with enemy. These men did good service in the Black Mountain; have done extremely well in Khyber, and may be well disposed towards Government. The work of years may be undone in a few days.[42]

The next day, Quarter-Master General Badcock wrote to Brigadier General Nicholson saying that he was not replying to the lieutenant-general commanding's wire, which he showed to Commander-in-Chief White, as the chief thought a demi-official would be best. The chief had seen the lieutenant governor of Punjab the previous day, and the latter was willing to have Udny's order cancelled, but the chief decided it best to leave the order alone.[43] It is interesting that the same day Elles wired the Army Headquarters that Udny was referring the question of occupying the Khyber with troops, and was ready to send one battalion to Landi Kotal and half battalion to Ali Masjid with 20 days' supply. White wrote at the bottom of the page, 'Dear Badcock, If this comes to Punjab it will not be approved. Don't however say so. You might answer—Chief will not consent. Yours G. S. W.'[44] White had seen the lieutenant governor Punjab the previous day, and had decided to let the Khyber go.

On 20 August, Wolseley again wired the Army Headquarters that the Khyber should not be abandoned:

> I am of opinion that abandonment of Khyber and Landi Kotal would be a grave Political mistake. From a military point of view also it seems essential to keep the road open. Further it is our duty to keep faith with those who hitherto have served us faithfully. I can see no reason why Captain Barton should not return to his duties, accompanied if thought desirable by a suitable military escort.[45]

White decided to ignore this telegram. When Quarter-Master General Badcock asked what reply should be sent, White responded:

> I do not like the proposal to send military garrisons now. I don't think you need say more. ... I don't know where the breach of faith alluded to in the L.G.C.'s telegram comes in. The Khyber Afridis undertake to keep open and protect the road for us, if

> by their own acts they upset this engagement I fail to see how it involves us in a breach of faith.[46]

In accordance to his orders, no reply was sent to the lieutenant-general commanding. In the same note White mentioned that now Commissioner Udny was in favour of sending troops into the Khyber, but White was irritated by this change in the commissioner's thinking.[47]

Finally, Wolseley made one last plea for the relief of Landi Kotal:

> At risk of being thought presumptuous, I would venture again to urge desirability of attempting to relieve Lanḍi Kotal Serai which is a strongly defensible post with reserve of water sufficient I understand for 400 men for one month. Considering our efforts to relieve Malakand it will I believe produce the worst effect to leave our auxilliaries, the Khyber Rifles, to do the best they can against a numerous enemy. The troops at Peshawar seem sufficient; and, so far, the enemy appears half hearted and probably a bold policy might disperse them. I recognise the difficulties in the way of an advance up the Khyber, still these are not insuperable and our defensive attitude is likely to encourage the Mullahs and the more fanatical among the tribesmen. We may lose men, but that is better than losing prestige and honour.[48]

In response he was sent a telegram from the Army Headquarters stating that the commander-in-chief could not trace in his telegrams any previous proposal to relieve Landi Kotal: 'You certainly did express an opinion on that date that it was inexpedient to abandon it, but this is very different from a proposal to relieve the place in the face of a large Afridi Lashkar a week later; a measure which requires carefully thought out plans.'[49] Wolseley responded by sending the following telegram:

> Question of relieving Landi Kotal Post has now unfortunately been settled by telegram 435 of same date from Commissioner Peshawar. The reason I hesitated to urge for a second time that the Khyber Rifles should receive military support was that my 250. P. to Q.M.G. of 18th instant remained unanswered while Q.M.G's 136. D. of same date addressed to General Officer Commanding Peshawar District, and dealing with the same subject seemed to indicate that Brigadier General Elles' proposal to abandon the Serai and leave the Khyber Rifles to defend our posts as best they

> could was accepted by Chief. I have not expressed my views on this and other points as freely as I might have done, but the fact that the General Officer Commanding Peshawar was reporting direct to Simla, copies being furnished to me .... and that orders were given him direct from Simla, ... led me to believe that the military action which was being taken at Peshawar had been considered and approved by His Excellency.[50]

However, the decision had already been made to let that prestige go, and by now preparations were under way to recover that prestige—these preparations called for an invasion of Tirah. Two months later, in a debate in the governor-general's council, the commander-in-chief stated ironically, if not duplicitously: 'I cannot help regarding the fall of the forts as a very grave blow at our prestige, and it has been so viewed by our neighbours. The Khyber Rifles, as they marched into Jamrud, taunted our soldiers, who turned out to cheer them, as poor comrades in arms.'[51] At the same time, he argued for the permanent annexation of Tirah.

The GoI still had to explain officially as to why the Khyber was lost, why Captain Barton had been recalled, and why the Khyber Rifles had been left behind to be massacred. The secretary of state asked for the views of the GoI and wanted supporting papers: 'The action taken in recalling Captain Barton is the point upon which primarily the Secretary of State desires to meet criticism and give papers to Parliament.'[52] Foreign Secretary Cuningham formulated a response which stated that the decision not to support the Khyber posts was arrived at on military grounds and it was the right decision; and the Government should 'uphold Sir R. Udny's action in recalling Captain Barton, because any other action would have created a situation in which the GoI would have been constrained to undertake military operations, the propriety of which had been condemned'.[53] Sir George White, in a minute on the subject, described the military situation at the time and again stated that the decisions undertaken were correct on military grounds: 'If the news were true, there would be 10,000 Afridis holding the Khyber on 18th August, and I consider that General Elles was justified in his opinion that, after providing for the safety of the Peshawar valley, he was not strong enough to force the pass....'[54] Whether they were strong enough or not was a military debate that never took place.

In conclusion, the British had news of the Afridi attack a few weeks in advance. But while the military men on the spot made preparations for the attack, Udny was eager to discredit this information while almost all other authorities in the region looked on his actions with surprise. Further, the man responsible for military affairs, the lieutenant-general commanding was not even consulted, neither by his superior the commander-in-chief nor by his subordinate, General Elles. In fact, the lieutenant-general commanding urged that the Khyber not be abandoned, but the commander-in-chief overrode him completely. It is clear that Udny and Elles were in direct communication with the Army Headquarters, and finally, even after Udny changed his mind and asked that troops might be sent to the Khyber (when the attack did not occur on 18 August), the commander-in-chief decided not to do so. What was to be gained by the loss of the Khyber? It provided the perfect justification for an invasion of Tirah, which otherwise would not have been approved by either the GoI or by Whitehall. As E. H. H. Collen, member of the governor-general's council who protested against the policy that had been followed, said, if the Khyber posts had been supported, then 'no Tirah campaign would have been necessary'.[55]

NOTES

1. The day the British lost the Khyber Pass, 25 August 1897, has been popularly described as the 'blackest' day for the British on the Frontier.

2. Udny himself mentioned how many reports he received: '...two or three days after the Shabkadar raid of the 7th August reports began to reach me that this proclamation [from Adda Mullah to the Afridis] was bearing fruit in the shape of attempts by the Afridi Mullahs to stir up their tribesmen to co-operate with the fanatical movement in Swat and the Mohmand country by attacking Jamrud and the posts held by garrisons of the Khaibar Rifles in the Khaibar Pass.' 'From—Sir R. Udny, K.C.S.I., Commissioner and Superintendent, Peshawar Division, To—The Officiating Chief Secretary to Government, Punjab', 3 October 1897, PGoI, Sec F, K.W., NAI, February 1898.

3. The question of water was important and would become an issue later.

4. 'From—Captain F. J. H. Barton, Commandant, Khaibar Rifles, To—The Political Officer, Khaibar', 9 September 1897, PGoI, Sec F, K.W., NAI, February 1898.

5. 'Secretary of State's Call for Papers Regarding the Withdrawal of Captain F. J. H. Barton from Landi Kotal on the Outbreak of the Afridis in the Khyber', PGoI, Sec F, K.W., NAI, August 1898.

6. E. H. H. Collen, 23-3-98, Khyber Affairs, Sec F, K.W., NAI.

7. A tribe that resides in Ningrahar, in Afghanistan. However, one clan of the Shinwaris, the Ali Sher Khel, lives in the Loargai valley above Landi Kotal in the Khyber.

8. 'From—Captain F. J. H. Barton, Commandant, Khaibar Rifles, To—The Political Officer, Khaibar', 9 September 1897, PGoI, Sec F, K.W., February 1898.

9. Ibid.

10. 'From—Captain F. J. H. Barton, Commandant, Khaibar Rifles, To—Sir R. Udny, K.C.S.I., Commissioner and Superintendent, Peshawar Division', 18 August 1897, PGoI, FF, October 1897.

11. Ibid.

12. 'From—Sir R. Udny, K.C.S.I., Commissioner and Superintendent, Peshawar Division, To—Captain F. J. H. Barton, Commandant of the Khaibar Rifles', 17 August 1897, PGoI, FF, October 1897.

13. 'From—Captain F. J. H. Barton, Commandant, Khaibar Rifles, To—The Political Officer, Khaibar', 9 September 1897, PGoI, Sec F, K.W., February 1898.

14. 'Secretary of State's Call for Papers Regarding the Withdrawal of Captain F. J. H. Barton from Landi Kotal on the Outbreak of the Afridis in the Khyber', PGoI, Sec F, K.W., August 1898.

15. Ibid.

16. W. Mackworth Young, 16 August 1897, 'Note or Precis: Disturbances in the Khaibar and on the Kohat and Kurram Borders', PGoP, K.W., Punjab Government Archives, Civil Secretariat, Lahore, 1897.

17. 'Secretary of State's Call for Papers Regarding the Withdrawal of Captain F. J. H. Barton from Landi Kotal ... Khyber', op. cit.

18. Ibid.

19. 'From—Sir R. Udny, K.C.S.I., Commissioner and Superintendent, Peshawar Division, To—The Officiating Chief Secretary to Government, Punjab', 3 October 1897, PGoI, Sec F, K.W., NAI, February 1898.

20. Ibid.

21. 'From—Lieutenant-Colonel Muhammad Aslam Khan, C.I.E., Political Officer, Khaibar, To—The Commissioner and Superintendent, Peshawar Division', 10 September 1897, PGoI, Sec F, K.W., DoA, February 1898.

22. Ibid.

23. Ibid.

24. Ibid.

25. Lord Roberts, 7 March 1898, *Parliamentary Debates*, Lords, IOR/BL.

26. 'From—Sir R. Udny, K.C.S.I., Commissioner and Superintendent, Peshawar Division, To—Captain F. J. H. Barton, Commandant of the Khaibar Rifles', 17 August 1897, PGoI, FF, NAI, October 1897.

27. 'From—The Commissioner and Superintendent, Peshawar Division, To—The Offg. Chief Secretary to the Government of the Punjab', 20 August 1897, PGoI, FF, NAI, September 1897.

28. Ibid.

29. Ibid.

30. 'From—Sir R. Udny, K.C.S.I., Commissioner and Superintendent, Peshawar Division, To—The Officiating Chief Secretary to Government, Punjab', 3 October 1897, PGoI, Sec F, K.W., NAI, February 1898.

31. Quoted by The Under Secretary of State for India, 7 March 1898, *Parliamentary Debates*, Lords, IOR/BL.

32. 'Extract from a Memorandum, Dated the 15th March 1898, by Sir R. Udny, K.C.S.I., Chief Political Officer, Tirah Expeditionary Force', PGoI, Sec F, K.W., NAI, August 1898.

33. 'Future Arrangements for the Control of the Khyber Pass', PGoI, Sec F, K.W., NAI, July 1898.

34. Colonel Aslam Khan, 31 August 1897, Miscellaneous Record, Samana File, Archives, Office of the Political Agent, Khyber Political Agency.

35. L. W. Dane, 15 August 1897, 'Note or Precis: Disturbances in the Khaibar and on the Kohat and Kurram Borders', PGoP, K.W., Punjab Government Archives, Civil Secretariat, Lahore, 1897.

36. L. W. Dane, 15 October 1897, ibid.

37. E. H. H. Collen, member of the governor-general's council, stated later that 'we have no information as to what passed between Elles and Army Headquarters...'. 'Secretary of State's Call for Papers Regarding the Withdrawal of Captain F. J. H. Barton from Landi Kotal on the Outbreak of the Afridis in the Khyber', PGoI, Sec F, K.W., NAI, August 1898.

38. 'From—The Commissioner, Peshawar, To—The Chief Secretary, Punjab Government, Simla', 18 August 1897, PGoI, Sec F, K.W., NAI, February 1898.

39. From—General Officer Commanding, Peshawar, To—Army Headquarters, Quarter Master General, India, 18 August 1897, White Mss., Mss.Eur.F.108/39, IOR/BL.

40. 'Afridi-Orakzai Expedition. Policy to be Adopted Towards the Tribes Who Rose Against Government on the North-West Frontier', PGoI, Sec F, K.W., NAI, February 1898.

41. Ibid.

42. From—Lt-Gen Commanding the Forces, Punjab, To—Army Headquarters, Quarter Master General, India, 18 August 1897, White Mss., Mss.Eur.F.108/39, IOR/BL.

43. 'Copy of a Demi-official Letter from Major General A. R. Badcock, C.B., C.S.I., Q.M.G. in I., to Br. Gen W. G. Nicholson, D.A.G., Punjab Command', 19 August 1897, White Mss., Mss.Eur.F.108/39, IOR/BL.

44. From—General Officer Commanding, Peshawar, To—Quarter Master General, India, 19 August 1897, White Mss., Mss.Eur.F.108/39, IOR/BL.

45. From—Lt-Gen Commanding the Forces, Punjab, To—Army Headquarters, Quarter Master General, India, 20 August 1897, White Mss., Mss.Eur.F.108/39, IOR/BL.

46. Note by White, 20 August 1897, White Mss., Mss.Eur.F.108/39, IOR/BL.

47. Ibid.

48. From—Lt-Gen Commanding the Forces, Punjab, To—Army Headquarters, Quarter Master General, India, 25 August 1897, White Mss., Mss.Eur.F.108/39, IOR/BL.

49. From—Army Headquarters, Quarter Master General, India, To—Lt-Gen Commanding the Forces, Punjab, 26 August 1897, White Mss., Mss.Eur.F.108/39, IOR/BL.

50. From—Lt-Gen Commanding the Forces, Punjab, To—Army Headquarters, Quarter Master General, India, 26 August 1897, White Mss., Mss.Eur.F.108/39, IOR/BL.

51. 'Secretary of State's Call for Papers Regarding the Withdrawal of Captain F. J. H. Barton from Landi Kotal on the Outbreak of the Afridis in the Khyber', PGoI, Sec F, K.W., NAI, August 1898.

52. Ibid.

53. Ibid.

54. Ibid.

55. Ibid.

6

CONCLUSION

The Limits of Empire

Through the preceding examination of the 1897 revolt, this study has attempted to reconstruct the colonial encounter in the North-West Frontier. This microhistorical approach offers insights into the complex ways in which imperial explanations are constitutive of Empire in the North-West Frontier. As examined in the three episodes of the 1897 revolt, we can see how imperial explanations have continued to dominate historiography and thus historical understandings of the revolt. Imperial explanations function at many levels. Immediately they work to disguise the continuous imperial military failures by misrepresenting the causes and history of those failures. By looking at the sub-imperial level, another layer of imperial explanations emerges where the limits of Empire first start to become visible. These involve patterns of misrepresentations of reality on the ground, civil–military tensions, collaborators and middle-men, all of which help us to begin to understand how imperialism functioned beyond the inconsistencies and contradictions present in the grand narratives of imperial history. Sub-imperialism is integrally tied to resistance because that is how the tribes responded to imperialism. The two, sub-imperialism and resistance, help explain Empire on the Frontier and demonstrate the limits of Empire.

Dominant imperial explanations are, as history, not sufficiently grounded in archival evidence. They lead to sloppy images of 'fanaticism'. They also inhibit us from asking questions and finding and probing patterns within the colonial archive of the disjunction between official explanations and how Empire actually operates. Empire is not good at representing its own failures as it has to maintain legitimacy and authority. However, the colonial archive reveals a sub-imperial face and does not corroborate the dominant imperial explanation.

Sub-imperial evidence (internal documents), oral accounts and recent history form a coherent, historical whole which dramatically annihilates official and enduring historiography. In contrast to the dominant imperial explanation, this study has shown that the 1897 revolt was not a 'sudden' and 'fanatical' explosion. The attack in Maizar and the uprising in Swat were the culmination of a resistance that had its origins in imperial military occupation. Sub-imperial evidence shows that in both cases relevant colonial officials realised and admitted this fact.

Both outbreaks also demonstrated British military failures. At Maizar, the British military party had to run away in the face of attack; in Swat, British troops were besieged and beleaguered and could only act on the defensive when attacked. The attack that led to the loss of the Khyber brought British military arrangements and the entire scheme of imperial defence even more into question. The attack was not sudden, and authorities on the spot and in India had several days to prepare for it. If we accept the official line that troops could not be spared to defend the Khyber, then despite the warning and the preparations undertaken, the British felt that they could not cope with the attack. However, this study revealed something else—that the Khyber was deliberately lost so it could justify a possible annexation of Tirah. The Tirah expedition, the largest military undertaking on the Frontier, was sanctioned to recover British prestige, which was lost due to the fall of the Khyber.

In the 1890s, the British undertook a new policy on the Frontier. The object of this Forward policy was imperial defence against Russia for which it was necessary to establish 'close and friendly relations' with the tribes between the administrative boundary and the Durand Line. However, there was a contradiction at the heart of this policy. Those who advocated this policy stated that they had no desire to interfere with the independence of the tribes. At the same time, they wanted to show these tribes that they were 'our men'. As already mentioned, the GoI emphatically stated when asking for approval from London for this policy:

> We wish it to be clearly understood that nothing is further from our intentions than the annexation of tribal country on our frontier. We believe, however, that without annexation, and without interference in the internal affairs of the tribes, it will be possible to bring them further within our influence, and to induce them to regard themselves as owing allegiance to us.[1]

The secretary of state approved this policy on the condition that the GoI in effecting this policy would abstain from extending its influence in such a manner 'which may tend to bring about a collision with the tribesmen, or to the establishment of fresh posts beyond the frontier which may require armed protection'.[2] The contradiction lay in the fact that the policy was one of interference and military occupation. As the voluminous mass of documents that lay out internal imperial debates shows, the Forward policy was undertaken ultimately because it outraged the GoI that the country beyond its administrative border was a 'terra incognita', and that the GoI was no longer content with the 'impenetrable wall' before it.[3] This contradiction is indicative of the internal limits of Empire. Imperial grappling with limits is splattered all over the colonial records as evidenced in different layers of imperial explanations and in Empire continuing to expand in opposition to its stated policy.

Prominent figures that advocated this policy, even while claiming no interference with the independence of the tribes, could not conceal their ultimate desire for annexation:

> I have always maintained that a condition of stable equilibrium is impossible as between a settled Government and contiguous savage tribes. The latter, if the stronger, must eventually overrun the country; if not, the endeavour to compel them to good behaviour must culminate in annexation. The only practical question in such a case is whether annexation— or its equivalent—should be effected at the first convenient opportunity, or should be delayed as long as the situation will admit of delay.[4]

Again, Lord Lansdowne, the Viceroy of India, in a farewell speech in 1894 stated:

> In political geography nature abhors a vacuum, and if one thing is certain it is that, under present circumstances, any space left vacant upon our frontiers will be filled up by others if we do not step in ourselves. And thus it has come to pass that districts which we could afford to regard with indifference as 'no man's land,' or as border Alsatias with which we need have no concern, have suddenly become of vital importance to us as forming part of the marches of the Empire.[5]

Or as the Commander-in-Chief in India, Sir George White, declared in a speech in 1897:

> ...the history of all times has shown that civilization and barbarism cannot exist conterminously, and at the same time peaceably, as independent neighbours. The savage will not subject himself to the restraining influences which enable communities more advanced in civilization to live at peace. This is more especially the case amongst our border tribes, who pride themselves on their individual liberty, on obeying no order, and on being no man's servants. ...History does indeed present a few lamentable instances in which barbarism has conquered civilization, but civilization had become effete, and I hope in this company, at all events, there is no Englander little enough to wish to terrible realization of his theories as regards England's great and civilizing mission in the East.[6]

Therefore, the policy that was undertaken was one of interference and occupation, and was viewed by the tribes as such. British internal documents and Pukhtun oral tradition establish this clearly in the case of Tochi and Malakand. In the case of the Khyber, the tribes themselves communicated their grievances to British authorities amongst which was the fact that they regarded British presence in the Khyber as occupation of their territory: '...you have taken possession of the Khaibar, and the Khaibar country is ours'.[7] The 1897 risings were part of a continuous struggle against this threat to the tribes' independence. The revolt demonstrated a complete failure of the Forward policy and showed up its contradictions. However, this ambiguity was reflected in the earlier period as well, starting in 1849 when the British took over the administrative boundary. Even though the independence of the trans-Frontier tribes was acknowledged, dozens of military expeditions were undertaken against them. Ultimately no government, whether it advocated a 'Forward', 'Stationary', or even a 'Backward' policy, could bring itself to retreat. Thus, holding the Frontier at the Indus was rejected, not because of its demerits as a Frontier, but because retreating from the administrative line would be a sign of weakness. As a member of Parliament declared during the debates on the Frontier risings:

> We maintain our Indian Empire entirely by prestige, backed up by a great military force, and if once the millions of natives who go to make up that nation should recognize that we were approaching a weak position, it would go very ill with our future maintenance of that country. Therefore it was recognized by great military experts at that time that the line of the Indus would be a fatal line to decide upon, and ultimately they decided that the only place where we could meet an invading force would be in the center of Afghanistan.[8]

This study has also revealed a complex network of sub-imperialism that entangled and drew the GoI on, even when that was not its stated objective. The GoI went along willingly (apart from a few voices of dissent), and Whitehall somewhat reluctantly. The local government of Punjab was a sullen bystander and attempted to provide a restraining hand at times, but was ultimately brushed aside. The question is why was the GoI continually drawn in, when that is the last thing it stated it wished to do? A. C. Lyall, in a secret Minute in 1897, acknowledged London and India's role in this pattern:

> The Government of India, indeed, have consistently developed a policy of advance; but at the India Office we have been content with according a dubious assent to each separate proposal. We confined ourselves to warnings, injunctions, expressions of misgiving, and record of general opinions; and when these have proved ineffective, we have accepted explanations, pleas of necessity, and other reasons of the same kind for disregarding our prudent observations. ...the Government of India excusing each expansion of the policy and increase of cost by fresh explanations and professions; the Secretary of State according

> a reluctant sanction coupled with admonitions, reserves, and formal instructions to avoid consequences that were manifestly unavoidable.[9]

The GoI continued to be drawn in, willingly or unwillingly, because the logic of this sub-imperialism coincided with the logic of the nineteenth-century (British) imperial state.[10] The GoI had two options before it in this case: to be drawn in (in one way or another), or to say that the Frontier and the Pukhtuns were beyond its grasp.

This revolt also brought into acute focus British military failures that further demonstrated not only the failure of the entire policy of imperial defence, but also the inadequacy of British defence against large-scale armed tribal resistance. The secretary of state asked the viceroy whether there was any

> foundation for rumours that British troops have failed during recent operations. Can you tell me whether failure has been in a few special cases admitting of explanation, or whether it has been general and attributable to youth of soldiers. Point is important because success of existing system in providing efficient Indian and colonial armies has, till now, been regarded as its strongest point.[11]

In Tochi and Swat the British were on the defensive and could not cope with the attacks, until reinforced. In the Khyber they did not even try. The commander-in-chief was forced to admit this when he stated the British military situation during the 1897 risings:

> At the present time we have found it necessary to mobilize 66,855 men. Our field army numbers roughly some 70,000 men. We therefore have now only 3,145, whom we could employ beyond the Durand line. An enemy that can occupy nearly all our effective military strength is evidently one that must be seriously reckoned with.[12]

Yet, with the almost complete mobilisation of its military strength, the British could not subdue the Pukhtuns. British military failures throw into doubt whether the British could have realistically undertaken annexation of the Frontier. Subsequently, internal limits that are built into empires, though not readily visible or readily admitted to, come into sharp focus.

Internal limits of Empire have to do with its resources, both human and material. External limits in this case came from resistance to imperial expansion. The sub-imperial zone is integral to Empire, it is always there, as are imperial explanations.[13] But often they do not reveal themselves so readily and extensively. In the case of the North-West Frontier they are dramatically revealed. Why? It is difficult to fully answer the question but perhaps once again the answer has something to do with continuous military failures on the Frontier and the ultimate failure to conquer or subdue the Pukhtuns. The point is important because, as demonstrated by the above quote by the secretary of state, military success was tied to Empire maintaining itself. The ideological belief that Empire should have won and the reality that it lost reflects an inner tension of Empire on the Frontier.

The British could not bring all of their imperial military strength to bear on the North-West Frontier and pacify it at any cost. This is an internal limit. At the same time, the external limits came from resistance to imperial expansion and occupation. Sub-imperialism reveals these limits and further demonstrates how Empire functions at its limits. Within imperial explanations these limits are not acknowledged, leading to unanswered questions, missing histories and what appear to be the persistent contradictions and inconsistencies of Empire. Sub-imperialism clearly reveals that acknowledging this history would have shown that the colonial encounter on the North-West Frontier, the resistance of its inhabitants to the expansion of Empire and their efforts to preserve their independence constituted the limits of Empire.

NOTES

1. 'From—GoI, To—The Secretary of State, 3rd Jan 1894', PGoI, Sec F, K.W., NAI, April 1894.

2. 'From—Secretary of State, To—GoI, 2nd February 1894', PGoI, Sec F, NAI, April 1894.

3. Lord Lansdowne, 'Proposed New Arrangements for the Administration of the N. W. Frontier Districts and the Management of the Trans-Frontier Tribes', PGoI, Sec F, NAI, 1889.

4. A. E. Macdonald, 8 June 1894, PGoI, Sec F, K.W., NAI, 1894.

5. Quoted in Colvin (1897: 858).

6. Ibid.: 859.

7. From—Officer on Special Duty, To—Simla and Punjab, 17 October 1897, PGoI, FF, NAI, 1897.

8. Sir J. Dickson Poynder, 14 February 1898, *Parliamentary Debates*, Commons, IOR/BL.

9. Minute by Sir A. C. Lyall on Frontier Affairs, L/P&S/18/A129, IOR/BL.

10. Charles Tilly's seminal argument about the relationship between states and violence is resonant here. 'The logic of international state making acts out on a large scale the logic of local aggrandizement' (Tilly 1985: 185). Here, in particular, the connection is highlighted between the imperial state and imperial expansion, of which war is an integral part. See Tilly (1985).

11. Hamilton to Elgin, 17 November 1897, Mss.Eur.D.508, IOR/BL.

12. G.S. White, 22 October 1897, PGoI, Sec F, K.W., NAI, February 1898.

13. An outstanding example of this within the history of colonial wars can be found in Belich (1986).

SELECT BIBLIOGRAPHY

ARCHIVES

India Office Records and Private Papers, British Library, London, England

Military Department

I. Military Department Library: North-West Frontier, Baluchistan (L/Mil/17)

North-West Frontier Policy, 1920.

Frontier Warfare, 1922.

Manual of Operations on the North-West Frontier of India, 1925.

A Record of the Expeditions Undertaken against the North-West Frontier Tribes, 1874.

A Record of the Expeditions against the North-West Frontier Tribes since the Annexation of the Punjab, 1884.

Frontier and Overseas Expeditions from India, 1907–11.

North-Western Frontier of India, 1898.

Report on the Hindustani Fanatics, 1895.

Military Operations on the North-West Frontiers of India, 1898.

List of Raids and Outrages Committed on the North-West Frontier and in Baluchistan from July 1899 to July 1906, 1906.

The Operations of the Malakand Field Force and the Buner Field Force 1897–98, 1900.

Proceedings of the Government of India Military Department: Chitral 1895–96, 1896.

Expedition against the Isazai Clans on the Hazara Border by a Force under the Command of Maj-Gen Sir William Lockhart in 1892, 1894.

Operations against the Orakzai Tribe on the Miranzai Frontier under the Command of Brig-Gen Sir William Lockhart in 1891, 1891.

Operations of the Mohmand Field Force in 1897, 1899.
Operations of the Tirah Expeditionary Force 1897–98, under the Command of Sir William Lockhart, 1900.
Report on the Engineer Operations of the Tirah Expeditionary Force 1897–98, 1898.
Operations of the Tochi Field Force in 1897–98, 1900.
Operations against the Mahsud Waziris by a Force under the Command of Lt-Gen Sir W. Lockhart in 1894–95, with a Short Account of the Events which Led up to the Expedition, 1897.
Mahsud-Waziri Operations, 1902.
History of the Blockade of the Mahsud Waziris in 1900–1901, 1904.
Waziristan and the Lessons of the Last 60 Years, 1921.
Military Report on Baluchistan, 1929–30 (2nd edn).
Proceedings of the Government of India Military Department: Quetta, 1885.
Operations of the Zhob Field Force under Maj-Gen Sir George White in 1890, 1892.
Expedition against the Black Mountain Tribes by a Force under Maj-Gen John Withers McQueen in 1888, 1889.
Expedition against the Hasanzai and Akazai Tribes of the Black Mountain by a Force under the Command of Maj-Gen William Kidston Elles in 1891, 1894.
An Official Account of the Chitral Expedition 1895, 1898.
The Value of Chitral, 1895.
Military Report and Gazetteer on Dir, Swat and Bajaur, 1928.
The Tribes of Waziristan, 1929.
The Mahsud-Waziri Expedition of 1881, 1884.
A General Report on the Yusufzais, 1864.
Summary of Measures Considered or Carried out in the Military Department of the Government of India during the Viceroyalty of the Earl of Elgin and Kincardine, January 1894 to December 1898, 1899.
Correspondence of Gen. Sir Frederick Roberts, 1877–1893.

II. Departmental Papers: Military Collections (L/Mil/7)
Coast and Frontier Defences of India: General Questions, 1881–1939.
Chitral Expedition 1895, 1895–1915.
Operations in Waziristan, 1881–1898.
Tochi Operations 1897, 1897–1898.
North-West Frontier Operations 1897, 1897–1920.

III. Department Papers: Military Correspondence, 1882–1948 (L/Mil/6)
L/Mil/6/35-37, 1897 (52 files)
L/Mil/6/38-39, 1898 (32 files)

IV. Correspondence with India (L/Mil/3)
L/Mil/3/152, 1897.
L/Mil/3/153, 1898.

Political and Secret Department

I. Political and Secret Memoranda (L/P&S/18)
Memorandum on the Reorganization of the Western and North-Western Frontiers, 1878.
Memorandum on the Rectification of the N-W Frontier of India, 1878.
Indian Frontier Policy, 1888.
Arrangements for the Control of Waziristan, 1895.
The Tochi Valley Cantonment, 1895.
Minute by Sir A. C. Lyall [on policy towards Afghanistan], 1896.
Minute by Sir A. C. Lyall on Our Policy in Regard to Afghanistan, 1896.
The Afghan Succession, 1896.
Memorandum on [North-West] Frontier Affairs by Mr. W. Lee-Warner, 1897.
Digest of North-West Frontier [Parliamentary] Papers, 1898.
External Relations with the Tribes on the Peshawar Border, 1898.
Minute on Correspondence with the Amir, 1897.
Baluchistan and Persia, 1899.
Darwesh Khel Torahs, 1900.
Punjab Frontier Administration, 1900.
Minute by the Viceroy on Frontier Administration, 1900.
Lord Curzon's Proposals Regarding the Administration of the N-W Frontier Districts, 1900.
Note by Sir Dennis Fitzpatrick on the Letter from the Foreign Secretary to the Government of India, 1896.
[Minutes on] Reorganization of the Frontier, 1877.
Formation of New Frontier Administration: Note by His Honour the Lt. Governor of the Punjab, 1901.
Collection of Agreements and Treaties with Afghanistan 1809–1893.
Frontier Disturbances, 1908.
Mohmand Delimitation, 1908.
The N-W Frontier of India, 1920.
[Chitral Affairs: Extracts From] 1904/5–1920/21.
Memorandum by Lieut-Col C E Bruce CIE on Policy in Waziristan, 1929.
Policy on the North-West Frontier, 1935.
Mohmand Affairs 1935–36, 1936.
A Survey of Anglo-Afghan Relations, 1947.

Reorganization of the [North-West] Frontier, 1877.
[The Afghan Question], 1878.
Minute by Sir A. C. Lyall on [North-West] Frontier Affairs, 1897.
Notes on the probable attitude of the Frontier tribes and of Afghanistan in the event of an attempted invasion of India by Russia and on the Frontier policy in connection therewith, 1907.

II. Political and Secret Letters and Enclosures Received from India, 1875–1911 (L/P&S/7)
L/P&S/7/90-110 (1897–98).
L/P&S/7/379 Box 23 (1897).
L/P&S/7/380 Box 24 (1897).
L/P&S/7/381 Box 25 (1898).
L/P&S/7/382 Box 26 (1898).
L/P&S/7/383 Box 27 (1898).

III. Demi-Official Correspondence, Secretary's Letters and Telegrams, 1862–1912 (L/P&S/8)
L/P&S/8/8 Vol. 8 1896–1897.
L/P&S/8/9 Vol. 9 1898–1912.
L/P&S/8/13 Vol. 4 1895–1898.

IV. Parliamentary Questions and Addresses, 1881–1911 (L/P&S/17)
L/P&S/17/4 June 1896–1902 Reg Nos 131-End.

V. Political and Secret Department Library (L/P&S/20)
A Dictionary of the Pathan Tribes on the North-West Frontier of India, 1910.
Memoranda of Information Received During the Month of ... Regarding Affairs on and Beyond the North-West Frontier of India, Jan 1896–Dec 1897.
Memoranda of Information Received During the Month of ... Regarding Affairs on and Beyond the North-West Frontier of India, Jan 1898–Dec 1900.
(a) Correspondence Relating to the Occupation of Chitral. (b) Agreement for Laying Down the Afghan Boundary. (c) Copy of Correspondence Relating to Afghan Proceedings in Kafiristan. (d) Kafiristan Question in House of Commons.
Digest of N-W Frontier of India [Parliamentary Papers], 1898 (in 3 vols).

Private Papers

Private Papers of Victor Alexander Bruce, 9th Earl of Elgin and 13th Earl of Kincardine (1849–1917) as Viceroy and Governor-General of India 1894–1898, Mss.Eur.F.84.

Private Papers of Sir George White as Commander in Chief India 1893–1898, White Mss, Mss.Eur.F.108.
Private Papers of Lord George Hamilton (Secretary of State 1895–1903), Mss. Eur.D.508.
Private Papers of Lord Curzon, Curzon Mss, Mss.Eur.F.111/F112.
Private Papers of Richard Isaac Bruce, Commissioner & Superintendent Derajat in Feb 1893 and British Joint Commissioner for Demarcation of the Afghan-Waziri Boundary from Oct 1894–April 1896, Mss.Eur.F.163.

Parliamentary Branch

Parliamentary papers.
Parliamentary journals.
Parliamentary Debates.

Proceedings

Proceedings of the Government of the Punjab in the Foreign and Foreign Frontier Department, 1871–1901.
Proceedings of the Government of India in the Foreign Department, Frontier Branch 1884–1921.
India Military Proceedings, 1897–1898.

National Archives of India, New Delhi, India

Proceedings of the Government of Punjab, Foreign Frontier.
Proceedings of the Government of India, Foreign Frontier
Proceedings of the Government of India, Secret Frontier.
Settlement Reports, 1879–1904.
Miscellaneous Records of the Foreign Department.
Miscellaneous Records of the Military Department.

Punjab Government Archives, Civil Secretariat, Lahore, Pakistan

Proceedings of the Government of Punjab, Foreign Frontier.
Proceedings of the Government of Punjab, Secret Frontier.
Northwest Frontier Agency Correspondence.

Directorate of Archives, Peshawar, Pakistan

Proceedings of the Government of Punjab, Foreign Frontier.
Proceedings of the Government of Punjab, Secret Frontier.
Darbari and Miscellaneous Records of NWFP, 1871–1902.
Secret Political Record of Police Department, 1895–1909.
Public Record 1st and 2nd List, Office of the Deputy Commissioner, Peshawar.

Reports of Various Departments

Administrative Report of Punjab.
Reports of Civil Justice Department in Punjab.
Reports of Criminal Justice Department in Punjab.
Files of Commissioner's Office, Peshawar.

OFFICIAL PUBLICATIONS

Aitchinson, C. U. 1909. *A Collection of Treaties, Engagements and Sanads Relating to India and Neighbouring Countries*. Calcutta: Superintendent Government Printing, India.

Bellew, H. W. 1864. *A General Report on the Yusufzai*. Lahore: Government Press.

Bolton, H. N. 1907. *Settlement Report on the Dera Ismail Khan District*. Lahore: Civil and Military Gazette.

Frontier and Overseas Expeditions from India [in 6 vols]. Simla: Government of India, 1907–13.

Griffin, Lepel. 1876. Memoranda Concerning the Tribes on the North-West Frontier. Calcutta: Superintendent of Government Printing, India.

——. 1883. *Punjab Frontier Memorandum*. Calcutta: Superintendent of Government Printing, India.

Howell, Evelyn. 1931. *Mizh: A Monograph on Government's Relations with the Mahsud Tribe*. Simla: Government of India Press.

Kemball, Major G. V., R. A. 1900. *Operations of the Tochi Field Force in 1897–98*. Simla: Intelligence Branch, Quartermaster General's Department.

King, L. W. 1900. *Monograph on the Orakzai Country and Clans*. Lahore: Punjab Government Press.

MacGregor, Charles. 1884. *The Defence of India: A Strategical Study*. Simla: Government Central Branch Press.

Merk, W. R. H. 1898. *Report on the Mohmands*. Punjab Government Civil Secretariat Press.

Paget, W. H. and A. H. Mason. 1885. *Record of Expeditions against the N.W.F. Tribes since the Annexation of the Punjab*. Calcutta: General Headquarters, India.

Temple, Richard. 1856. *Report Showing the Relations of the British Government with the Tribes, Independent and Dependent, on the North-West Frontier of the Punjab, from Annexation in 1849 to the Close of 1855*. Calcutta.

PUBLISHED WORKS TO 1947

Books

Adye, John. 1867. *Sitana: A Mountain Campaign on the Borders of Afghanistan in 1863*. London: Richard Bentley.

____. 1897. *Indian Frontier Policy*. London: Smith Eldar.

Andree, N. P. 1878. *India and Her Neighbours*. London: Allen & Co.

Andrew, William Patrick. 1880. *Our Scientific Frontier*. London: Allen & Co.

____. 1885. *The Advance of Russia: Letters Re-printed from 'The Times'*. London: Waterlow.

Andrews, C. F. 1937. *The Challenge of the North-West Frontier*. London: Allen & Unwin.

Atteridge, A. H. 1899. *The Wars of the Nineties*. London: Cassell & Co.

Barton, W. 1939. *India's North-West Frontier*. London: John Murray.

Bellew, H. W. 1879. *Reprint of Four Articles on the North-West Frontier and Afghanistan Contributed to the Calcutta 'Englishman'*. Lahore.

Bernays, R. H. 1931. *Naked Fakir*. London: Victor Gollancz.

Beynon, W. G. L. 1896. *With Kelly to Chitral*. London: Edward Arnold.

Biddulph, C. E. 1890. *Afghan Poetry of the Seventeenth Century*. London: Kegan Paul, Trench, Trubner & Co.

Bird, W. D. 1909. *Some Principles of Frontier Mountain Warfare*. London: Hugh Rees.

Blood, Sir Bindon. 1933. *Four Score Years and Ten: Sir Bindon Blood's Reminiscences*. London: G. Bell & Sons.

Boulger, Demetrius C. 1879. *Ought We to Hold Candahar?* London: Allen & Co.

Bruce, Richard Isaac. 1900. *The Forward Policy and Its Results: Or Thirty-Five Years' Work amongst the Tribes of the North-Western Frontier of India*. London: Longmans, Green Co.

Burnes, Alexander. 1843. *Cabool: A Personal Narrative of a Journey to, and Residence in that City, in the Years 1836, 7, and 8*. London: John Murray, Albemarle St.

Callwell, C. E. 1911. *Campaigns and Their Lessons: Tirah. 1897*. London: Constable & Co. Ltd.

Campbell, G. 1879. *The Afghan Frontier*. London: Edward Stanford.

Churchill, W. S. 1898. *The Story of the Malakand Field Force*. London: Longmans, Green.

Collen, Sir Edwin. 1906. *The Defence of India*. London: Harrison and Sons.

Coxe, H. 1878. *The Panjab and North-West Frontier of India*. London: Kegan Paul.

Curzon, Lord. 1908. *Frontiers*. Oxford: Clarendon.

Dacosta, J. 1891. *A Scientific Frontier*. London: W. H. Allen.

Davies, C. C. 1915. *The Life of Field Marshall Sir George White*. London: William Blackwood & Sons.

——. 1932. *The Problem of the North-West Frontier, 1890–1908, with a Survey of Policy since 1849*. Cambridge: Cambridge University Press.

Dilke, C. W. and S. Wilkinson. 1892. *Imperial Defence*. London and New York.

Egerton, C. C. 1899. *Hill Warfare on the North-West Frontier of India*. Allahabad: *The Pioneer*.

Enriquez, C. M. D. 1910. *The Pathan Borderland*. Calcutta: Thacker, Spink & Co.

Ewart, J. M. 1930. *The Story of the North-West Frontier Province*. Peshawar: Government Printing.

Fincastle, V. C. Viscount and P. C. Elliot-Lockhart. 1898. *A Frontier Campaign: A Narrative of the Operations of the Malakand and Buner Field Forces, 1897–1898*. London: Methuen & Co.

'Frontier' pseud. 1921. *Frontier Warfare*. Bombay: Thacker.

Gibbs, N. H. 1955. 'The Origins of Imperial Defence: An Inaugural Lecture Delivered Before the University of Oxford on 8 June'. Oxford: Clarendon Press.

Hamley, E. B. 1879. *The Strategical Conditions of our Indian North-West Frontier*. London: W. Mitchell.

Hanna, H. B. 1895. *Indian Problems* (3 volumes). Westminster: Archibald Constable & Co.

——. 1898. *The Defence of India's North-West Frontier*. Petersfield: A. W. Childs.

——. 1899, 1904, 1910. *The Second Afghan War* (3 volumes). Westminster: Archibald Constable & Co.

Hobson, John Atkinson. 1902. *Imperialism: A Study*. London: James Nisbet.

Holdich, Colonel Sir T. 1901. *The Indian Borderland, 1880–1900*. London: Methuen & Co.

——. 1910. *The Gates of India*. London: Macmillan.

——. 1916. *Political Frontiers and Frontier Making*. London: Macmillan.

Hutchinson, H. D. 1898. *The Campaign in Tirah, 1897–1898*. London: Macmillan.

James, L. 1895. *With the Chitral Field Force*. Calcutta: 'Englishman' Press.

____. 1898. *The Indian Frontier War: Being an Account of the Mohmund and Tirah Expeditions*. London: Heinemann.

Keppel, Arnold. 1911. *Gun-running and the Indian North-West Frontier*. London: John Murray.

Lenin, Vladimir Ilich. 2013. *Imperialism, the Highest Stage of Capitalism: A Popular Outline*. New York: New York International Publishers, reprint.

Lumsden, P. S. 1897. *Lumsden of the Guides*. London: John Murray.

Macfall, C. 1895. *With the Zhob Field Force, 1890–91*. London: Heinemann.

MacMunn, G. F. 1931. *The Romance of the Indian Frontiers*. London: Jonathan Cape.

Malmesbury, James Howard Harris, Earl of. 1885. *Memoirs of an Ex-minister: An Autobiography*. London: Longmans, Green & Co.

Miles, C. V. 1909. *The Zakka Khel and Mohmand Expeditions*. Rawalpindi: Egerton.

Mills, H. W. 1897. *The Pathan Revolt in North-West India*. Lahore: *Civil and Military Gazette*.

____. 1898. *The Tirah Campaign, being the Sequel to the Pathan Revolt in North-West India*. Lahore: *Civil and Military Gazette*.

Morison, J. L. 1936. *From Alexander Burnes to Frederick Roberts: A Survey of Imperial Frontier Policy*, Raleigh Lecture on History, Read 15 July 1936, British Academy Proceedings.

Nevill, H. C. 1912. *Campaigns on the North-West Frontier, 1849–1908*. London: John Murray.

Newman, H. 1897. *Umra Khan and the Chitral Campaign of 1895*. Lahore: *Civil and Military Gazette*.

Oliver, E. E. 1890. *Across the Border, or Pathan and Beloch*. London: Chapman and Hall.

Pennell, T. L. 1909. *Among the Wild Tribes of the Afghan Frontier*. London: Seeley & Co.

Richard, Henry. 1878. *The Afghan Question*. London: Hodder & Stoughton.

Roberts, Frederick Sleigh Roberts, Earl. 1897. *Forty-one Years in India: From Subaltern to Commander-in-Chief by Field-Marshal Lord Roberts of Kandahar*. Guildford: Billing and Sons, Printers.

Robertson, George S. 1899. *Chitral: The Story of a Minor Siege*. London: Methuen & Co.

Shadwell, L. J. 1898. *Lockhart's Advance through Tirah*. London: W. Thacker Spink.

Shadwell, L. J. 1902. *North-West Frontier Warfare*. Calcutta: Thacker, Spink & Co.

Skeen, General Sir Andrew. 1932. *Passing It On: Short Talks on Tribal Fighting on the North-West Frontier of India*. London: Gale & Polden.

Slessor, A. K. 1900. *The 2nd Battalion Derbyshire Regiment in Tirah*. London: Swan Sonnenschein.

Sykes, Sir Percy. 1926. *Sir Mortimer Durand: A Biography*. London: Cassell & Co.

The Risings on the North-West Frontier. 1898. 'Compiled from the Special War Correspondence of the *Pioneer*'. Allahabad: *The Pioneer*.

Thomson, H. C. 1895. *The Chitral Campaign*. London: William Heinemann.

Thorburn, S. S. 1876. *Bannu; or Our Afghan Frontier*. London: Trubner & Co.

Thomsett, R. G. 1899. *With the Peshawar Column, Tirah Expeditionary Force*. London: Digby, Long.

Tolstoy, Leo. 1904. *War and Peace*. Boston: Dana Estes & Co.

Tucker, Louis H. 1871. *Umbeylah: A Poem*. Lahore: Punjab Printing Company.

Warburton, Robert. 1900. *Eighteen Years in the Khyber, 1897–98*. London: John Murray.

Wylly, H. C. 1912. *From the Black Mountain to Waziristan*. London: Macmillan.

Yate. C. E. 1888. *Northern Afghanistan: Letters from the Boundary Commission*.

Younghusband, G. J. 1898. *Indian Frontier Warfare*. London: Kegan Paul, Trench, Trubner & Co.

Younghusband, G. J. and F. E. Younghusband. 1895. *The Relief of Chitral*. London: Macmillan.

Articles

Barrow, E. G. 1881. 'Tirah and the Afridi Question'. *Proceedings of the United Services Institution of India*, 10.

Bromhead, Sir B. 1900. 'Tribal Control on the Frontier'. *U. S. I. India Journal*, July.

——. 1940. 'The Future of the Tribal Areas'. *U. S. I. India Journal*, October.

Colvin, Sir Auckland. 1897. 'The Problem beyond the Indian Frontier'. *The Nineteenth Century*, 42, December.

Griffin, Sir Lepel. 1897. 'The Breakdown of the "Forward" Frontier Policy'. *The Nineteenth Century*, 42.

Holdich, Col. Sir T. H. 1899. 'Swatis and Afridis'. *Journal of the Anthropological Institute*, 2.

Howell, Sir E. 1934. 'Some Problems of the Indian Frontier'. *Journal of Royal Central Asian Society*, April.

Pearse, Maj. H. 1897–98. 'Former Campaigns against the Afridis'. *United Services Magazine*, 16.

Raverty, H. G. 1895. 'Afghan Waziris and Their Country'. *Asiatic Quarterly Review*, January.

Simpson, F. C. 1944. 'Review of N-W Frontier Policy'. *U. S. I. India Journal*, January, July and October.

Slessor, Capt. A. K. 1899–1900. 'Why and How the Afridis Rose'. *United Services Magazine*, 18.

BOOKS (1947 TO PRESENT)

Adas, Michael. 1979. *Prophets of Rebellion: Millenarian Protest Movements against the European Colonial Order*. Chapel Hill: University of North Carolina Press.

Ahmed, Akbar S. 1976. *Millennium and Charisma among the Pathans: A Critical Essay in Social Anthropology*. London: Routledge & Kegan Paul.

____. 1980. *Pukhtun Economy and Society*. London: Routledge & Kegan Paul.

____. 1983. *Religion and Politics in Muslim Society: Order and Conflict in Pakistan*. Cambridge: Cambridge University Press.

Alder, G. 1963. *British India's Northern Frontier*. London: Longmans.

Anderson, David and David Killingray, eds. 1991. *Policing the Empire: Government, Authority and Control, 1830–1940*. Manchester: Manchester University Press.

Barth, Fredrik, ed. 1965. *Political Leadership among Swat Pathans*. London: Athlone Press, 1965.

____. 1969. *Ethnic Groups and Boundaries*. London: George Allen & Unwin.

Barthorp, Michael and Douglas N. Anderson. 1996. *The Frontier Ablaze: The North-West Frontier Rising, 1897–98*. London: Windrow & Greene.

Bayly, C. A. 1996. *Empire and Information: Intelligence Gathering and Social Communication in India, 1780–1870*. Cambridge: Cambridge University Press.

Bayly, Martin J. 2016. *Taming the Imperial Imagination: Colonial Knowledge, International Relations, and the Anglo-Afghan Encounter, 1808–1878*. Cambridge: Cambridge University Press.

Beattie, Hugh. 2002. *Imperial Frontier: Tribe and State in Waziristan*. Richmond and Surrey: Curzon.

Beckett, I. F. W. 2003. *The Victorians at War*. London and New York: Hambledon & London.

Bejen, Peter and Katherine Tiedemann, eds. 2013. *Talibanistan: Negotiating the Borders between Terror, Politics, and Religion*. Oxford: Oxford University Press.

Belich, James. 1986. *The Victorian Interpretation of Racial Conflict: The Maori, the British, and the New Zealand Wars*. Montreal and Kingston, London, Buffalo: McGill-Queen's University Press.

Blyth, Robert J. 2003. *The Empire of the Raj: India, Eastern Africa and the Middle East, 1858–1947*. Houndsmill: Palgrave Macmillan.

Bond, Brian. 1967. *Victorian Military Campaigns*. London: Hutchinson.

Burroughs, P. 1999. 'Defense and Imperial Disunity'. In *History of the British Empire, Volume III: The Nineteenth Century*, ed. A. Porter, 320–45. Oxford and New York: Oxford University Press.

Caroe, Sir Olaf. 1958. *The Pathans*. London: Macmillan.

Christensen, R. O. 1987. 'Tribesmen, Government and Political Economy on the North-West Frontier'. In *Development Studies and Colonial Policy*, eds Barbara Ingham and Colin Simmons, 175–92. London: Frank Cass & Co. Ltd.

Cohn, Bernard S. 1996. *Colonialism and Its Forms of Knowledge: The British in India*. Princeton: Princeton University Press.

Comaroff, John L. and Jean Comaroff. 1997. *Of Revelation and Revolution, Volume 2: The Dialectics of Modernity on a South African Frontier*. Chicago: University of Chicago Press.

Darwin, John. 2009. *The Empire Project: The Rise and Fall of the British World-System, 1830–1970*. Cambridge: Cambridge University Press.

Davies, L. E. 1986. *Mammon and the Pursuit of Empire: The Political Economy of British Imperialism, 1860–1912*. Cambridge: Cambridge University Press.

Davis, Natalie Z. 1983. *The Return of Martin Guerre*. Cambridge, MA: Harvard University Press.

Dichter, David. 1967. *The North-West Frontier of West Pakistan: A Study in Regional Geography*. Oxford: Clarendon Press.

Docherty, Paddy. 2008. *The Khyber Pass: A History of Empire and Invasion*. New York: Union Square Press.

Edwards, David B. 1996. *Heroes of the Age: Moral Fault Lines on the Afghan Frontier*. Berkeley: University of California Press.

Elliot, J. G. 1968. *The Frontier*. London: Cassell.

Elridge, C. C. 1978. *Victorian Imperialism*. New Jersey: Humanities Press.

Ewan, Martin. 2010. *Securing the Indian Frontier in Central Asia: Confrontation and Negotiation, 1865–1895*. New York: Routledge.

Farrington, A. J. 1981. *British Army Casualties in Tirah, 1897–98* (Extract from Medals International, Vol. 5, No. 3).

Farwell, B. 1972. *Queen Victoria's Little Wars*. New York: Harper and Row.

Galbraith, John Semple. 1963. *Reluctant Empire: British Policy on the South African Frontier 1834–1854*. Berkeley: University of California Press.

Gillard, D. R. 1977. *The Struggle for Asia, 1828–1914: A Study in British and Russian Relations*. London: Methuen & Co.

Gilmartin, David. 2015. *Blood and Water: The Indus River Basin in Modern History*. Berkeley: University of California Press.

Ginzburg, Carlo. 1976. *The Cheese and the Worms: The Cosmos of a Sixteenth-Century Miller*. London: Routledge & Kegan Paul.

Gordon, Donald C. 1965. *The Dominion Partnership in Imperial Defense, 1870–1914*. Baltimore: Johns Hopkins University Press.

Gott, Richard. 2011. *Britain's Empire: Resistance, Repression and Revolt*. London: Verso.

Gough, General Sir Hubert. 1954. *Soldiering On*. London: Arthur Baker.

Guha, Ranajit. 1983. 'The Prose of Counter-Insurgency'. In *Subaltern Studies II*, ed. Ranajit Guha. New Delhi: Oxford University Press.

____. 1997. *Dominance without Hegemony: History and Power in Colonial India*. Cambridge, MA: Harvard University Press.

Hanifi, Shah Mahmoud. 2011. *Connecting Histories in Afghanistan: Market Relations and State Formation on a Colonial Frontier*. New York: Columbia University Press.

Harris, John. 1975. *Much Sounding of Bugles: The Siege of Chitral, 1895*. London: Hutchinson.

Hevia, James Louis. 2012. *The Imperial Security State: British Colonial Knowledge and Empire-Building*. Cambridge: Cambridge University Press.

Hopkins, Benjamin D. 2008. *The Making of Modern Afghanistan*. New York: Palgrave Macmillan.

Hopkirk, P. 1992. *The Great Game: The Struggle for Empire in Central Asia*. New York: J. Murray.

Ingram, E. 1979. *The Beginning of the Great Game in Asia, 1828–1834*. Oxford: Oxford University Press.

____. 1981. *Commitment to Empire: Prophecies of the Great Game in Asia*. Oxford: Oxford University Press.

Isaacman, Allen F. 1977. *The Tradition of Resistance in Mozambique: The Zambesi Valley, 1850–1921*. Berkeley: University of California Press.

Johnson, R. A. 2006. *Spying for Empire: The Great Game in Central and South Asia, 1757–1947*. London: Greenhill.

Johnson, Robert A. 2009. *The 1897 Revolt and Tirah Valley Operations from the Pashtun Perspective*. Tribal Analysis Center. Available at http://www.tribalanalysiscenter.com/PDF-TAC/The%201897%20Revolt%20and%20Tirah%20Valley%20Operations.pdf (accessed on 18 December 2019).

Johnson, Robert. 2011. *The Afghan Way of War: How and Why They Fight*. New York: Oxford University Press.

Johnston, Franklyn Arthur. 1960. *Defence by Committee: The British Committee of Imperial Defence, 1885–1959*. London: Oxford University Press.

Jones, Seth G. 2010. *In the Graveyard of Empires: America's War in Afghanistan*. New York: W. W. Norton & Co.

Keay, John. 1979. *The Gilgit Game*. London: John Murray.

Kennedy, G., ed. 2008. *Imperial Defence: The Old World Order, 1856–1956*. London and New York: Routledge.

Khan, Munawwar. 1964. *Anglo-Afghan Relations, 1798–1878: A Chapter in the Great Game in Central Asia*. Peshawar: University Book Agency.

Killingray, D. 1999. 'Imperial Defence'. In *The Oxford History of the British Empire, Volume V: Historiography*, ed. Robin Winks, 342–53. Oxford and New York: Oxford University Press.

Levi, Giovanni. 1991. 'On Microhistory'. In *New Perspectives on Historical Writing*, ed. Peter Burke, 97–119. Cambridge: Polity Press.

Long, Roger D., ed. 1995. *The Man on the Spot: Essays on the British Empire*. Westport, CT: Greenwood Press.

Mason, P. 1974. *A Matter of Honour*. London: Papermac.

Maxwell, Robert, ed. 1989. *Villiers-Stuart on the Frontier, 1894–1914*. Edinburgh: Pentland.

Menon, K. S. 1957. *The 'Russian Bogey' and British Aggression in India and Beyond*. Calcutta: Priyadarshi Banerji, Eastern Trading Co.

Metcalf, Thomas R. 2007. *Imperial Connections: India in the Indian Ocean Arena, 1860–1920*. Berkeley: University of California Press.

Meyer, K. E. and S. Brysac. 1999. *Tournament of Shadows: The Great Game and the Race for Empire in Central Asia*. Washington, D.C.: Counterpoint.

Miller, C. 1977. *Khyber, British India's North-West Frontier: The Story of an Imperial Migraine*. New York: Macmillan.

de Moor, J. A. and H. L. Wesseling, eds. 1989. *Imperialism and War: Essays on Colonial War in Asia and Africa*. Leiden: Universitaire pers Leiden.

Moreman, T. R. 1998. *The Army in India and the Development of Frontier Warfare, 1849–1947*. London: Macmillan.

Nichols, Robert. 2001. *Settling the Frontier: Land, Law and Society in the Peshawar Valley, 1500–1900*. Karachi: Oxford University Press.

Noelle-Karimi, Christine. 1997. *State and Tribe in Nineteenth-Century Afghanistan: The Reign of Amir Dost Muhammad Khan (1826–1863)*. London: Routledge.

Omissi, D. E. 1990. *Air Power and Colonial Control: The Royal Air Force, 1919–1939*. Manchester: Manchester University Press.

——. 1994. *The Sepoy and the Raj: The Indian Army 1860–1940*. London: Macmillan.

Parsons, Tim. 1999. *The British Imperial Century, 1815–1914*. Lanham: Rowman & Littlefield.

Peers, Douglas. 1995. *Between Mars and Mammon: Colonial Armies and the Garrison State in India, 1819–1835*. London: I. B. Tauris.

Popplewell, R. J. 1995. *Intelligence and Imperial Defence: British Intelligence and the Defence of the Indian Empire, 1904–1924*. London: Routledge.

Preston, Adrian. 1976. 'Wolseley, the Khartoum Relief Expedition and the Defence of India, 1885–1900'. In *Swords and Covenants*, eds Adrian Preston and Peter Dennis, 89–122. London: Croom Helm.

Rand, Gavin. 2018. 'From the Black Mountain to Waziristan: Culture and Combat on the North-West Frontier'. In *Culture, Conflict and the Military in Colonial South Asia*, eds Kaushik Roy and Gavin Rand. London and New York: Routledge.

Ranger, Terence O. 1967. *Revolt in Southern Rhodesia, 1896–97: A Study in African Resistance*. Evanston: Northwestern University Press.

Reed, Graham F. 2010. *Walks in Waziristan: A Young Officer's Guide to Dealing with Cock-Ups on the Front Line*. Bloomington: Author House.

Richards, D. L. 2003. *The Savage Frontier: A History of the Anglo-Afghan Wars*. London: Pan Books.

Robinson, Ronald and John Gallagher with Alice Denny. 1961. *Africa and the Victorians: The Official Mind of Imperialism*. London: Macmillan.

Robson, B. 1993. *Roberts in India*. London: Alan Sutton.

Roe, A. W. 2010. *Waging War in Waziristan: The British Struggle in the Land of Bin Laden, 1849–1947*. Kansas: University Press of Kansas.

Roque, Ricardo and Kim A. Wagner, eds. 2012. *Engaging Colonial Knowledge: Reading European Archives in World History*. London: Palgrave Macmillan.

Roy, Kaushik. 2008. *Brown Warriors of the Raj: Recruitment and the Mechanics of Command in the Sepoy Army, 1859–1913*. New Delhi: Manohar Publishers.

——. 2015. *War and Society in Afghanistan: From the Mughals to the Americans, 1500–2013*. Delhi: Oxford University Press.

Roy, Kaushik and Gavin Rand, eds. 2018. *Culture, Conflict and the Military in Colonial South Asia*. London and New York: Routledge.

Said, Edward. 1978. *Orientalism*. New York: Pantheon Books.

Sergeev, Evgeny. 2013. *The Great Game, 1856–1907: Russo-British Relations in Central and East Asia*. Baltimore, MD: John Hopkins University Press.

Siegel, J. 2002. *Endgame: Britain, Russia and the Final Struggle for Central Asia*. London and New York: I. B. Tauris.

Singer, A. 1974. *Lords of the Khyber*. London: Faber & Faber.

Singhal, Damodar P. 1963. *India and Afghanistan, 1876–1907: A Study in Diplomatic Relations*. Brisbane: University of Queensland Press.

Spain, J. 1962. *The Way of the Pathans*. London: Robert Hale.

——. 1963. *The Pathan Borderland*. The Hague: Mouton & Co.

Stewart, George R. 1959. *Pickett's Charge: A Microhistory of the Final Attack at Gettysburg, July 3, 1863*. Boston: Houghton Mifflin.

Stewart, Jules. 2005. *The Khyber Rifles: From the British Raj to Al Qaeda*. Stroud and Gloucestershire: Sutton.

——. 2007. *The Savage Border: The History of the North-West Frontier*. Stround: Sutton.

Sunderland, Willard. 2004. *Taming the Wild Field: Colonization and Empire on the Russian Steppe*. Ithaca: Cornell University Press.

Swinson, A. 1967. *North-West Frontier: People and Events, 1839–1947*. London: Hutchinson.

Tilly, Charles. 1985. 'War Making and State Making as Organized Crime'. In *Bringing the State Back In*, eds Peter Evans, Dietrich Rueschemeyer and Theda Skocpol. Cambridge: Cambridge University Press.

Toynbee, Arnold. 1961. *Between Oxus and Jumna*. London: Readers Union.

Tripodi, C. 2011. *Edge of Empire: The British Political Officer and Tribal Administration on the North-West Frontier, 1877–1947*. Surrey and Burlington: Ashgate.

Wallerstein, Immanuel Maurice. 2006. *World-systems Analysis: An Introduction*. Durham, London: Duke University Press.

Warren, Alan. 2000. *Waziristan, the Faqir of Ipi, and the Indian Army*. Oxford: Oxford University Press.

Wilkinson-Latham, R. 1977. *North-West Frontier: 1837–1947*. London: Osprey.

Woodruff, P. 1965. *The Men Who Ruled India*. London: Jonathan Cape.

Wyatt, C. M. 2011. *Afghanistan and the Defence of Empire: Diplomacy and Strategy during the Great Game*. London and New York: I. B. Tauris.

Yapp, M. E. 1980. *Strategies of British India: Britain, Iran and Afghanistan, 1798–1850*. Oxford: Oxford University Press.

ARTICLES (1947 TO PRESENT)

Allina-Pisano, Eric. 2003. 'Resistance and the Social History of Africa'. *Journal of Social History* 37(1): 187–98.

Beckett, I. F. W. 2005. 'Soldiers, the Frontier and the Politics of Command in British India'. *Small Wars & Insurgencies* 16(3): 280–92.

Burroughs, Peter. 1986. 'Imperial Defence and the Victorian Army'. *Journal of Imperial and Commonwealth History* 15(1): 53–72.

Catignani, Sergio. 2012. '"Getting COIN" at the Tactical Level in Afghanistan: Reassessing Counter-Insurgency Adaptation in the British Army'. *Journal of Strategic Studies* 35(4): 513–39.

Chappell, David A. 1993. 'Ethnogenesis and Frontiers'. *Journal of World History* 4(2): 267–75.

Chin, Warren. 2007. 'British Counter-Insurgency Operations in Afghanistan'. *Defense & Security Analysis* 23(2): 201–25.

Christiansen, R. 1982. 'Tradition and Change on the N-W Frontier'. *Modern Asian Studies* 16(1): 159–66.

Condos, Mark. 2016. 'Licence to Kill: The Murderous Outrages Act and the Rule of Law in Colonial India, 1867–1925'. *Modern Asian Studies* 50(2): 479–517.

Darwin, John. 1997. 'Imperialism and the Victorians: The Dynamics of Territorial Expansion'. *The English Historical Review* 112(447): 614–42.

Egnell, Robert. 2010. 'Winning "Hearts and Minds"? A Critical Analysis of Counter-Insurgency Operations in Afghanistan'. *Civil Wars* 12(3): 282–303.

Galbraith, John S. 1960. 'The "Turbulent Frontier" as a Factor in British Expansion'. *Comparative Studies in Society and History* 2(2): 150–68.

———. 1961. 'Myths of the "Little England" Era'. *American Historical Review* 67 (1): 34–48.

Gallagher, John and Ronald Robinson. 1953. 'The Imperialism of Free Trade'. *The Economic History Review* 6(1): 1–15.

Ginzburg, Carlo. 1993. 'Microhistory: Two or Three Things That I Know About It'. *Critical Inquiry* 20(1): 10–35.

Harris, Leslie. 1966. 'A Scientific Frontier for India: Background to the Forward Policy of the Nineties'. *Canadian Journal of History* 1(1): 46–71.

Hilali, A. Z. 2013. 'Contemporary Geopolitics of FATA: An Analysis of the Afghanistan-Pakistan Border Region'. *Small Wars and Insurgencies* 26(4): 595–638.

Hoffman, Bruce. 2009. 'A Counterterrorism Strategy for the Obama Administration'. *Terrorism and Political Violence* 21(3): 359–77.

Hopkins, Benjamin D. 2015. 'The Frontier Crimes Regulation and Frontier Governmentality'. *The Journal of Asian Studies* 74(2): 369–89.

Iqbal, Khuram and Sara de Silva. 2013. 'Terrorist Lifecycles: A Case Study of Tehrik-e-Taliban Pakistan'. *Journal of Policing, Intelligence and Counter Terrorism* 8(1): 72–86.

Jackson, Isabella. 2012. 'The Raj on Nanjing Road: Sikh Policemen in Treaty-Port Shanghai'. *Modern Asian Studies* 46(6): 1672–704.

Jagadish, Vikram. 2009. 'Reconsidering American Strategy in South Asia: Destroying Terrorist Sanctuaries in Pakistan's Tribal Areas'. *Small Wars and Insurgencies* 20(1): 36–65.

Johnson, R. A. 2003. '"Russians at the Gates of India"? Planning the Defence of India, 1885–1900'. *Journal of Military History* 67(3): 697–744.

Johnson, Thomas H. 2013. 'Taliban Adaptations and Innovations'. *Small Wars and Insurgencies* 24(1): 3–27.

Knox, Bruce. 1986. 'The Concept of Empire in the Mid-Nineteenth Century: Ideas in the Colonial Defence Inquiries of 1859–61'. *Journal of Imperial and Commonwealth History* 15(3): 53–72.

Lindholm, C. 1979. 'Contemporary Politics in a Tribal Society: Swat District, NWFP, Pakistan'. *Asian Survey* 19(5): 485–505.

———. 1980. 'Images of the Pathan: The Usefulness of Colonial Ethnography'. *European Journal of Sociology* 21(2): 350–61.

———. 1981. 'The Structure of Violence among the Swat Pukhtun'. *Ethnology* 20(2): 147–56.

Marini, Ruy Mauro. 1965. 'Brazilian Interdependence and Imperialist Integration'. *Monthly Review* 17(7): 10–29.

Moreman, Tim. 1992. 'The British and Indian Armies and NW Frontier Warfare, 1849–1914'. *Journal of Imperial and Commonwealth History* 20(1): 35–64.

Mustafa, Daanish and Katherine E. Brown. 2010. 'The Taliban, Public Space, and Terror in Pakistan'. *Eurasian Geography and Economics* 51(4): 496–512.

Ortner, Sherry B. 1995. 'Resistance and the Problem of Ethnographic Refusal'. *Comparative Studies in Society and History* 37(1): 173–93.

Peceny, Mark and Yury Bosin. 2011. 'Winning with Warlords in Afghanistan'. *Small Wars and Insurgencies* 22(4): 603–18.

Peers, Douglas M. 2005. 'Colonial Knowledge and the Military in India, 1780–1860'. *Journal of Imperial and Commonwealth History* 33(2): 157–80.

Qazi, Shehzad H. 2011. 'Rebels of the Frontier: Origins, Organization, and Recruitment of the Pakistani Taliban'. *Small Wars and Insurgencies*, 22(4): 574–602.

Rand, Gavin. 2006. '"Martial Races" and "Imperial Subjects": Violence and Governance in Colonial India, 1857–1914'. *European Review of History* 13(1): 1–20.

Roberts, A. D. 1962. 'The Sub-Imperialism of the Baganda'. *Journal of African History* 3(3): 435–50.

Simpson, George L. 1996. 'Frontier Banditry and the Colonial Decision-making Process: The East Africa Protectorate's Northern Borderland Prior to the First World War'. *International Journal of African Historical Studies* 29(2): 279–308.

Stacey, C. P. 1950. 'The Myth of the Unguarded Frontier, 1815–1871'. *American Historical Review* 56: 1–18.

Stoler, Ann Laura. 2002. 'Colonial Archives and the Arts of Governance'. *Archival Science* 2: 87–109.

Striegher, Jason-Leigh. 2013. 'Early Detection of the Lone Wolf: Advancement of Counter-Terrorism Investigation with an Absence or Abundance of Information and Intelligence'. *Journal of Policing, Intelligence and Counter Terrorism* 8(1): 35–53.

Surridge, K. 2008. 'The Ambiguous Amir: Britain, Afghanistan and the 1897 North-West Frontier Uprising'. *Journal of Imperial and Commonwealth Studies* 36(3): 417–34.

Thruelsen, Peter Dahl. 2010. 'The Taliban in Southern Afghanistan: A Localised Insurgency with a Local Objective'. *Small Wars and Insurgencies* 21(2): 259–76.

Tripodi, C. 2008. 'Peacemaking through Bribes or Cultural Empathy? The Political Officer and Britain's Strategy towards the North-West Frontier, 1901–1945'. *Journal of Strategic Studies* 31(1): 123–51.

Varynen, Raimo and Luis Herrera. 1975. 'Subimperialism: From Dependence to Subordination'. *Instant Research on Peace and Violence* 5(3): 165–77.

Watt, D. C. 1963. 'Imperial Defence Policy and Imperial Foreign Policy, 1911–1939: A Neglected Paradox'. *Journal of Commonwealth Political Studies* 1(4): 266–81.

Williams, Brian Glyn. 2008. 'Talibanistan: History of a Transnational Terrorist Sanctuary'. *Civil Wars* 10(1): 40–59.

———. 2010. 'CIA's Covert Predator Drone War in Pakistan, 2004–2010: The History of an Assassination Campaign'. *Studies in Conflict and Terrorism* 33(10): 871–92.

Winks, Robin. 1976. 'On Decolonization and Informal Empire'. *American Historical Review* 81(3): 540–56.

Wong, J. Y. 1997. 'British Annexation of Sind in 1843: An Economic Perspective'. *Modern Asian Studies* 31(2): 225–44.

UNPUBLISHED THESES

Baha, Lal. 1968. 'The Administration of the North-West Frontier Province, 1901–1919', Ph.D. diss., SOAS, University of London.

Christiansen, R. 1989. 'Conflict and Change among the Khyber Afridis'. Ph.D. diss., University of Lester.

Harris, Leslie. 1960. 'British Policy on the North-West Frontier of India 1889–1901'. Ph.D. diss., SOAS, University of London.

Hussain, Gul. 1985. 'The Political and Administrative Development of Tribal Areas (FATA) of Pakistan'. M. Phil. thesis, Area Study Centre, Peshawar University.

Rehman, Sarfur. n.d. 'Mulla Powinda'. M. Phil. thesis, Area Study Centre, Peshawar University.

Singhal, Damodar P. 1955. 'Indian External Policy, with Special Reference to the North-Western and Eastern Frontier, 1876–1898'. Ph.D. diss., University of London.

Zaffar, Zahida. 1985. 'Peshawar under the British Rule'. Ph.D. diss., Area Study Centre, Peshawar University.

Appendix A

QUESTIONS TO H. W. GEE AND HIS REPLIES

Dated Camp Dera Ismail Khan, the 12th December 1897.
From—H. W. Gee, Esq.,
To—R. E. Younghusband, Esq.

I return your enclosures with the information you require as far as I can give it.

I have no wish to give evidence in person, for the main reason that I have already given the facts fully as far as I know them, and the rest is more a matter of argument and opinion. It should be remembered that the opinions I gave were based on such evidence as I had then been able to collect, and I have not wish to press them unduly.

Dated Dera Ismail Khan, the 13th December 1897.
From—H. A. Anderson, Esq.,
To—R. E. Younghusband, Esq.

I send on this letter from Gee with its enclosures. He sent them to you through me and asked me to look at them.

1. We understand that the 'bach'[1] of Honde Ram's fine was not *finally* settled either at the jirga in February or at any other time. Is this so? Can you remember whether any jirga was held to discuss this subject *after* February 1897?	1. See my No. 94-C, paragraph 4. The question of Mirdad's share was left over. That was the only matter which they could not agree about, Alambe taking one side and Sadda Khan the other.

(contd)

Table (contd)

	When sanction to the reduction was received, I told the maliks when they were in at Datta Khel, and as they still differed on this point and continued to do so, it was then that I said we would discuss it on my visit to Maizar, when the gathering would be representative. No formal jirga was held about the fine then; but no other point was raised, and I should, therefore, say I regarded the rest of the bach as settled. Some money was paid up before 10th June. It must be remembered that the Maizarwals agreed to the bach. (?) It should never in any case interfere authoritatively in the bach of a tribal fine, but only help the maliks through Assistant District Superindendent of Police as far as possible.
2. If so, how was it that the arrest of the Tarmor men on an unsubstantiated charge of theft was used in order to make them (or their friends) pay up their share of the fine before the actual bach was settled?	2. I object to this form of question. A baramta[2] was made of Shiranna Madda Khels to put pressure on the maliks to act up to their engagements and settle the case. Baramtas of this kind are always made in such cases where the chance occurs.
3. Can you remember exactly what you said to Sadda Khan on the 8th June, when you told him you were going to pay a visit to Maizar with the troops, what answer he made and who was present?	3. No; I cannot. I saw all the maliks who were in at Datta Khel, probably more than once, and they all knew I was going to visit Maizar in the same way as I had done the Kazha. Sadda Khan certainly made no particular reply to me in the matter.

(contd)

Table (contd)

4. Some of the evidence recorded before you is to the effect that angry and excited marakkas had been held at Maizar when it was known that you intended to go there, and that the Maizarwals had resolved in certain eventualities to fight rather than pay the fine. One of the difficulties in the way of believing these statements is that, if these statements are true and if (as is alleged) the fact that the Maizarwals were in this frame of mind was well known to everybody, no report should have been made to you by any one, either the Khidder Khel maliks or Kotan Khan or Shekh Jamal or the Kazha maliks or by your own levies (Alam Shah and others), who had been at Maizar helping Sadda Khan. Can you explain this?	4. How much of this evidence is true and how much exaggerated can perhaps better be judged now than at the time I wrote my report. I don't think my expressing any opinion at this stage would be of much use.
5. Besides Sadda Khan and Alambe, do you remember the names of any of the Sheranni or Maizar maliks that you saw at Maizar, i.e., can you personally identify any of those who were there?	5. Namwar Khan, Pyall, and Zar Muhammad.
6. Do you think that, if an attack had been settled on beforehand, the women and children would have been left in the villages? Is it not possible that something may have happened during the troop's stay at Maizar that may have, taken with the state of dissatisfaction the Maizarwals appear to have been in, led to the sudden attack being made on the troops? If so, what was it?	6. This is a matter of opinion. The Commissioner, I believe, considers that the women and children would have been sent away in such a case. I know of no sudden cause which would have accounted for the outbreak, nor has one ever been suggested to me. If there was such, I presume it must have been in the jirga itself, which was not visible from the place where we were sitting.

(contd)

Table (contd)

7. When did the troops open fire? Was it after the first shot or after the irregular volley was fired from the direction of the village?	7. It was after Seton Browne had been wounded. That I will swear to. Beyond that I don't think I personally can say with any accuracy.
8. In your letter No. 95-C you state that Ghulam Muhammad Khan came to you and said that the marakka had come to an amicable arrangement amongst themselves, and that it was only necessary for them to come up and make a formal statement. Ghulam Muhammad Khan now denies this, and says he only said that they were still discussing the matter. Can you recollect exactly what Ghulam Muhammad Khan said to you?	8. I can only repeat what I said in my letter. I went over to him with the intention of having the jirga up, and naturally should have done so had I not been told that the points still undecided had been amicably settled. The Assistant District Superintendent of Police said that they had asked for a few days' time to pay in, which I told him they would of course be given.
9. Your telegram about feeding the troops?	9. Sadda Khan was never ordered to prepare food, nor he did offer to before me. He may have done so to Colonel Bunny when I was away. The first I knew of it was the appearance of the food.

H. W. GEE
12th December 1897

Source: 'From—Major-General G. Corrie Bird, To—The Secretary to the Government of India', 28 December 1897, Proceedings of the Government of India, Foreign Department, Secret Frontier, National Archives of India.

NOTES

1. 'Bach' referred to distribution or the share of fine that different clans would pay.
2. 'Baramta' is reprisal or forcible seizure of people or property.

Appendix B

CORRESPONDENCE BETWEEN THE MULLAHS

Translation of a Letter to the Mullah Saheb (of Adda), dated the 2nd Rabi-us-Sani 1315 H. (31st August 1897).

After compliments—I beg to inform you that, in the first fight which the Afridis had in the Khyber, the Khyber was conquered by the aid of God. All the forts, particularly the fort at Loargai (Landi Kotal), were destroyed. Some of the Mujahid Moslems were slain, and the infidels lost more than 300 men in killed.

I have directed the 'lashkar' of the Orakzais to be engaged in fight at Samana and along the whole of the frontier, since the last twelve days. They have destroyed four forts there. The villainous infidels have lost many persons in killed. At the Ublan, an English Subedar-Major was killed; and his head was severed and brought. There is one fort alone which remains untaken on the top of the Samana. The 'lashkar' of the Orakzais has surrounded it; it is hoped that it will be taken by the grace of God.

I have again prepared another Afridi 'lashkar', and have ordered them to attack Jam (Jamrud) and the cantonment of Peshawar. I hope that God will grant a permanent victory. I trust that you also have been praying for the success of the 'lashkar' of this side.

On receipt of this note you should prepare the lashkar on that side, so that they may begin to fight from that side, and we, from this side, so that God may be pleased to turn out the infidels from the Moslem country. You should send a letter to Swat, so that the

Mian Guls may also use their endeavours and fight, so that the enemy may be destroyed, according to the word of God:-

'Verily, the victory of God is at hand.'

Accept most sincere salaams and best wishes from Muntasar, inhabitant of the shrine of Kaka Saheb of the Akhunzada Khel.

Source: 'From—Major H. A. Deane, Political Agent for Dir, Swat, and Chitral, To—The Secretary to the Government of India, Foreign Department', 24 September 1897, Proceedings of the Government of India, Foreign Department, Secret Frontier, National Archives of India.

Note: Seal not legible.

Translation of a Letter from Mulla Adda to the Mian Guls, Swat, dated the 4th Rabi-us-Sani 1315 H. (2nd September 1897).

After compliments—I have to inform you that I am doing well, and I pray always for the health and welfare of you all. The news about the Moslems in Tirah and the Khyber as regards their relations with the villainous infidels is as follows:-

All the 'thanas' of the infidels, above Jam (Jamrud) in the Khyber, have been, by the grace of God, burned and destroyed, and the property seized. All thanas in the direction of Kohat have also been plundered and burned. 'Thana' of Lowargai (Landi Kotal) contained every kind of articles including ammunition, rifles, cash, etc. The whole of the above property has been taken away, and the Moslems have been satiated with the plunder. Now all the Moslems, having regard to the religion of the Prophet, have prepared themselves for a 'jehad'. They intend to attack the cantonment of Peshawar and Jam. I am going to join the jehad. His Highness replied that we should wait; that His Highness would consult all the military officers, Khans and Maliks of His Highness's territory, and then write again in reply, telling me the arrangements and preparations for jehad. His Highness gave 100 rupees to the Sheikh, who carried my letter to His Highness, for his road expenses. This has been a great kindness of His Highness. I have told the tribesmen to wait, telling them to be ready by the time the second letter comes, and that on receipt of this letter arrangements for a jehad would be made.

I therefore write to you to be patient, and to let no anxiety enter your mind, because all the Moslems, with great zeal for the religion of the Prophet, and the honour of the people of Islam, have raised a general disturbance against the infidels.

I hope that God may be pleased, for the sake of the holy Sheikhs, to keep Swat safe, and that it may be left alone (by the English).

Please God, His Highness the Amir will make arrangements for the jehad, and issue a notification to that effect.

On receipt of the second reply, I shall let you know the contents. You asked me to inform the Sipah Silar about the state of your affairs. My friends, the Sipah Silar cannot do anything without the orders of His Highness the Amir. Your affairs will be arranged in accordance with the directions which His Highness the Amir will issue.

Further, I pray for your welfare under every circumstance.

FAKIR-I-HADDA

Source: 'From—Major H. A. Deane, Political Agent for Dir, Swat, and Chitral, To—The Secretary to the Government of India, Foreign Department', 24 September 1897, Proceedings of the Government of India, Foreign Department, Secret Frontier, National Archives of India.

Appendix C

PETITIONS OF MALIKS

Translation of a Letter from the Khans and Khan Khels of Thana and Khans of Aladand, Deri, Bat Khela, &c., &c., to Major H. A. Deane, Chief Political Offier, Chitral Relief Force.

After compliments—We, the Khans and Khan Khels of Thana, and the Khans of Aladand, Deri, Bat Khela, Khar, Derai, Jawalgiram, Totakan and Mata-kanarai, beg to request that the British Government may be pleased to keep in our country a strong body of troops, for the following two reasons:-

1stly—That we may not suffer injury at the hands of other tribes. Most of the tribes think that we have done services to the Government, and when the Government troops leave the country they will perhaps do us injury. The road goes from Peshawar to Kashkar (Chitral), and we shall thus be helped in its protection. It will be difficult to protect the road without the aid of Government troops; and the presence of the troops will secure our safety; we shall be benefited in every way in the matter of mercantile transactions, &c., and instead of mischief and disturbance, we shall have peace and quiet in our country.

2ndly—We beg to submit that we will, with the greatest pleasure, give to Government whatever land may be required for the purpose of road, forts and posts.

It will be a matter of favour if the Government gives us compensation for the land; otherwise, we do not want any compensation. Because of our demand for compensation, the Government should not take away their troops from us.

3rdly—We beg to state that we will, with the greatest pleasure, produce our tribesmen for service and protection of the road, so that there may be no harm done by wicked people. We will first offer for service our near relatives. We are very grateful to Government, because they have furnished us with employment in our own country.

We are unable to adequately render our thanks for this favour of Government. We beg most respectfully to solicit that a strong body of troops may be posted at the Malakand, because it is a dangerous place.

At whatever place in Swat, *i.e.*, within our limits, the Government may desire to erect forts, they can do so.

SWAT VALLEY, CHAKDARA
11th September 1895

Source: 'From—Major H. A. Deane, Political Officer, Chitral Relief Force, To—The Chief Staff Officer, Chitral Relief Force', 13 September 1895, Proceedings of the Government of India, Foreign Frontier, National Archives of India.

Translation of a Letter from the Adinzais to Major H. A. Deane, Chief Political Officer, Chitral Relief Force, dated the 18th Rabi-ul-awal 1313 H. (8th of September 1895).

After compliments—We, on behalf of all the Adinzais, beg first to solicit that the British Government should take our country in their own possession, and not hand it over to any other party. We will with the greatest pleasure pay whatever taxes the Government may impose on us. We desire that the Government troops should remain in our country, so that no disturbance may occur in it. The Government troops are necessary for two objects in this country:-

1stly—That they may put a stop to all the internal mischiefs, such as murder, theft, robbery and other crimes, as well as all the riots which occur in regard to lands, women, &c., leading to conflict and slaughter.

2ndly—That they may protect us against the attacks, violence and high handed proceedings of other tribesmen. Since the time the British troops have come to our country, we have rendered services to Government to the best of our ability. It is therefore possible that the other tribesmen may be displeased with us, and that they may do us injury. We sincerely solicit that the Government should not leave our country. If the Government do not take taxes from us for their own use, but hand us over to some Khan, we beg to request that the taxes should be collected by Government servants, and then Government may retain the money for themselves or hand it over to any other person they like. Even then we beg that the Government troops should remain in our country, so that we may live in peace and quiet under the shadow of Government. We shall also be thus aided in the protection of the road which extends from Peshawar to Kashkar (Chitral); and the presence of Civil and Military officers will prove of great help to us.

We beg further to state that, if you are unable to grant our request, we may be permitted to send our petition to Lahore and Simla to the authorities there, who can grant our request. We beg most respectfully to earnestly solicit Government that our country should be under the control and jurisdiction of Government. During the past six months that the Government troops have been in our country, we have been benefited. Previous to that time we were suffering from hardship and distress—our women used to be submitted to insults of every kind and lands used to be taken by force from us.

Although a large army of Government is located in our country, our villages have suffered no injury whatever; and our women go about where they like, without receiving any insult. They pass by the big camp, but no bad words are addressed to them.

The Government officers who are appointed to our country have duly enquired into our complaints, whether from high or low people, in accordance with the custom of the country.

We, the Maliks and all the other people, big and small, beg to solicit that our petition may be heard and granted.

SWAT VALLEY, CHAKDARA
11th September 1895

Source: 'From—Major H. A. Deane, Political Officer, Chitral Relief Force, To—The Chief Staff Officer, Chitral Relief Force', 13 September 1895, Proceedings of the Government of India, Foreign Frontier, National Archives of India.

Translation of a Petition in Urdu from Muhammad Ibrahim Khan of Swat, Servant of Mian Gul Khan, to the Foreign Secretary, dated nil.

Before the disturbance took place I had brought the matter to the notice of Government through Mr. Clarke and Abdur Rahim Khan Sahib at Simla verbally as well as by a letter, but I have not been made aware of the result of my communication. I have had to spend much for road expenses. I wished to do good to Government. I stated before that the disturbance is due to Muhammad Sharif Khan of Dir and Mian Rahim Shah, Kaka Khel. On account of their oppression this great disturbance arose. Major Deane does not listen to any complaints against them. If you be kind enough, give me a note for Major Deane, and give me hopes of not burning the villages and not putting us to death, then we will, everyone of us, present ourselves with the Khans to the Government and agree to submit. Mian Gul says that all that has occurred is the consequence of the above named two persons' wickedness. Should they leave the place, no disturbance would take place. By my agreeing to do service to Government I have placed myself in a dangerous position on account of them, because they will complain that I have reported them to Government. It is now desirable that Government should write promising us protection, so that I may do what Government would wish. Had I proved a liar in my previous statements, I would be considered one in making this statement. It is desirable that Government should show us kindness.

* * *

P.S.—I shall wait for a reply to this letter at this place with a letter at the Mardan Post Office. The reply should be sent by a letter or a telegram.

Source: Proceedings of the Government of India, Foreign Frontier, September 1897, National Archives of India.

INDEX